"From the title to the last word, Ziegler expounds God's gracious apocalyptic advent in human history, and its outworking: a faith that is 'militant in love.' Bracing, erudite, passionate, exegetical, provocative—*Militant Grace* is destined to become a classic. Read this book."

—**Susan Eastman**, Duke Divinity School

"This remarkable volume establishes Ziegler as the leading figure in shaping Christian theology in Pauline apocalyptic mode. Anchored by two programmatic opening chapters and six theses on apocalyptic in contemporary theology, the writings gathered here combine to form something far more powerful than the sum of its parts. Drawing on Martyn and Käsemann, Barth and Bonhoeffer, Calvin and Kierkegaard, Ziegler presents a clear, coherent, compelling vision of dogmatics and ethics 'funded by a fresh hearing of New Testament apocalyptic.' This is a serious work, and demands to be taken seriously by all who would be faithful theologians in our time."

—**Douglas Harink**, The King's University, Edmonton, Alberta

"In a day when the word 'apocalyptic' is popularly used for the worst news of cosmic proportions, it may come as a surprise to discover that in the gospel of the New Testament, most decidedly in the testimony of Paul, it is used precisely for the best news. Nothing less than a new creation, empowered against all opposition by what happens with Jesus Christ, is said to be 'apocalypsed' as the turn of the ages. Ziegler provides a brilliant account, unsurpassed in expositional depth and clarity, of what this good news entails and how realistic it is today. For those familiar with the subject, this valuable text is an encyclopedic compendium of the major thinkers. For students new to the issues, it offers a most inviting place to become informed and engaged. Such is the author's exemplary tribute 'in memory of and gratitude to J. Louis Martyn.'"

—**Christopher Morse**, Union Theological Seminary, New York

"Rigorous, deep, rich, scholarly, judicious, clear, but most of all exciting, *Militant Grace* is the very best of systematic theology. Bridging the gap between systematics, ethics, and biblical studies through its serious engagement with the apocalyptic turn and its significance for thinking about the Christian faith and the Christian life, this book offers exciting new angles on traditional theological questions and figures. For students of theology at all levels, it is a must!"

—**Tom (**

MILITANT
GRACE

The Apocalyptic Turn
and the Future of Christian Theology

PHILIP G. ZIEGLER

BakerAcademic
a division of Baker Publishing Group
Grand Rapids, Michigan

Published by Baker Academic
a division of Baker Publishing Group
PO Box 6287, Grand Rapids, MI 49516-6287
www.bakeracademic.com

Printed in the United States of America

Library of Congress Cataloging-in-Publication Data
Names: Ziegler, Philip Gordon, author.
Title: Militant grace : the Apocalyptic turn and the future of Christian theology / Philip G. Ziegler.
Description: Grand Rapids : Baker Academic, 2018. | Includes bibliographical references and index.
Identifiers: LCCN 2017041926 | ISBN 9780801098536 (pbk. : alk. paper)
Subjects: LCSH: End of the world. | Eschatology. | Theology.
Classification: LCC BT877 .Z54 2018 | DDC 236—dc23
LC record available at https://lccn.loc.gov/2017041926

18 19 20 21 22 23 24   7 6 5 4 3 2 1

In memory of and gratitude to

J. Louis Martyn

Contents

Part 3   Living Faithfully at the Turn of the Ages

Acknowledgments

I am grateful to Dr. Taido Chino for his help in the early stages of preparing the typescript and pursuing the necessary permissions. I am also grateful to the Department of Theology and Religion of the University of Durham for electing and hosting me as Alan Richardson Fellow during the Epiphany Term of 2016/2017, during which time I was able to finish preparing the text.

I owe an unpayable debt to my close colleagues in divinity at the University of Aberdeen for their friendship and encouragement. Many thanks too to all those who have participated over the years in the "Explorations in Theology and Apocalyptic" working group during annual meetings of the AAR/SBL, and in particular to Professor Doug Harink for his leadership and encouragement of this common work.

I am grateful to Francis Boutle Publishers for permission to reproduce in fair use the final lines of Jack Clemo's poem "The Awakening" in *The Awakening: Poems Newly Found*, edited by J. Hurst, A. M. Kent, and A. C. Symons (London: Francis Boutle, 2003).

The chapters of this book represent revised versions of previously published essays and articles. I am very grateful to the publishers noted here for their kind permission to make use of them in this volume:

Chapter 1 revises "Eschatological Dogmatics: To What End?," in *Escha-tologie-Eschatology*, ed. H.-J. Eckstein et al., Wissenschaftliche Un-tersuchungen zum Neuen Testament 272 (Tübingen: Mohr Siebeck, 2011), 348–59.

Chapter 2 revises "Some Remarks on Apocalyptic in Modern Chris-tian Theology," in *Paul and the Apocalyptic Imagination*, ed. Ben C.

Blackwell, John K. Goodrich, and Jason Maston (Minneapolis: Fortress, 2016), 199–216.

Chapter 3 revises "Love Is a Sovereign Thing: The Witness of Romans 8:31–39 and the Royal Office of Jesus Christ," in *Apocalyptic Paul: Cosmos and Anthropos in Romans 5–8*, ed. Beverly Gaventa (Waco: Baylor University Press, 2013), 111–30.

Chapter 4 revises "'Christ Must Reign': Ernst Käsemann and Soteriology in an Apocalyptic Key," in *Apocalyptic and the Future of Theology: With and beyond J. Louis Martyn*, ed. Joshua B. Davis and Douglas Harink (Eugene, OR: Cascade, 2012), 202–20.

Chapter 5 revises "*Nisi per Spiritum Sanctum*—The Holy Spirit and the Confession of Faith," *Journal of Reformed Theology* 8, no. 4 (2014): 247–56.

Chapter 6 revises "*Veniat Regnum Tuum!* Christology, Eschatology and the Christian Life," in *Game Over? Reconsidering Eschatology*, ed. C. Chalamet et al., Theologische Bibliothek Töpelmann 180 (Berlin: Walter de Gruyter, 2017), 407–23.

Chapter 7 revises "The Enmity of Death and Judgment unto Life," in *Eternal God, Eternal Life: Theological Investigations into the Concept of Immortality*, ed. P. G. Ziegler (London: T&T Clark, 2016), 131–48.

Chapter 8 revises "Creation, Redemption and Law—Toward a Protestant Perspective on the Question of Human Law," in *Explorations in Christian Theology and Ethics: Essays in Conversation with Paul L. Lehmann*, ed. P. G. Ziegler and M. Bartel (Aldershot, UK: Ashgate, 2009), 63–78.

Chapter 9 revises "The Fate of Natural Law at the Turning of the Ages," *Theology Today* 67, no. 4 (2011): 419–29.

Chapter 10 revises "The Adventitious Origins of the Calvinist Moral Subject," *Studies in Christian Ethics* 28, no. 2 (May 2015): 213–23.

Chapter 11 revises "The Christian Life of Discipleship," in *The T&T Clark Companion to Kierkegaard*, ed. A. Edwards and D. Gouwens (London: T&T Clark, forthcoming).

Chapter 12 revises "Dietrich Bonhoeffer—An Ethics of God's Apocalypse?," *Modern Theology* 23, no. 4 (October 2007): 579–94.

Chapter 13 revises "Discipleship," in *Sanctified by Grace: A Theology of the Christian Life*, ed. K. Eilers and K. Strobel (London: T&T Clark, 2014), 173–86.

Abbreviations

General

§(§)	section(s)	NABRE	New American Bible, revised (2010) edition
alt.	altered		
art(s).	article(s)	q(q).	question(s)
b.	Babylonian Talmud	RSV	Revised Standard Version
cf.	compare	rev.	revised
esp.	especially	s.v.	under the word
et al.	*et alii*, and others	vol(s).	volume(s)
n(n).	note(s)		

Bibliographic

CD	*Church Dogmatics*, by Karl Barth	PC	*Practice in Christianity*, by Søren Kierkegaard
DBWE	Dietrich Bonhoeffer Works in English	PL	Patrologia Latina, edited by J.-P. Migne
Institutes	*Institutes of the Christian Religion*, by John Calvin	SV	*Søren Kierkegaards samlede værker*. Edited by A. B. Drachmann, J. L. Heiberg, and H. O. Lange. 14 vols. Copenhagen: Gyldendalske boghandels forlag, 1901–6
JLPL	*Juridical Law and Physical Law*, by T. F. Torrance		
JP	*Journals and Papers*, by Søren Kierkegaard		
Pap.	Søren Kierkegaard's Papers (Danish manuscripts)		

Introduction

Grace is God's sovereign realm.
—Karl Barth, *Holy Spirit
and the Christian Life*

An informal working group of theologians and biblical scholars committed to undertaking some "Explorations in Theology and Apocalyptic"
first met at the American Academy of Religion / Society of Biblical Literature
annual meetings in Montreal in 2009. At that first gathering we took as our
theme the significance of J. Louis Martyn's Pauline scholarship for contemporary theology and biblical studies. The expanding conversation has continued
ever since. It has been a privilege and an education for me to participate in this
work alongside so many fine colleagues. This book represents something of my
own modest contribution to that conversation to date. Its ambition is simply
to share with readers some of the insights and perspectives that have opened
up for me in the course of my recent thinking concerning the significance of
Paul's apocalyptic gospel for contemporary Protestant theology.

The apocalyptic eschatology, language, and imagery of the New Testament is integral to its witness to the accomplishment of God's salvation in
Jesus Christ, representing a primary idiom by which faith sought to attest the
gospel and conceive its consequences. As the Scottish divine James Stewart
remarked already half a century ago, "however we may interpret it," when we
confront the apocalyptic eschatology of the New Testament "we are dealing,
not with some unessential . . . scaffolding, but with the very substance of the
faith."[1] Some of the most important reconsiderations of apocalyptic in this

1. Stewart, "On a Neglected Emphasis in New Testament Theology," 300.

spirit have been undertaken in recent Pauline scholarship: Ernst Käsemann, J. Christiaan Beker, J. Louis Martyn, Martinus de Boer, Beverly Gaventa, Susan Eastman, John Barclay, Douglas Campbell, Alexandra Brown, and others besides have labored at length to discern, display, and better understand the apocalyptic character of Paul's evangelical witness.[2] While this body of biblical scholarship is, of course, not uniform, its collective insight coalesces around Paul's apprehension of the profound depth and immense scope of the consequences of God's own saving advent in Christ. As Gaventa concisely puts it, "Paul's apocalyptic theology has to do with the conviction that in the death and resurrection of Jesus Christ, God has invaded the world as it is, thereby revealing the world's utter distortion and foolishness, reclaiming the world, and inaugurating a battle that will doubtless culminate in the triumph of God over all God's enemies (including the captors Sin and Death). This means that the Gospel is first, last, and always about God's powerful and gracious initiative."[3] Inasmuch as it is an expression of specifically Christian faith, "apocalyptic theology always and everywhere denotes a theology of liberation in an earth that is dying and plagued by evil powers."[4]

In the words of Donald MacKinnon, its subject matter is nothing less than "God's own protest against the world He has made, by which at the same time that world is renewed and reborn."[5] Undoubtedly there are all manner of other "apocalyptic" sensibilities, postures, and even theologies abroad that stand at a distance from all this. Whether the product of "overenthusiastic misinterpreters" within the churches, or a trace left by the manifold cultural diffusion and refraction of biblical concepts and images now floating free of the determinative interpretative context once provided by the New Testament itself, we can be sure that any "apocalyptic reduced to a mood of world ruin and promoting desperate anxiety has nothing to do with the gospel."[6] In the mouth of a Christian theologian, the nominal adjective "apocalyptic" does

---

2. In addition to the work of these authors themselves, much of which is engaged in this book, there are a number of works that provide a useful entrée into this Pauline scholarship, including Blackwell, Goodrich, and Maston, *Paul and the Apocalyptic Imagination*; Gaventa, *Apocalyptic Paul*; and concisely in Lewis, *What Are They Saying about New Testament Apocalyptic?*, 38–52. For recent critical appraisal of representative work in this area, see J. Davies, *Paul among the Apocalypses*; and more briefly in J. Frey, "Demythologizing Apocalyptic?," esp. 502–27. There is rather more vigorous criticism on offer in N. T. Wright, *Paul and His Recent Interpreters*, esp. part 2, "Re-Enter Apocalyptic," 135–220, as well as the earlier work of Matlock, *Unveiling the Apocalyptic Paul*.

3. Gaventa, *Our Mother Saint Paul*, 81.

4. Käsemann, "Beginning of the Gospel," 8.

5. MacKinnon, "Prayer, Worship, and Life," 247–48.

6. Käsemann, "Beginning of the Gospel," 8. The phrase "overenthusiastic misinterpreters" is taken from Gaventa, *Our Mother Saint Paul*, 84.

not give voice to an anxious and resigned pessimism. Rather, it denotes the distinctive form of "God's eschatological activity" displayed in the gospel, and proclaims the unrivaled and salutary divine activity that "*generates* what it determines" and "*effects* the judgment which it presents."[7]

This book ventures to begin to take renewed theological responsibility for just this kind of hearing of the Christian gospel and its entailments. In this it is distinct—and in many ways even remote—from other cultural projects as well as theological programs to which the term "apocalyptic" might be affixed.[8] The overarching argument of this book is that in pursuit of renewed accountability to the apocalyptic gospel, theology is required to think again about its own forms, methods, and foci precisely in virtue of its distinctively eschatological *content*. Indeed, a range of Christian doctrines—centrally, those concerning sin, grace, salvation, and the character of the Christian life—invite reconsideration in light of an understanding of the gospel of Jesus Christ as the announcement of God's eschatological overturning of the "old and passing age," that "shattering message of the Kingdom of God drawn near, and the consequent end of all mediating philosophy, theosophy and cosmology,"[9] as Karl Barth once put it. For theology to take an "apocalyptic turn" of this kind means undertaking to discern and inhabit forms of thought that eschew conformity with the schema of that old "world which is passing away" because they seek to accord with the world graciously remade by God in Christ. It means working to conceive and to articulate what it means that by grace Christians suffer the loss of that same world, that in faith they own that loss, and that by the Spirit's power they may know and exercise the dizzying freedom of those who have been won from captivity to—and complicity with—powers antithetical to God. For while we are "still in the sphere of that evil ambivalence," Barth observes, "we are already in the very different sphere of the Holy Spirit who awakens, enlightens, comforts and impels us."[10] To pursue an "apocalyptic turn" in Christian dogmatics is thus simply to learn

---

7. The final phrase is from Jüngel, "Emergence of the New," 55. De Boer, "Apocalyptic as God's Eschatological Activity in Paul's Theology," gives a pellucid account of the meaning of "apocalyptic" understood in this way.

8. One might think here of the "apocalyptic" mindsets and political ideologies that are the target of the critical theological writing of Catherine Keller in her works *Apocalypse Then and Now* and *God and Power*. The work undertaken here is also at some remove from the style of the "apocalyptic theology" advanced by Thomas J. J. Altizer under the rubric of "radical theology," which concentrates on tracing and creatively amplifying the modern philosophical and literary transformations of ancient Christian apocalyptic concepts and images: see his *Call to Radical Theology*, 17–30.

9. K. Barth, CD III/1:53.

10. K. Barth, CD IV/4:172.

anew what it means to "never boast of anything but the cross of our Lord Jesus Christ, by which the world has been crucified to me, and I to the world," as Paul wrote (Gal. 6:14). The effort, in short, is to do theology in a manner both shaken and disciplined by the "elemental interruption of the continuity of life" that the gospel is and brings about.[11]

The argument of the book is developed in three parts. Part 1, "The Shape and Sources of an Apocalyptic Theology," consists of two programmatic chapters in which I make a case for the kind of theological endeavor I would like to recommend as "apocalyptic theology." These essays outline the sources, themes, and tasks that I take to be fundamental to that work. Part 2, "Christ, Spirit, and Salvation in an Apocalyptic Key," encompasses five chapters that together explore cardinal themes in soteriology, arguing in turn for a renewed understanding of the distinctive doctrinal importance of Christ's royal office, the primacy of redemption in our understanding of salvation, the eschatological character of the Spirit's gift of faith, the Kingdom of God as the object of prayer, and the last judgment as the final victory of divine grace. Following on from this, the six chapters of part 3, "Living Faithfully at the Turn of the Ages," examine different aspects of the Christian life. The first two chapters consider the difference an apocalyptic theological understanding makes for the way in which we conceive of our relation to natural, moral, and positive law. The next three chapters undertake what might be thought of as apocalyptic "readings" of aspects of the theologies of John Calvin, Søren Kierkegaard, and Dietrich Bonhoeffer in order to illumine in turn the nature of our existence as moral agents, the fundamental posture of Christian existence in humility and gratitude, and the nature of Christian ethics. In the final chapter, I argue that an apocalyptic theology naturally sees the whole of the Christian life as *discipleship*, that is, as a free and faithful venture to inhabit—and so to attest—the world being remade by the living lordship of Christ.

D. Stephen Long has observed that apocalyptic has particular currency among "some ardently Protestant theologians."[12] Perhaps not all who are working in relation to the rubric would characterize themselves in this way.[13] For my own part, I am certainly drawn to the task of envisaging an apocalyptic

11. Jüngel, "Value-Free Truth," 205.
12. Long, *Hebrews*, 198–211, at 207. At the end of an excursus reflecting on apocalyptic as a tone in contemporary thought (with Derrida and Žižek as exemplars), Long comments critically on Nathan Kerr's book, *Christ, History and Apocalyptic*, worrying about the "anti-ecclesiocentric" posture deriving from the fact that Kerr advocates for "a pleromatic christological apocalyptic with a kenomatic ecclesiology" (211).
13. In addition to Kerr's work, for an indication of the kind of theological work already being done under these auspices, see the programmatic essays by Walter Lowe: "Prospects for a Postmodern Christian Theology" and "Why We Need Apocalyptic," as well as Harink, *Paul*

theology for "ardently Protestant" reasons. For it seems to me that, understood as it is here, apocalyptic is a discursive idiom uniquely suited to articulate the radicality, sovereignty, and militancy of adventitious divine grace; just so it is of real import to the dogmatic work of testing the continued viability of Protestant Christian faith. The chapters that follow can be read as an attempt to vindicate this intuition materially and, in the case of my interpretation of other theologians, also heuristically. The apocalyptic idiom starkly illumines at one and the same time both the drastic and virulent reality of human captivity and complicity in sin, and the extraordinary power of saving divine grace that outbids it, reminding us that things are at once much worse yet also paradoxically far, far better than we could possibly imagine them to be. For just this reason, Jörg Frey is undoubtedly right to suggest that "neutralizing apocalyptic is . . . a dangerous way of weakening the Christian message."[14] Perhaps, for the sake of the gospel, Protestant theology has a peculiar vocation today to resist any such weakening of Christian witness precisely by keeping its sails close-hauled into the strong winds of apocalyptic Paulinism.

---

among the Postliberals, and the wide-ranging and exploratory essays collected in Davis and Harink, eds., *Apocalyptic and the Future of Theology.*

14. J. Frey, "Demythologizing Apocalyptic?," 524, though I am perhaps less anxious than he is that such neutralization is, as he continues, "as dangerous as making apocalyptic the center of everything." For in the perspective pursued in this volume, apocalyptic discourse is precisely a medium by means of which to acknowledge and attest that (and how) God's saving advent in Christ is, in fact, the center of everything.

PART 1

The Shape and Sources
of an Apocalyptic Theology

1

An Eschatological Dogmatics
of the Gospel of Grace

Do not be afraid; I am the first and the last, and the living One.
I was dead, and see, I am alive for ever and ever
and I have the keys of Death and of Hades.

—Revelation 1:17–18

The present day ought to be the best of times for eschatological theology. Since the early years of the twentieth century, generations of theologians have struggled in various ways to "do full justice to the distinctive priority given to the eschatological future in primitive Christian eschatology."[1] And during the decades since Klaus Koch declared that we moderns are "baffled by apocalyptic,"[2] scholars have endeavored to explain it to us at length. The fruits of such efforts are by now conveniently distilled into encyclopedias and comprehensive handbooks.[3] Further, at hand we have the substantive legacies of Jürgen Moltmann, Wolfhart Pannenberg, Gerhard Sauter, and others whose labor since the 1960s has been to shift eschatology from being merely one dogmatic locus among others to being instead the decisive register in

---

1. Pannenberg, *Systematic Theology*, 3:595. Helpful surveys of developments in eschatology over this period are offered by Sauter, *What Dare We Hope?*; Schwartz, *Eschatology*, 107–72; Runia, "Eschatology in the Second Half of the Twentieth Century"; Paulson, "Place of Eschatology in Modern Theology"; Schwöbel, "Last Things First."

2. Koch, *Ratlos vor der Apokalyptik*, translated into English as *Rediscovery of Apocalyptic*.

3. See Collins, McGinn, and Stein, *Encyclopedia of Apocalypticism*; Walls, *Oxford Handbook of Eschatology*.

which all theological loci are set. There have been important impulses from the "theology of hope," from thinking of "revelation as history," and from receiving the "future as promise," as well as a honing of the valuable technical concepts of *prolepsis* (effective anticipation of the future in the present), *adventus* (arrival of the future), and *novum* (sheer, unanticipated novelty) that attend them. These impulses have in no small measure contributed to bringing us to wherever it is that we currently are theologically.[4] The enterprise of eschatological dogmatics may never have been as well capitalized as it is now.

And yet, at precisely this same juncture, there are other, strongly countervailing trends afoot in Christian theology, trends that aim to draw a closing parenthesis around the era of eschatological dogmatics. As the lead editorial of a major English-language theology journal has suggested firmly, "It is time to give eschatology a rest, a time-out."[5] Eschatological dogmatics, it is said, is rendered untenable by postmodern criticism of hegemonic master narratives; it is corroded by our despair of any progressive interpretation of history; and it is fatally undermined by the scientific view of the entropic nature of the cosmos.[6] Furthermore, a thoroughgoing historicism has recently reemerged as a serious program in contemporary theology, and it is as allergic to the eschatological as were its precursors. In English-language theology, it involves a vigorous "cultural turn" in which theology is to be understood, says Dutch thinker Mieke Bal, as "a specialization within the domain of cultural analysis that focuses . . . on those areas of present-day culture where the religious elements from the past survive and hence 'live.'"[7] While its intellectual mainsprings, including American neopragmatism and variants of postliberalism, are not altogether identical with those driving the current Troeltsch revival in Europe, the aspirations and form are similar.[8] Both these theological movements are historicist all the way down, operating on the assumption that in theology, as in all other discourses, there is "nothing but history."

4. Moltmann, *Theologie der Hoffnung*; Pannenberg, *Offenbarung als Geschichte*; Sauter, *Zukunft und Verheißung*.

5. Steckel, "Confessions of a Post-Eschatologist," 144.

6. For careful and provocative exploration of this last particular point, see Tanner, "Eschatology without a Future?"

7. Bal, "Postmodern Theology as Cultural Analysis," 6; cf. the programmatic collection of essays in D. Brown, Davaney, and Tanner, *Converging on Culture*; Tanner, *Theories of Culture*.

8. See Rendtorff, *Theologie in der Moderne*; Renz and Graf, *Troeltsch-Studien*; Grab and U. Barth, *Gott im Selbstbewußtsein der Moderne*; and centrally Troeltsch, *Kritische Gesamtausgabe*. Translations of Troeltsch's *Christian Faith* and key essays in *Religion in History* have been followed by studies on Troeltsch: Chapman, *Ernst Troeltsch and Liberal Theology*; Pearson, *Beyond Essence*. More directly programmatic is the work of Shelia Greeve Davaney in *Historicism* and in *Pragmatic Historicism*. Contemporary North American historicists in this line acknowledge as a mainspring the theological project that Gordon D. Kaufman began in earnest in his *Systematic Theology*.

American theologian William Dean gave definitive articulation to the challenge of this new historicism:

> What would it mean if theology were to treat the event of history as that beyond which there was no recourse—and to treat the creatures of history as in new ways crucially powerful in shaping history—and to do that because all trans-historical imports, even the abiding reality of the modernists, have been embargoed? The interpretive imagination is utterly historical; it reinterprets nothing other than history; and it, and it alone, in human and nonhuman creatures, creates history. It is historical communication about historical communication, creative of historical communication. Might this imagination give to theology a somewhat different meaning?[9]

Indeed it might. Such historicism insists that theology exhausts its mandate in the practice of cultural analysis and criticism, being distinguished from other such efforts only by its concern with those tracts of human culture called "religious" or "similar cultural configurations that give meaning and direction to human existence." As such, it must be disciplined away from any misguided "pretensions of timeless truth" and immunized against "the assumption that in theology humans traffic with some nonhistorical realm."[10]

Of course, a previous explosion of eschatological dogmatics in the early twentieth century itself occurred on the playground of a self-consciously historicist theology. And now, as then, proponents of the latter complain that eschatological theology "severs the knot which centuries, with good reason, have tied"[11]—as Troeltsch once put it—unwinding the muddle of daily religious life with its complicated social and cultural entanglements and accommodations that constitute Christianity as an actual historical phenomenon.[12] Eschatological dogmatics, it is said, threatens to forget that while "the radical slaying of the 'the old man' corresponded to the birth of 'the new man,'" this new human being has "to work out his relationships to the 'world.'"[13] For the historicists, then, the very possibility of an intelligible Christianity trades on the essential continuity of the human person across this moment, and on the determinative priority given in Christianity's theological self-understanding to the history of the accommodation and mediation between faith and world, indeed of faith *by* and *to* world. The slaying and making alive, the death of the old and the birth of the new, the aeonic work of God to save, which constitutes so central

---

9. Dean, "Challenge of the New Historicism," 265.
10. Davaney, *Historicism*, 161–62.
11. Troeltsch, "Apple from the Tree of Kierkegaard," 314.
12. Cady, *Religion, Theology, and American Public Life*, 145.
13. Troeltsch, "Apple from the Tree of Kierkegaard," 313.

a part of the scriptural portrait of Christian faith—all this can only be taken to describe modulations within an order of things finally left undisturbed, a collection of dramatic tropes for "naming and symbolizing what we take to be of significance in existence" in an "outsideless" world that, for all its flux, is ever essentially just one damn thing after another.[14] If they were taken in any other sense, eschatological categories would simply have to be adjudged category mistakes, since on this view everything is and must be firmly knotted into the horizontal weave of human culture without remainder.[15]

Now, an eschatological dogmatics will inevitably press hard on precisely *this* neuralgic point, resisting historicism's seeming evacuation of genuine transcendence. Here in this first chapter I explore one particular example of such resistance, that offered by the work of American Lutheran theologian Gerhard Forde († 2005). Forde's theology is a bold defense of the transcendent radicality of divine grace. It discerns that the prospects for an eschatological dogmatics turn on whether the historicist knot can be persuasively cut at precisely the point Troeltsch himself identified: in the account of salvation being accomplished in Christ. For should we finally be forced to admit that salvation "can signify nothing other than the gradual emergence of the fruits of the higher life," then closing time will truly have come to the bureau of eschatology, and the world will be left—falsely—to suffer under the chilling laws of its own aimless contingency.[16]

Justification and the Turning of the Ages

While other theologians have certainly noted the eschatological valences of a radically evangelical account of justification,[17] few have pursued their signal

---

14. Davaney, *Historicism*, 164. She cites (at 158) the term "outsideless" from Cupitt, *Life, Life*. Lord Stratford is credited with announcing the view that history is merely "a patternless succession of one damn thing after another."

15. The term "category mistake," coming from the work of Gilbert Ryle, denotes an instance where one thing is talked about in terms that are fitting only for something of a radically different sort. From a historicist perspective, thinking that eschatological claims are not fully exhausted by historical reference and explanation mistakes their logical form, on the premise that no form of discourse is simply reducible in this way. For a detailed and nuanced study of the interconnected careers of historicism and transcendence in early twentieth-century theology, see Wolfes, *Protestantische Theologie und moderne Welt*.

16. The citation is from Troeltsch, *Christian Faith*, 38, at which point he also alludes to his famous quip "The bureau of eschatology is generally closed these days."

17. Gerhard Sauter signals this in *What Dare We Hope?*, 166–69, identifying this as the sole place in which the Reformers were "revolutionary" in eschatological matters (168). The prominence of the theme of justification as "new creation" in the work of Oswald Bayer reflects a similar insight. See his "Theses on the Doctrine of Justification," esp. theses 4, 5, 24.

importance with such sustained attention and vigor as did Gerhard Forde.[18] In essence, Forde gives an account of justification that republishes the "microcosmic apocalyptic" discerned by Luther to be the heart of personal salvation.[19] Key is an appreciation of how the juridical language of justification is explicated materially by the description of salvation as strictly a matter of death and life: of the judgment of the old unto death, and in Christ the gift of life to the new. Paul's announcement that "if anyone is in Christ, there is a new creation: everything old has passed away; see, everything has become new!" (2 Cor. 5:17) distills the point: reconciliation occurs by way of death and new creation.[20] The aim is to connect talk of justification so closely with talk of death and life along these lines that they become identified, as indeed they were by Luther.[21] As Forde contends, when we grasp that "justification by faith alone *is* death and resurrection, then one has a potent theological explosive."[22] Only with such an explosive can all moralism, legalism, and religious distortions of the freedom of the Christian life under the promise of the gospel be sapped. The ambition is to undercut what J. Louis Martyn in his work on Paul has styled the "two ways" or "two-step dance" view of salvation, a view that pivots around claims for the continuity of the self and unvitiated human capacity for choice of the good.[23]

The matter of justification properly arises against the dramatic-dualistic background of the New Testament witness. This certainly is not an absolute dualism of origin, yet it is marked by a "radical opposition between the forces of evil and the creator God." Set in this apocalyptic context, the death and resurrection of Jesus Christ together constitute an event by which the new age breaks in on the old: God's decisive and salutary contradiction of all that is opposed to him.[24] Death and resurrection are not merely fanciful tropes

18. In what follows I draw on a number of Forde's writings: *Law-Gospel Debate*; *Where God Meets Man*; *Theology Is for Proclamation*; "Work of Christ"; *Justification by Faith*; *More Radical Gospel*; *Captivation of the Will*; and *Preached God*.

19. I take this phrase from Jones, "Apocalyptic Luther," 312.

20. Forde also looks to Rom. 6:1–11 as a concise statement of this, observing that Paul meets moralistic incredulity at the radical nature of grace—"Should we continue in sin in order that grace may abound?" (Rom. 6:1)—precisely by commenting at length on the sinner's dying and rising in and with Christ.

21. "Baptism signifies two things: death and resurrection, that is, full and complete justification" (Luther, "Babylonian Captivity of the Church," 67). Cf. Forde, *Justification*, 16–18.

22. Forde, *Justification*, 4.

23. Martyn contends that such a view is at the heart of the message of Paul's opponents in Galatia (the "Teachers") and is met by Paul's proclamation of the apocalyptic gospel; see Martyn, *Galatians* and *Theological Issues in the Letters of Paul*. For a summary statement of the position see Martyn, "Apocalyptic Gospel in Galatians."

24. Forde, "Work of Christ," 36–37, 40.

for other processes that are really taking place within the stable ambit of the self. Rather, as Forde explains,

> Death and resurrection is the primary reality, . . . [and this] posits a radically different understanding of the way of salvation. Under the legal metaphor, the subject is a continuously existing one who does not die but is merely altered by grace. Salvation, you might say, is something of a repair job. . . . Death and resurrection as a real event, however, proposes quite a different way. . . . The subject does not survive intact on its own steam, undergoing only certain "alterations." What is involved is rather a matter of death and life. There is new life. That the subject is made new is due to the action of God, the resurrection in Christ, not to repairs made according to the legal scheme.[25]

In keeping with such a view, Forde cannot do enough to emphasize the radical *discontinuity* that salvation entails. As another later statement makes plain, the event of Christ's cross and resurrection is not

> "just one of those things" because it is God who is at work here, who intends to bring us to our end, to put all things "out of joint," and make a new start. It means that everything and everyone stands under the judgment, that God has found a way here, so to speak, to do what he would not quite do in the flood—wipe out everyone and start anew. Here he has found a way to do it so as truly to save and not to destroy. There is a new creation in Jesus, the risen one. . . . So it is that the accident becomes the point of departure . . . for something absolutely new: faith in the God who calls into being that which is from that which is not.[26]

With this emphasis, Forde stands in close continuity with the early Barth, who insisted that the *eschaton* is "*not* the extension, the result, the consequence, the next step in following out what has gone before, *but* on the contrary, it is the radical break with all that has gone before, but also precisely as such its original significance and motive power."[27] Notice how both Barth

---

25. Forde, *Justification*, 17–18; cf. "Work of Christ," 96: "If, however, atonement is the actual event, the accident that happens to us from without, it affects us profoundly subjectively. It ends the old life and begins a new one. It means death and resurrection. The old subjective views [of atonement] were partially right. They simply were not radical enough. They thought of a modification of the subject, not its death and resurrection." With the word "accident," Forde emphasizes the contingent, eventful, uncontrolled, and uncontrived character of salvation that befalls us from beyond our own willing and doing.

26. Forde, *Theology Is for Proclamation*, 128–29.

27. My translation of K. Barth, "Der Christ in der Gesellschaft," 35, emphasis original. Cf. K. Barth, "Christian's Place in Society," 324. The congruence is also noted in Mattes, "Gerhard Forde on Revisioning Theology," 376.

and Forde locate the salutary character of the eschatological in its *discontinu-ity*: it is from this discontinuity that eschatology draws its significance and power to move events, as Barth says; or in Forde's idiom, when Christ, who is killed, is then raised to new life by God for the sake of his slaughterers, "something else happens: ultimate judgment, a full stop, and grace."[28] The cross of Christ is not, as Albert Schweitzer once styled it, just another turn of the bone-crushing wheel of history.[29] It is rather the start of "something else," another kind of turning in which an unfathomably gracious Divinity accomplishes the salvation of the world. For Forde, the cross is the instrument by which God brings to naught that which is, certainly; but more important still, it is at the same time the instrument by which God brings into being that which has not yet been: it is the instrument of the new creation in Christ. For this reason we must acknowledge that Christ dies, Forde argues, not "instead of us" but rather *"ahead of us,"* drawing sinful flesh into and through his own death to the place it must die, so as to remake it anew.[30]

There is more than a touch of apocalyptic sensibility in an account of salvation that so stresses the salutary power of radical disjunction. The escha-tological word of the cross saves precisely because it "kills the old Adam and Eve." This is salvation by catastrophe—like the flood of Noah, but salutary. Its very unconditional character contains "the uncompromising apocalyptic 'no' to all human religious aspiration within itself."[31] Forde is of the view that God inaugurates a new reality in the present through "creative negation" when, by cross and resurrection, the vital eschatological future invades the passing age and conquers it from within, effecting a "neo-genesis beyond the last negation of life."[32] When Christ is understood in his work, as he is here, as the inbreaking of the eschaton, and the love of God is identified as "the *power* which in resurrection wins the victory in the actual historical battle on the cross," then the cry of the Crucified, "It is finished" (John 19:30),

---

28. Forde, "Work of Christ," 94. Cf. Minear, *Kingdom and the Power*, 119: "The new Day with this new opportunity is not simply the third factor in the succession of tenses—past, pres-ent, future. It is a new creation which permeates and interrupts the apparently self-perpetuating series of days. The new Day is a projection of God's purpose from the future into the present; it is a heavenly future that judges and redeems whatever the earthly future may hold."

29. Cf. A. Schweitzer, *Quest of the Historical Jesus*, 370–71.

30. Forde, *Where God Meets Man*, 28. Cf. Mattes, "Gerhard Forde on Revisioning Theology," 279. This line of argument is central to Forde's critical evaluation of the Anselmic tradition of atonement theology set forth at length in "Work of Christ" and *Theology Is for Proclamation.* Christoph Schwöbel notes that acknowledgment of a discontinuity countered only by the con-tinuity provided by the "faithfulness of God who raises Jesus from the dead" is a pattern that "forms a central part of the gospel"; see Schwöbel, "Last Things First," 239–40.

31. Forde, "Apocalyptic No and the Eschatological Yes," in *More Radical Gospel*, 31.

32. See Braaten, "Significance of Apocalypticism for Systematic Theology," 491, 493.

becomes the epitaph of the old age, while the angelic word that "He is not here; for he has been raised" (Matt. 28:6) stands as the rubric over the advent of the new.[33] In these events, and by way of their subsequent proclamation, God "who is our end . . . does it to us": God does this by putting "an end to us both negatively and positively" as the salvation brought by the gospel both "ends us as old beings and gives us a new end."[34] This new thing that the Lord does proves definitive; it will not forfeit its novelty because, as an incursion of God's future, it stands as the unsurpassable basis of everything for which faith now hopes and waits, the permanently sharp edge of the coming age set against our present.[35]

In a late essay Forde himself summarizes very nicely the way in which soteriology is thoroughly eschatological. Eschatology, he writes, concerns

> how the future will come to us in Jesus, how the end and the new beginning breaks in upon us in Jesus' life and deeds among us, especially his death and resurrection. Here, the end comes to meet us. The eschatological "yes" invades our present. To be sure, it is clothed in the "no," in the hiddenness of the cross and even the utter unconditionality of its graciousness. It is the story of how God's sovereign future invades our present, ending the old and the beginning of the new. The apocalyptic clash of ages remains, but is now christologically anchored and done to us in the living present.[36]

We noted above that eschatological dogmatics pitches itself into a struggle for transcendence in theological reflection. We are now in a position to specify this rather broad claim further. What makes Christian dogmatics eschatological is, first, a proper preoccupation with understanding salvation as the advent of the radically new, and only thus as a *divine* act. An eschatological grammar is required to explicate the sense of the Christian gesture of pointing to Jesus and uttering, "*God. God* did this new thing for us." This is the abiding truth in Barth's assertion that Christianity must be utterly eschatological if it in fact arises from the *coming of God* to save.[37] Forde concurs, claiming that the cross is a saving event because, and only because, in it *God* conquers our dissolution and "ends it *for us* by *coming.*"[38] We might say that dogmatics

---

33. Forde, "Fake Theology," in *Preached God*, 215; Forde, *Law-Gospel Debate*, 189.
34. Forde, "Karl Barth on the Consequences of Lutheran Christology," in *Preached God*, 85.
35. For the eschatological logic of this, see Jüngel, "Emergence of the New," esp. 49–58; Forde, *Law-Gospel Debate*, 207.
36. Forde, "Apocalyptic No and the Eschatological Yes," in *More Radical Gospel*, 21.
37. K. Barth, *Epistle to the Romans*, 314: "In Jesus Christ the wholly Other, unapproachable, unknown, *eternal power and divinity* (1:20) of God has entered into our world."
38. Forde, "Work of Christ," 73.

is eschatological first and foremost because it conceives of and emphasizes salvation as God's very own action.

Second, Christian theology requires an eschatological grammar because the outworking of salvation in Christ is a matter of *ends*. Following the contours of Paul's apocalyptic gospel rather closely,[39] the cross, for Forde, proves to be the axis for the turning of the ages, a macrocosmic revolution that is also iterated in the microcosm of human being. The *finality* of this revolution and the creative *force* of the new thing it inaugurates can only come to full expression in an eschatological register, for when "God quickens, he does so by killing," as Luther famously put it.[40] So too, it seems, must the once-for-all character of salvation's accomplishment—what Forde denotes as its "christological anchor"—be articulated in eschatological terms. For only if what takes place in cross and resurrection is unsurpassable in time—only as Christ's person and work is the "unsurpassably new which does not grow old and which therefore makes all things new"[41]—can it be the final ground of Christian faith and future hope.[42] The decisiveness of the passion and resurrection of Christ is signaled fully when set forth as the "invasion of God's sovereign future" into time, the preemptive deliverance unto a destiny not of creation's own making. The resurrection of Jesus Christ is truly "a first swing of the sickle" (cf. 1 Cor. 15:23).[43] Dogmatics is also eschatological in that it acknowledges and bespeaks the finality, singularity, and unsurpassable effectiveness of the saving judgment that God renders in Jesus Christ.

Third and finally, Christian dogmatics must be eschatological if it is to do justice to the very logic and form of divine grace as such. This is a particularly strong emphasis in Forde's work: "The question about grace—whether it is a quality in the soul or the sheer divine promise—is a question of ontology versus eschatology. Is 'grace' a new eschatological reality that comes *extra nos* and breaks in upon us bringing new being to faith, the death of the old and the life of the new, or is it rather to be understood in ontological terms as an infused power that transforms old being?"[44]

It is the very *graciousness* of grace that is at stake here. The full force of the classical Reformation devices that serve to emphasize this—for example,

---

39. See de Boer, "Paul, Theologian of God's Apocalypse."

40. Luther, *Bondage of the Will*, 101. Luther himself sets 1 Sam. 2:6 as a superscription over the gospel of salvation in Christ: "The Lord kills and makes alive; He brings down to the grave and raises up."

41. Ebeling, *Dogmatik des christlichen Glaubens*, 3:129.

42. For extended reflection on this point, see Kreck, *Die Zukunft des Gekommenen*, 187–88, 203–20.

43. Dunn, *Jesus and the Spirit*, 159.

44. Forde, "Apocalyptic No and the Eschatological Yes," in *More Radical Gospel*, 32.

the logic of imputation, the alien character of the righteousness that grace delivers, the *unconditional* character of the divine promise that "while we still were sinners, Christ died for us" (Rom. 5:8), the insistence that grace comes on us from outside (*ab extra*) so that we are justified by *faith alone (sola fide)*—is only fully acknowledged when they are understood eschatologically. Nothing militates against synergism as fully and finally as the reality of the death of the sinner; and nothing affirms the divine monergism of salvation as fully and finally as its designation as "new creation." If, as Forde discerns, God's grace is pronounced in Christ so as to "establish an entirely new situation," if it is nothing less than "a re-creative act of God, something he does precisely by speaking unconditionally,"[45] then such a thing must be set forth in an eschatological discourse or not at all. Dogmatics is finally eschatological because and as it admits and articulates the victorious grace of the God of the gospel.

Concluding Remarks

What might be learned about the eschatological character of Christian dogmatics from all this, and what precisely is at stake in the contest with other contemporary options in theology generally, and resurgent historicism in particular?

First, we may ask whether it is possible to uphold the affirmations involved in Forde's account of the work of salvation that we have enumerated—summarily, that salvation worked out in Christ's cross and resurrection is an unsurpassable and utterly gracious act of God—in anything other than an eschatological register. Forde clearly thinks not; he sees his program as a contemporary re-iteration of Luther's own combat against theologizing *ad modum Aristotelis* (in the speculative manner of Aristotle), which is to say attempting to think the gospel in categories antithetical to its very character. Might we agree that the eschatological categories provided by the New Testament—casting forward to the future while anchored christologically—are finally the only ones adequate to trace the lineaments of the gospel and to "render to reality its due," as Käsemann once put it?[46]

Second, an eschatological dogmatics situates its practitioner in a peculiar way. To say that theology done in this mode is self-involving is too weak an assertion. Any account of salvation in Christ unfolded in an eschatological mode involves claims about the very constitution of present reality itself; it seeks to answer the questions "Where am I?" and "What time is it?" in ways

---

45. Forde, *Justification*, 29–30.
46. Käsemann, "On the Subject of Primitive Christian Apocalyptic," 137.

that simultaneously acknowledge that the theologian is decisively placed—not only conceptually, but also actually—by the gospel.[47] An eschatological dogmatics traffics in a new "definition of situation" that orients faith, life, and thought in view of God's "redefinition of reality despite the paradoxes of life."[48] The theologian qua believer is found in the world so described. One lives in the present under the promise and in the expectation of new life, acknowledging that one has been "inserted into the situation before God that is opened up by God's condemning and saving judgment." The world remade by the saving action of God simply *is* the site of this human life. And as Gerhard Sauter puts it, its reality is for us a "categorical indicative": "Your life *is* hidden with Christ in God" (Col. 3:3).[49] Sauter's use of the term "categorical" signals that the events of the cross and resurrection, the God of Jesus Christ who is their prime agent, and the situation they inaugurate are together absolutely *normative* for Christian faith and life, and so also for the reflective and critical work of Christian dogmatics. And they do not simply exercise the formative claim of a historical past received in the present as a compelling tradition or inheritance; rather, their normativity is a function precisely of their eschatological character: as events that are "unsurpassably new," they continually render the form of the old age past as they make all things new.[50] "This invisible pull of God's future," Paul Minear argues, determines the potential meaning of every other prospect that stands open to human beings, bringing to bear upon the present "an order of priorities that the world would reverse."[51]

Third, and finally, important epistemological matters are raised by the practice of eschatological dogmatics. Insisting that salvation in Christ entails a graciously sovereign incursion of God's future of unsurpassable consequence, an eschatological dogmatics demands a particularly robust concept of divine revelation. Indeed, because he characterizes the cross–resurrection sequence in eschatological terms, Barth identifies it *as* revelation: "This triumph, this act of victory in which the victor already exists and the vanquished likewise still

47. See Lowe, "Prospects for a Postmodern Christian Theology," 23: "Reason spontaneously seeks to contextualize that with which it deals. But Christian theology proceeds upon the quite different premise that we ourselves have been contextualized; and not just conceptually, but actually. It is we who have been inscribed."
    48. C. Frey, "Eschatology and Ethics," 74.
    49. Sauter, *Eschatological Rationality*, 197–98.
    50. When historicism despairs of the authority of the past because of its inescapable "contingency and fallibility (and with these plurality, diversity, and contestability)," it is left to take the present as "the normative site for decisions" and to appeal to pragmatic norms and criteria tuned to consequences—so Davaney, *Historicism*, 158.
    51. Minear, *Kingdom and the Power*, 117.

exist, this transition . . . from the old aeon that ends with the cross of Christ to the new one that begins with His resurrection—this transition is *revelation*, . . . the light of fulfilled time."[52] The catastrophic invasion of God's saving love from the future must register epistemically. The category of "revelation" is admittedly a rather abstract cipher on which to hang the full implications of such a claim, implications that Paul himself, at significant points in his letters, was working out in detail (e.g., Rom. 12:1–2; 2 Cor. 5:16–17).[53] But the term "revelation" does announce the very peculiar character of theological knowledge considered within an eschatological rendering of the gospel. The thought experiment with which Kierkegaard opens *Philosophical Fragments* has abiding value in signaling some of the epistemic issues ingredient in an eschatological account of Christ as the advent of divine and saving truth, and only just so as revelation.[54]

Last, it is also theology's duty to observe that just such epistemic issues accompany the work of biblical exegesis itself. The matter was winsomely explored by Minear in a volume titled *The Bible and the Historian: Breaking the Silence about God in Biblical Studies*.[55] Minear puts the central question in this way:

> What happens, then, when we discover in the Bible attitudes toward time which not only claim to be true, but which also commend themselves to us with increasing power? The entire hermeneutical system is placed in question. . . . The conception of endless, unilinear, one-way time must be modified if we are to accept the apostolic testimony. . . . If the end has actually been inaugurated, then historical time is capable of embracing simultaneously both the old age and the new. No methodology whose presuppositions on time are limited to the old age will be adequate to cope with the historicity of the new age or with the temporal collision between the two times.[56]

What should follow for historical study of the Scriptures and for hermeneutics when one is overpowered by the evangelical claim that the cross is "simply that

---

52. K. Barth, *CD* I/2:56.

53. See Martyn, "Epistemology at the Turn of the Ages" and "Apocalyptic Antinomies," in *Theological Issues in the Letters of Paul*, 89–120, 111–24.

54. Kierkegaard, *Philosophical Fragments, Johannes Climacus*, 7–36. The prominent place of eschatological categories is notable here, e.g., the Teacher brings about a "break" within the life of the student (19): the "moment" of teaching effects and makes one aware of having undergone a "new birth" from nonbeing to being (21–22); as the moment of permanent necessity and significance, the Teacher represents nothing less than the "fullness of time" (18).

55. Minear, *Bible and the Historian*; cf. Deines, "God's Role in History"; S. Adams, *Reality of God and Historical Method*.

56. Minear, *Bible and the Historian*, 54–55.

apocalyptic event which changes both the world and our perceptions of it"?[57] Such questions must forthrightly be put to all our labors over the Scriptures.

We can safely say that a thoroughly historicist theology will finally consider eschatological dogmatics nothing but a sustained and elaborate misconception, or perhaps at best an extended exercise in "strong poetry."[58] Either way it will be intellectually suspect. Conversely, a properly eschatological dogmatics will consider historicism to be an intellectually sophisticated mode of unbelief, and precisely for that reason also, if differently, rationally suspect. Is the relation between eschatological and historicist theology then an either-or, the former committed to seeing history as a function of revelation, the latter to understanding revelation to be a function of history?[59] As Christian theology pursues these matters in an eschatological or apocalyptic key—as does Gerhard Forde in his provocative and wayfinding work—its content and its form must be unfolded in a way that makes patent faith's venture that "what is going on in what takes place"[60] in Jesus Christ is in fact the Archimedean point of divine salvation and the axis on which the ages are turning. For if it is not, then it is really nothing with which we need trouble ourselves (1 Cor. 15:14).

---

57. See Duff, "Pauline Apocalyptic and Theological Ethics," 281.

58. The term is from Richard Rorty in his *Objectivity, Relativism and Truth*, 7.

59. The particular terms here are Karl Barth's: "Revelation is not a predicate of history, but history is a predicate of revelation" (CD I/2:58).

60. The phrase is from John Marsh, *Gospel of St. John*, 19–20 and 118, where it is used to characterize the particular form of Johannine historiography.

2

Apocalyptic Theology

Background, Tone, and Tasks

The end is beginning, signifies the apocalyptic tone.

—Jacques Derrida, "Of an Apocalyptic
Tone Recently Adopted in Philosophy"

We are living in apocalyptic times without an apocalyptic faith
and theology.

—Carl Braaten, "Recovery of Apocalyptic Imagination"

Apocalyptic as Theological Problem and Prospect

When the intractable presence of New Testament apocalyptic was rediscovered around the start of the twentieth century, it was acknowledged to be at once a historical fact and a theological impossibility. The parousiac Jesus and his adventist Kingdom of God, the agonistic dualism of "the ages" and its imminent catastrophic final resolution, the mythic cosmic imaginings and martial metaphysics of salvation—while all of this was, no doubt, the very stuff of primitive Christian faith and witness, it was also now, as Feuerbach had earlier said of Christianity as such, "nothing more than a *fixed idea*, in flagrant contradiction with our fire and life assurance companies, our

17

railroads and steam-carriages, our picture and sculpture galleries, our military and industrial schools, our theatres and scientific museums."[1] Contemporary theology found itself simply *at a loss* regarding biblical apocalyptic: such ancient forms of thought—adjudged "an excrescence . . . rank and wild" and something properly "left behind in the gothic nursery of the human imagination"[2]—are simply uninhabitable by us moderns; their concepts and idioms are a thoroughly devalued currency, with no purchase in or upon the present.[3] "Eschatology in the strict sense, with all its apocalyptic features," it was agreed, "has long ago passed out of our view of the world."[4] For these reasons, Christianity's original eschatological density and its contemporary dogmatic credibility stood in strictly inverse proportion to each other.[5]

The start of the twenty-first century has brought with it the suggestion that the relation between the original eschatological density of the New Testament witness and the contemporary credibility of Christian dogmatics can and must be fundamentally reset. In view is a new kind of "apocalyptic theology" that overturns the high modern view of apocalyptic as a merely antiquarian curiosity while, at the same time, repudiating the weaponized eschatologies of soothsaying doomsday calendarists, often associated with popular varieties of "apocalypticism."

This new sensibility is evident when graduating mainline seminarians are instructed that they must appropriate an apocalyptic "attitude" and "movement of mind," because their ministry and the churches they will serve "can never make do or be legitimate . . . without the themes of the radical sovereignty of God and the exercise of that sovereignty through the cross and resurrection of [God's] royal agent, Jesus Christ."[6] It is also on display where academic theologians are openly advised that they "should press forward to a robust recovery of apocalyptic teaching and preaching" precisely because such is

---

1. Ludwig Feuerbach, from the preface to the second German edition of his *Essence of Christianity*.

2. Sanday, "Apocalyptic Element in the Gospels," 104; Jennings, "Apocalyptic and Contemporary Theology," 54.

3. The German title of Klaus Koch's book *Rediscovery of Apocalyptic* expresses this clearly: modern theology finds itself *Ratlos vor der Apokalyptik* (baffled by apocalyptic), at sea in the presence of apocalyptic. The "currency" metaphor is Johannes Weiss's own; see Weiss, *Jesus' Proclamation of the Kingdom of God*, 59–60. For a concise and critical assessment of this trope and its significance, see Morse, "'If Johannes Weiss Is Right . . . ,'" 137–53.

4. So Walter Lowrie in his introduction to A. Schweitzer, *Mystery of the Kingdom of God*, 40.

5. So thought Weiss, Schweitzer, Troeltsch, et al. "If the Kingdom of God is an eschatological matter, then it is a useless concept as far as dogmatics is concerned," claimed Julius Kaftan as reported by Rudolf Bultmann, introduction to Weiss, *Jesus' Proclamation of the Kingdom of God*, xi.

6. Gillespie, "Studying Theology in Apocalyptic Times," 7.

"pressed upon us by the character of the New Testament witnesses themselves" in texts that deliver a gospel that is "apocalyptic to the core."[7] Indeed, it has been suggested that we *need* apocalyptic as a "pertinent, perhaps essential" contemporary discourse if we are to rise to meet the theological challenges of the present day.[8] Over the course of a century, something decisive has shifted in our discernment of the proper relation between biblical apocalyptic and contemporary Christian faith, life, and theology.

Essential to any telling of the story of this reversal of sensibility is the emerging conviction that the apocalyptic idiom of the New Testament is itself an indispensable *theological* vocabulary and is recognizable as such despite its strangeness.[9] It represents an originary theological discourse with which Christians have described the world, and we in it, with relentless formative reference to the sovereign God of the gospel of salvation in Jesus Christ. The recovery of apocalyptic in theology begins when we discern that this disquieting evangelical idiom is not only a historic fixture of early Christian witness, but also something that can and must, in some sense, be recovered as a permanent feature of Christian faith and theology so long as we are about the business of the gospel. The force of Käsemann's famous dictum about apocalyptic being the "mother of Christian theology" at least suggests that "apocalyptic narrative and apocalyptic expectation are integral to the logic of the gospel" itself, and thus indispensable to any genuinely evangelical theological reflection.[10] One might say that in Easter's wake, among the tongues that came upon an early church in receipt of the Spirit was the language of Christian apocalyptic, a tongue that theologians may yet learn to speak and to interpret.

From among the many things that can and should be done to further elucidate these claims and to fill out the wider theological context within which the "apocalyptic turn" in contemporary theology might be understood, I undertake only two in this chapter. First, I more directly address the question of where to place the figure of Karl Barth, paying particular attention to the important yet somewhat ambivalent role played by his work in recent

---

7. Hays, "'Why Do You Stand Looking Up toward Heaven?,'" 133.

8. Lowe, "Why We Need Apocalyptic," 41.

9. For various tellings of the story, see Jennings, "Apocalyptic and Contemporary Theology"; J. Davis, "Challenge of Apocalyptic to Modern Theology"; and from a notably different perspective, O'Regan, *Theology and the Spaces of Apocalyptic*.

10. Käsemann's original paper, "Beginnings of Christian Theology," is collected together with a range of responses in Funk, *Apocalypticism*. The quoted words are from Hays, "'Why Do You Stand Looking Up toward Heaven?,'" 116. Here, as throughout, I use the term "evangelical" in its primary sense to characterize that which is "evoked, governed and judged by the gospel," as John Webster succinctly put it in his "Self-Organizing Power of the Gospel of Christ," 69.

apocalyptic theological reflection. Second, and in a different mode, I present a series of six tersely annotated dogmatic theses. The aim of these theses is to signal concisely something of what I take to be at stake in the ongoing business of appropriating New Testament—and in particular Pauline—apocalyptic impulses. In identifying the distinctive character, foci, and most pressing tasks of Christian theology undertaken in this mode, they anticipate the key arguments I develop across the remaining chapters of this book.

Karl Barth—Pioneering Pauline Apocalyptic?

> Paul is the proper name for a ferment in the history of Christianity.
>
> —Simon Critchley, *Faith of the Faithless*

The emerging apocalyptic sensibility in theology with which we are concerned is particularly inspired by a fresh hearing of the evangelical witness of Paul. Perhaps unsurprisingly, the name of Karl Barth is often encountered in the work of its advocates. For Barth's early theology, as crystallized around the second edition of the *Romans* commentary, was marked by a volatile conjunction of themes that together fill out the meaning of the *Krisis* (the radical crisis) that Paul's gospel represents: the radical *priority* of divine agency in salvation, the uncompromisingly "vertical" or transcendent nature of God's action, the real evangelical *power* of God—a theme taken up from the Blumhardts—the inviolate *particularity* of the incarnation, and the sharp *contrast* between the old on which God's grace and Spirit fall, and the *new* thing brought into being thereby.[11] Barth swept all these themes up into the meaning of the term "eschatology" as it appears in his famous declaration that "if Christianity be not altogether eschatology, there remains in it no relationship whatever with Christ."[12] It is often suggested that the dialectical character of Barth's early eschatology is more Platonic than not, signaling a merely negative relation between a timeless eternity and temporal reality.[13] Yet it is also true that under the formative weight of Paul's own concepts, categories, and arguments, Barth

11. A concise and direct treatment of these motifs is offered by Thompson, "From Invisible Redemption to Invisible Hopeful Action in Karl Barth," esp. 50–54. On the influence of the Blumhardts for Barth's developing theology, see Collins Winn, *"Jesus Is Victor!,"* esp. 155–207, chap. 4.

12. K. Barth, *Epistle to the Romans*, 314.

13. For typical criticism of Karl Barth's "transcendent eschatology" in this vein, see Moltmann, *Theology of Hope*, 50–58; cf. Beker, *Paul the Apostle*, 142–43, where Barth is summarily treated as an instance of a "neo-orthodoxy" that evacuates future eschatology into overrealized Christology that is utterly tangential to historical reality.

was steadily driven to recast his eschatology in the form of a christological objectivism that offered an arguably "apocalyptic supplement" to received Protestant accounts of the gospel of salvation.[14]

In taking inspiration from the Pauline scholarship of Ernst Käsemann and J. Louis Martyn in particular, contemporary apocalyptic theology draws upon thinkers who themselves readily admit Barth's notable influence. Käsemann did not need Barth to introduce him to Paul's apocalyptic gospel, of course. Yet by his own admission, the German exegete devoured Barth's writings "ravenously" during a formative period.[15] As David Way observes, Barth's hermeneutical program announced in the several prefaces to his *Romans* was "of the greatest importance for the formation of Käsemann's views of the task of interpretation," cementing his conviction that Paul must be read in light of his controlling subject matter: God in his coming.[16] Käsemann did draw on Barth at various individual points in his interpretation of Paul's letter; but Barth's influence was most significant in relation to two comprehensive concerns central to Käsemann's exegetical theology as a whole: the lordship of Christ and the "theological appropriation of Paul's eschatology."[17] Like Barth's analysis, Käsemann's reading of Paul is funded by an acknowledgment that the apostle, his vocation, his communities, and his witness to the gospel, all "exist from the very first within the eschatological parameter"; Käsemann identifies that parameter as Christ's salutary reign unto God.[18]

Influenced in turn by Käsemann, Martyn's pathbreaking Pauline scholarship also manifests what Bruce McCormack has styled "a self-conscious affinity" with the theological vision Barth displays in the second edition of his *Romans* commentary.[19] McCormack goes on to argue that for Martyn and his "school"—"those who read Paul as an 'apocalyptic theologian' these

14. On this, see McCormack, "Can We Still Speak of 'Justification by Faith'?," 177–83; and more extensively, McCormack, "Longing for a New World"; cf. Smythe, "Karl Barth in Conversation with Pauline Apocalypticism," for reflections on the broad congruence of aspects of Barth's theology, with key features of the apocalyptic reading of Paul.

15. Käsemann, "Theological Review," xv.

16. Way, *Lordship of Christ*, 40.

17. Ibid., 41–42. Beverly Gaventa has observed that "what is most disturbing about Galatians has less to do with Marcion than with Barmen," explaining that Paul's singular announcement of the lordship of Christ, which "knows no boundaries and permits no limits"—taken up by Karl Barth as the theme of art. 2 of the Barmen Theological Declaration—represents the sharp edge of the gospel in Paul, a theme relentlessly emphasized by Käsemann as well. See Gaventa, "Singularity of the Gospel Revisited," esp. 199.

18. Käsemann, *Commentary on Romans*, 3. The ubiquity of invocation of hope and the present transformative pressure of the *futurum resurrectionis* in Karl Barth's *Romans*—esp. in his exegesis of chap. 6—hold out the place of the future even in his early eschatology.

19. McCormack, "Can We Still Speak of 'Justification By Faith'?," 162.

days"—Barth's commentary is "regarded not as a (largely) defensible piece of exegesis but as opening up an approach for understanding Paul which they too embrace."[20] There is little enough direct discussion of Barth in Martyn's own writing, though he does ask readers of his *Galatians* commentary to remember that "Barth was an exegete as well as a systematic theologian" who consistently argued—rightly in Martyn's judgment—that Paul's soteriology only conceives of its "problem" retrospectively, considering "Adam in the light of Christ, sin in the light of grace, and so on."[21] It is also possible, I suggest, that Martyn discerned a true echo of Paul's radical gospel of the turning of the ages in the work of his Union Theological Seminary colleague Paul Lehmann, who himself argued that Barth be embraced as a "theologian of permanent revolution"—that is, a practitioner of "Archimedean" rather than culturally reactive theology—for whom the gospel persistently unsettles all received truths of our present age, being ever "a hinge" and never "a door."[22] Certainly, Barth's vigorous registration of the "menace and the promise of the Kingdom of God" comports with Martyn's reading of the disruptive advent of a salvation that is also, at once, God's own self-revelation.[23] Be that as it may, McCormack's considered view is that Martyn's vision of a pattern of "cosmological apocalyptic eschatology" (in Martinus de Boer's phrase) captures and characterizes Barth's early reading of Paul very well; however, he also argues that Barth's later and decidedly *forensic* account of salvation, as rendered in the fourth volume of the *Church Dogmatics*, corrects this early reading and amounts to a better understanding of Paul. Implied is a judgment that apocalyptic readings of Paul of the sort advanced by Martyn might suffer certain theological weaknesses ingredient in Barth's 1922 presentation of the apostle and in fact might fare much better as interpretations of Barth on Paul than they do as readings of Paul as such.[24]

20. McCormack, "Longing for a New World," 144. He later suggests that if we look to understand the present popularity of Karl Barth's theology in the English-speaking world, to begin with, his current positive reception precisely among apocalyptic readers of Paul "would not be a bad place to start" (149).

21. Martyn, "God's Way of Making Right What Is Wrong," 144n8; Martyn reiterates this remark in his *Galatians*, 95, 163. Cf. K. Barth, *Christ and Adam*.

22. Lehmann, "Karl Barth, Theologian of Permanent Revolution," esp. at 77 and 72, where Lehmann is citing K. Barth, *Römerbrief*, 11, via his own translation. Cf. Rose, *Ethics with Barth*, 8–9, where he provides a catena of readings of Barth that associate him with a radical repudiation of the theological significance of the created order's stabilities that one associates with the radical logic of apocalyptic disjuncture. Rose himself cites these readings, including Lehmann's, in order to contest their validity.

23. The phrase is Barth's from his commentary on Philippians, cited in Gorringe, *Karl Barth*, 94.

24. McCormack, "Longing for a New World," 146–48; McCormack, "Can We Still Speak of 'Justification By Faith'?," 179. For a concise presentation of the matter, see de Boer, "Paul

But what of the invocation of Barth in the work of those who are continuing to develop "apocalyptic theology" at present? Walter Lowe's important programmatic essays look to Barth as a uniquely generative source. Lowe argues that Barth's *Romans*—a work that "throbs with an apocalyptic urgency" and is acutely alert to the perpetual crises of the age—instantiates a distinctively Christian postmodern turn, communicating a vision of "apocalyptic postmodernism" whose prospects have not yet been fully explored, let alone realized.[25] This vision conceives of history with decisive reference to God's gracious and sovereign delimiting, overreaching, and determining of all things in and by the scandalous particularity of his eschatological coming in Christ. Christian theology begins from a recognition of this divine seizure of reality, and in its tasks, tone, and tempo it must register that the God of the gospel is *"closing in."*[26] In this, it resists the quintessential move of modern rationality to contextualize, historicize, and thereby relativize and domesticate all things, the apocalyptic gospel included. Lowe suggests that pursuit of an "unqualified apocalyptic" posture in theology turns the tables on modernity: "Christian theology proceeds upon the quite different premise that we ourselves have been contextualized; and not just conceptually, but actually. It is we who have been inscribed. It may be that, whatever else it does, apocalyptic stands as a primary means by which scripture effects or announces such inscription."[27]

To the question "Why do we need apocalyptic?" Lowe replies that a Christian theology fit for purpose needs, first and foremost, to recover precisely this recognition of being contextualized by a comprehending divine reality that "presses in upon us." Apocalyptic is a scriptural idiom uniquely qualified to deliver this, to impress upon us that we are at once utterly chastened and kept "appropriately off balance" by the gospel while also entrusted to the fact that we are "suspended within the event of Jesus Christ" and that *that* is enough.[28] As he explicates this vision, Lowe looks not only to Barth's commentary on Romans but also to his *Church Dogmatics*, finding there a developed "eschatological realism" that sees the very fullness of God himself revealed—literally, "apocalypsed"—upon the world in Jesus Christ, the full "secondary objectivity . . . of God's ownmost reality—without loss, without diminution."[29]

---

and Apocalyptic Eschatology." For extended analysis and discussion of Karl Barth's theology on this score see Smythe, *Forensic Apocalyptic Theology*.

25. Lowe, "Prospects for a Postmodern Christian Theology," 19.
26. Ibid., 20, emphasis original.
27. Ibid., 23. Cf. Lowe, "Why We Need Apocalyptic," 48–50.
28. Lowe, "Why We Need Apocalyptic," 51–52.
29. Ibid., 53. The phrase "eschatological realism" is drawn from Dalferth, "Karl Barth's Eschatological Realism," a text to which Lowe himself appeals as an ally.

Nate Kerr's widely discussed study *Christ, History and Apocalyptic* also opens its engagement with Barth with a reading of the second edition of the Romans commentary. Barth's early thought emerges in Kerr's interpretation as an anti-ideological project, set firmly and expressly against theology's historicist captivity and funded by a recovery of the radical apocalyptic crisis that is the gospel. Kerr goes on to argue that Barth deploys the grammar of apocalyptic discourse—emphasizing as it does the interruptive, alien, extrinsic, miraculous, unconditioned, and *negative* character of divine activity on the world—in the service of a species of "metaphysical idealism" whose necessary counterpart is a "nihilistic description of bare 'historicity' such as we find it in Troeltsch" that evacuates the very reality of history as such.[30] Kerr's contention is that the historicity of Jesus of Nazareth himself falls victim to this project, leaving Barth bereft of any way to imagine how divine revelation can actually reach and transform us *"in our historicity."*[31]

Yet this critical assessment of Barth's early apocalyptic theology gives way to a somewhat more positive evaluation of his later treatment of history within the christological doctrine of his *Church Dogmatics*. Following leads from Douglas Harink and Joseph Mangina, Kerr lifts out the "still discernible apocalyptic 'logic'" of Barth's later theology, in which the particular historicity of Jesus Christ comes to serve as a critical ingredient in specifying the mode of God's eschatological action.[32] The transcendence of the interruptive Word of God is now specified in terms of its gracious priority and *singularity*: revelation is never a predicate of history, but history is made a predicate of revelation (as Barth puts it) precisely where and when the lordship of Christ is effectively realized in the midst of the creation and for its sake. Yet Kerr remains convinced that the metaphysical investments that structure and shape Barth's mature thinking still ultimately efface the genuine contingency of Christ's history and thus abstract his person and work from "the hard core of real history, the tragic contradictions and intricate complexities of history's broken pathways." Kerr's own ambition is to press beyond Barth on just this score, looking to repair this shortcoming by pursuing what he calls an "apocalyptic *historicism*" that is able to do better justice to the claim that "Christ is made to be Lord precisely *in* the flux and contingency of history, and that it is *through* such flux and contingency that we are made to be 'contemporaneous' with him."[33]

30. Kerr, *Christ, History and Apocalyptic*, 64–73.

31. Ibid., 73, emphasis original.

32. Ibid., 74–79. In this regard Kerr appeals to Harink, *Paul among the Postliberals*, 45–56; and Joseph Mangina, *Karl Barth*, 124–29.

33. Kerr, *Christ, History and Apocalyptic*, 91–92. Kerr's concerns about Barth's seemingly congenital inability to "take history seriously" echo those that G. C. Berkouwer expressed in his *Triumph of Grace in the Theology of Karl Barth*.

As with Lowe, so also in Kerr's account Barth figures as a theologian who crucially inaugurates an apocalyptic "turn" in Christian theology and then significantly develops its contours. But Kerr in particular adjudges Barth's work in this regard to be incomplete: it remains tethered to certain defining features of the intellectual milieu in which it was forged as well as to categories and forms inherited from the longer theological tradition that serve to frustrate its fuller advance. In both readings, however, Barth stands as a critical pivot, pathbreaker, and pioneer of apocalyptic theology because he espies and displays—even if he does not fully realize—the revolutionary theological promise of a renewed reception of Paul's eschatological gospel. Barth's tempestuous early work has pride of place in both these accounts; nevertheless, they also espy important developments of the apocalyptic sensibility in Barth's later dogmatic theology. Indeed, as Doug Harink summarizes,

> Perhaps the most remarkable imprint of Pauline logic on Barth's theology . . . is surely to be discerned in the very structure of the *Church Dogmatics*. The entire project begins with the "apocalypse," that is, with the doctrine of revelation which is determined from beginning to end by the world-dissolving and world-constituting event of God's advent in the cross and resurrection of Jesus Christ. This apocalypse epistemologically precedes and in turn determines everything that Barth will go on to say about the knowledge of God, the reality of God, the election of God, and the command of God. . . . [And he] will not treat the doctrine of creation and humanity apart from God's apocalypse in Jesus Christ, for we do not finally know their true shape and destiny apart from that revelation.[34]

Robert Jenson has argued that "modernity's great theological project was to suppress apocalyptic, and to make messianism into guru-worship."[35] Barth's comprehensive and bracing recollection that the "Gospel is the power of God, . . . the 'miraculous warfare' (Luther)" that God wages so that the old world might be "dissolved and overthrown by the victory of Christ," represents a repudiation of precisely *this* ambition of modern theology.[36] As such, it seeded a movement in theology in which eschatology moved from the obscure margins in toward the center of the theological endeavor. We have good reason to see contemporary efforts to win through to a form of Christian theology that is particularly alert to and shaped by Paul's apocalyptic gospel, as—at least in part—a ripening fruit of that particular sowing.

---

34. Harink, *Paul among the Postliberals*, 54.
35. Jenson, "Apocalypticism and Messianism in Twentieth Century German Theology," 12.
36. The citations are from remarks on Rom. 5:12–21 by K. Barth, *Epistle to the Romans*, 166.

Some Theses on Apocalyptic in Contemporary Theology

I now turn to set out a series of programmatic doctrinal theses concerning apocalyptic and contemporary theology. My aim is to suggest that the focus, form, and substance of Christian theology itself are all at issue in the effort to reappropriate the fundamental impulses of Pauline apocalyptic into the heart of our practice of theology.

1. A Christian theology funded by a fresh hearing of New Testament apocalyptic will discern in that distinctive and difficult idiom a discourse uniquely adequate both to announce the full scope, depth, and radicality of the gospel of God, and to bespeak the actual and manifest contradiction of that gospel by the actuality of the times in which we live.

Hearing the apocalyptic gospel confronts us with the claim that the divine work of salvation remakes the world as such: it is a work of cosmic scope, metaphysical depth, and universal human concern. It is a work performed by God in acts of sovereign and adventitious grace that "tear down and build up," that "kill and make alive." The apocalyptic idiom strains to articulate the gratuity of divine sovereignty and the sovereignty of divine grace. Where and when God so acts—as manifest in singular concentration in the life and death of Jesus Christ—the invasion of sovereign love and mercy is met with open and covert opposition, whose outworking threatens to belie the gospel itself. Lived faith knows all too well the experience of the manifold contradiction of the gospel. An "apocalyptic theology" indexed to the paradox of the divine victory on the cross furnishes categories that in fact well "match the realities of the present" by which faith may grasp and endure this agonistic "time between the times."[37] Thinking in this way, as Barth says, leads "straight to the place where light and darkness are locked in a grueling but victorious struggle, . . . into the kingdom of grace, into Christ, where life in its entirety becomes complicated and gets called into question, but is, nonetheless, filled with promise."[38]

2. A Christian theology funded by a fresh hearing of New Testament apocalyptic will turn on a vigorous account of divine revelation in Jesus Christ as the unsurpassable eschatological act of redemption; its talk of God and treatment of all other doctrines will thus be marked by an intense christological concentration.

37. Braaten, *Christ and Counter-Christ*, 16.
38. K. Barth, "Christian in Society (1919)," 60–61.

Hearing the apocalyptic gospel rivets our attention to the events of incarnation, crucifixion, and resurrection as the hinge on which the "ages turn." The concrete outworking of the vocation of the Son sent "in the fullness of time," these events are confessed to be the very parousia of God who draws near to save. Created, arrested, and summoned by sovereign grace, faith meets, acknowledges, and so is given to know God in and through this salutary "apocalypse of the Son" (cf. Gal. 1:16). In Christ, we are met by a revelation that acquaints us with the "*dunamis*, the meaning and power of the living God who is creating a new world."[39] The concrete form, specific intention, and particular ends of this effective self-disclosure of God in Christ provide apocalyptic theology with a positive "pleromatic space" of knowledge and substantive ethical orientation.[40] This is because "the situation between God and the world has been altered in such a fundamental and absolute way that our being in Christ radically governs the attitude we take toward life."[41] Apocalyptic theology done in this mode has its center of gravity firmly in the second, christological article of the ancient creeds of the church.

3. A Christian theology funded by a fresh hearing of New Testament apocalyptic will stress the unexpected, new, and disjunctive character of the divine work of salvation that comes on the world of sin in and through Christ. As a consequence, in its account of the Christian life, faith, and hope, it will make much of the ensuing evangelical "dualisms."

Hearing the apocalyptic gospel demands that we acknowledge that salvation is accomplished at "the end of the law" and "apart from the law," a salvation consisting in a "*new* covenant" that overreaches the distinction between pagan and Jew, a salvation whose outworking by way of juridical murder in the flesh of a marginal Jewish criminal can, by any and all available measures, be only a scandalous folly (1 Cor. 1:18). An apocalyptic theology will hold Christian faith and thought hard by such claims, demanding that it register the unexpected and disjunctive newness of the good news: the newness of the new creation, the new and second Adam, and the new covenant. It also demands that Christian faith and thought own the radical character of salvation expressed in the apocalyptic tropes of death and resurrection, the ending of the old age and the onset of the new, the overthrow of the "god of this age" by the God who is God, a new and second creation, a world "turned upside

---

39. Ibid., 40.
40. O'Regan, *Theology and the Spaces of Apocalyptic*, 29.
41. K. Barth, "Christian in Society (1919)," 53.

down," in which all things are to be "made new": these are not images of mere repair, development, or incremental improvement within a broadly stable situation. The content of Jesus's teaching, as much as Paul's testimony, bespeaks a salvation whose advent involves an unanticipated divine action that marks a radical break with what has gone before, its overturning, its revolution, its displacement. As Carl Braaten observes, "The apocalyptic God approaches history with oppositional power, in order that through crisis and conflict the existing reality may give way to a counter-reality" such that theology must reckon with "the eschatological otherness of a God who makes himself manifest first of all as the power of contradiction, of criticism, in crisis on the cross, and not in smooth continuity as the consummator and converging center of a continuing creation."[42] Correspondingly, an apocalyptic theology will insist on the standing importance of the new "dualisms"—such as that between Flesh and Spirit—that the gospel enjoins as "militant antinomies born of apocalypse."[43]

4. A Christian theology funded by a fresh hearing of New Testament apocalyptic will provide an account of salvation as a "three-agent drama" of divine redemption in which human beings are rescued from captivity to the anti-God powers of sin, death, and the devil. In addition to looking to honor the biblical witness, this is also, it is wagered, an astute and realistic gesture of notable explanatory power.

Hearing the apocalyptic gospel drives us to an account of salvation, whose fundamental form is "creative negation" of the present age, whose consequence is deliverance, and whose substance is an exchange of lordships. Such redemption from Sin represents a comprehensive account of salvation able to encompass other soteriological motifs such as atonement, guilt, and forgiveness. Apocalyptic theology will advocate for "the revolution of Life against the powers of death that surround it, the powers in which we ourselves are caught."[44] Faith in the reality of the resurrection of Jesus Christ warrants hope for a divinely wrought "future which negates the life-negating power of death."[45] This apocalyptic theological idiom may be adjudged uniquely adequate to discerning the realities of our age. Is anything less fantastical

---

42. Braaten, *Christ and Counter-Christ*, 14. He continues, pointedly, "Theology still must decide whether Aristotle or Jesus is the teacher of God and how he relates or dis-relates to the world."
43. Martyn, *Galatians*, 101.
44. K. Barth, "Christian in Society (1919)," 47.
45. Braaten, "Significance of Apocalypticism," 493.

to us than the autonomous, rationally transparent, and well-buffered self of bourgeois modernity? A soteriological discourse that speaks of our captivity, complicity, and gracious liberation into the hands of another genuine and genuinely philanthropic Lord—that discourse is able to illumine how it is that we are, in fact, played by powers, structures, and systems of all kinds (political, technological, etc.), subjected to effective discursive and disciplinary regimes (which, having been conjured by us as the outworking of sin, now prosecute us with a kind of "downward causation" all their own), and moved by unfathomable drives and obscure impulses, both psychological and social, all of which amounts to so many modes of repudiation of God's grace and freedom. Apocalyptic categories might be thought of as crucial tools of faith's historiographical discrimination—or, if you rather, faith's "bifocals"—by which we orient ourselves in the work of discerning just "what is going on" in what is taking place in the contested world in which the life of faith is now lived.[46]

> 5. A Christian theology funded by a fresh hearing of New Testament apocalyptic will acknowledge that it is the world and not the church that is the ultimate object of divine salvation. It will thus conceive of the church as a creation of the Word, a provisional and pilgrim community gathered, upheld, and sent to testify in word and deed to the gospel for the sake of the world. Both individually and corporately, the Christian life is chiefly to be understood as militant discipleship in evangelical freedom.

Hearing the apocalyptic gospel drives us to see the cosmic scope of divine salvation in the recovery, liberation, and transformation of the whole of creation. It is in the service of the salvation of this our world that the Christian community is an *ecclesia militans* (a church that struggles). "Once we have become conscious of the Life in life, we can no longer bear living in the land of death, in an existence whose forms cause us most painfully to miss the meaning of life."[47] The congregation will ever be active and forthright in its public witness and service to attest the Life that is coming to the world and seek to see God's reign justified, even now, before that world. Such discipleship involves an enactment of radical Christian freedom and love that actively denies and resists the false lordship of sin and death in open and courageous

---

46. The trope of "bifocal vision" is taken over from Martyn, "From Paul to Flannery O'Connor," 284.

47. K. Barth, "Christian in Society (1919)," 45.

testimony to the truth of the lordship of Christ, even now in *this* or *that* particular place and circumstance. Such a life of faith has Christ's own present exercise of his royal office and the ongoing empowerment of the Spirit as its basis, its media, and its hope. As Barth explains, those who hear and own the apocalyptic gospel "are not disinterested observers. We *are* moved by God. We do know God. The history of God is happening in us and toward us. The last word . . . [and thus] our 'given' is the advancing rule of God."[48] All this amounts to a distinctively Christian witness, worship, and service that takes shape in a life of *revolt*, one whose imagination is furnished and fired by the "socially aggressive and politically aggravating" apocalyptic concepts and images in which the gospel comes to us from the first.[49]

> 6. A Christian theology funded by a fresh hearing of New Testament apocalyptic will adopt a posture of prayerful expectation of an imminent future in which God will act decisively and publicly to vindicate the victory of Life and Love over Sin and Death. The ordering of its tasks and concentration of its energies will befit the critical self-reflection of a community that prays, "Let grace come and let this world pass away."[50]

Hearing the apocalyptic gospel drives us to receive the theological vocation as a call to serve the mission and service of the pilgrim church in the time that remains. In this, theology will cultivate Christian unease with the present world by calling to mind the advent of the Kingdom, lamenting its present contradiction, discerning and calling out its contemporary parables where they are to be found, and hanging all of its faith and hope on its knowledge of the God of Jesus Christ.[51] Apocalyptic theology will be a nonspeculative, concrete, and practical form of knowing, committed to the work of discerning the signs of the times by Scripture and Spirit. It will itself be a militant discourse, always on the verge of tipping over into proclamation, offering at most a kind of urgent and sufficient traveling instruction for pilgrims, and as such will be lovingly impatient with more contemplative theological postures. Its primary service will always be to serve the vital clarification of the Christian witness to the present salutary agency of the crucified and risen One, to whom faith owes allegiance and obedience.

48. Ibid., 51.
49. Braaten, *Christ and Counter-Christ*, 17–18. That the Christian life as a whole might be properly set under the rubric of "revolt" is a claim advanced late in life by Karl Barth in *CD* IV/4, *Christian Life*, esp. 205–13.
50. *Didache* 10.6.
51. See Lowe, "Why We Need Apocalyptic," 52.

Reading over and reflecting upon these theses, one might well ask whether such "apocalyptic theology" is possible at all, or whether, by its own accounting, there is really no time for such an undertaking. Does the very existence of the intellectual, institutional, and personal "space" to pursue such theology belie its seriousness and reality?[52] Or is the writing of such theology itself part of the faithful business of "waiting in action," the "anticipating and hastening" (2 Pet. 3:12) required of Christians and their congregations in this time? This project goes forward on the basis that the latter is the case. Just so, theologians must harbor no illusions about the entirely provisional and transitory character of their dogmatic labors. For the apocalyptic gospel ever reminds us that on the horizon of all our theological endeavors—as indeed, of all things—there stands,

> In the new Day's reversal of values, the decree
> That every mouth be stopped
> While grace invades, abases and destroys,
> And with each shoot of mortal skill and wisdom lopped
> In total loss,
> Christ holds the Sum of joys,
> No tree upon our land except his Cross.[53]

---

52. One might take such questions as echoes of the searching criticisms of modern Christian theology *as such*, as once ventured by Franz Overbeck; see his *On the Christianity of Theology*.
53. Clemo, "Awakening," 69.

PART 2

Christ, Spirit, and Salvation in an Apocalyptic Key

A Sovereign Love

The Royal Office of Christ the Redeemer

O LORD our God,
> other lords besides you have ruled over us,
> but we acknowledge your name alone.

> —Isaiah 26:13

The Spiritual Character of the *Munus Regnum Christi*

The doctrine of Christ's offices has long served Protestant theology as an important device by which to organize exposition of his saving work.[1] In its best-known form—that of the *munus triplex*, or "threefold office"—Jesus Christ is acknowledged as the prophet, priest, and king of divine salvation,

---

1. Bornkamm, "Amt Christi." Though it does not originate in the work of the Reformers, the threefold office came to particular prominence in Calvin's work (see his *Institutes* 2.15) and went on to provide the scheme through which to analyze the work of Christ in both Lutheran and Reformed orthodoxy. See Heppe, *Reformed Dogmatics*, 481–82; Schmid, *Doctrinal Theology*, 370–71. Alongside its close study of Luther's theology of the "twofold office," Karin Bornkamm also provides extensive historical discussion of ideas regarding Christ's offices in the ancient, medieval, and early modern periods in *Christus—König und Priester*. The formative role of this teaching is evident by its appearance in Protestant catechetical texts, including Calvin's Geneva Catechism, arts. 37–38; the Heidelberg Catechism, qq. 31–32; Luther's Small Catechism, q. 132; and the Westminster Catechism, qq. 23–26.

the singular concentrated fulfillment and antitype of these roles as they are depicted in the scriptural history of ancient Israel. By means of this scheme, the manifold character of his saving activity as the "one Mediator between God and humankind" is ordered and displayed. The scheme of the threefold office has been subject to sustained criticism since the nineteenth century on various grounds, chief among which are its alleged failure to do justice to the historical reality and activity of Jesus of Nazareth and the inappropriateness of applying the titles of prophet, priest, and king to him when these are understood in rigorously *religionsgeschichtliche* (history-of-religions) terms.[2]

Not all historical-critical scholarship supports such a judgment, and recent Christian theology has shown itself willing to continue to work with the scheme on the far side of such criticism. The most significant example of this is Karl Barth's creative use of a variant of the *munus triplex* as the essential architecture of his massive account of the doctrine of reconciliation, where it affords a means by which to overcome what the Swiss theologian considered deeply unhelpful divisions between Christology, soteriology, and hamartiology, which have dogged the theological tradition.[3] Others working since Barth have also continued to find the formula valuable in ordering comprehensive accounts of Christ's saving work.[4]

So it is still largely with reference to this scheme that doctrinal reflection on Christ's lordship—his *munus regnum*, "royal or kingly office"—has been undertaken and continues to take place. The theme of the lordship of Christ, together with its wide-ranging ecclesial and political consequences, was a central preoccupation of ecumenical theology within the World Council of Churches in its first two decades.[5] Extended treatments of the theme from the postwar period were typically advanced as correctives to long-standing

2. Albrecht Ritschl wrote of the "purely arbitrary analysis of the word 'Christ'" and "superficial formalism," which underwrote the traditional account of the *munus triplex* with the result that modern theology must adjudge that "the doctrine of the three offices spells failure" (*Christian Doctrine of Justification and Reconciliation*, 427, 431). On related grounds, the doctrine was rejected by Wolfhart Pannenberg in his *Jesus-God-Man*, 212–25. In vol. 2 of his more recent *Systematic Theology*, 445–49, he reiterates the earlier criticism that "the historical Jesus, then, was neither priest, nor king nor, in the strict sense, prophet" (445). But he now also sees more dogmatic value in the teaching of the threefold office on the basis of the significant admission that "the earthly activities [of Jesus] have contexts other than those that appear on a purely historical approach" (446).

3. See K. Barth, *CD* IV/1–3.

4. For three examples of quite different kinds, see Berkouwer, *Work of Christ*, 58–87; Wainwright, *For Our Salvation*, 99–186; and more extensively Sherman, *King, Priest, and Prophet*.

5. Indicatively, see the working paper prepared by the Division of Studies of the World Council of Churches, "Lordship of Christ over the Church and the World"; cf. Hasselmann, "Lordship of Christ in Ecumenical Discussion."

neglect of the royal motif in Protestant soteriology, a neglect rooted in nearly exclusive concentration on Christ's priestly or prophetic work, and so also on substitutionary atonement or salutary teaching respectively.[6] Yet already around the start of the twentieth century, when Johannes Weiss and Albert Schweitzer were putting the centrality of the Kingdom of God as a specifically *apocalyptic* reality back on the christological agenda, others were also moving in a parallel way to reassert the primacy of the *munus regnum* within the threefold scheme. So E. F. Karl Müller, writing just before the outbreak of the First World War, concluded his brief article on the doctrine by asserting that "the permanent union and simultaneous exercise of the three functions do not exclude, however, a fixed aim, namely the kingdom. To this as the organizing purpose of the whole points before everything the Biblical basis of the formula, the starting-point and essential content of the Messianic office is royal dominion over and for God's people, the peculiar modification of which is described by the other titles."[7]

It can be argued that the substance of this claim was already borne out in Calvin's own seminal account of the threefold office in the 1559 edition of his *Institutes of the Christian Religion*, where it is the *munus regnum* that in fact dominates the compressed presentation of the doctrine of the threefold office.[8] And Calvin's teaching here could be characterized as "messianic" inasmuch as he acknowledges that Christ combines in his person the roles of king and pastor as the one through whom God wills to protect, direct, bless, and secure the "everlasting preservation" of his covenant people the church. Moreover, Calvin argues expressly that "Christ was called Messiah especially with respect to, and in virtue of, his kingship."[9] In support of this understanding of Christ's kingship and in order to display, as he says, its "efficacy and benefit for us, as well as its whole force and eternity," Calvin is at great pains to emphasize its *spiritual* character. Calvin's glosses on the meaning of "spiritual" concern the eternal, incorruptible character of Christ's reign and focus on the distribution of the gifts and power of the Holy Spirit by means of which he secures victory for his people over "the devil, the world,

---

6. See, e.g., Bosc, *Kingly Office of the Lord Jesus Christ*; and Visser 't Hooft, *Kingship of Christ*.

7. Müller, "Jesus Christ, Threefold Office of"; cf. Bosc, *Kingly Office of the Lord Jesus Christ*, 10: "Without doubt, the character which dominates the eschatological Messiah is that of the King."

8. Calvin, *Institutes* 2.15.1–6, where §§3–5 treat of the royal office. In his *Christian Doctrine of Creation and Redemption* (314), Emil Brunner remarks, "The fact that in his presentation the largest part is given to the office of King, is in harmony with the whole of Calvin's outlook, and also with that of the earliest creed of the Church, *Kyrios Christos*."

9. Cf. Calvin, *Institutes* 2.6.3.

and every kind of harmful thing." The spiritual work of Christ's reign is to "share with us all that he has received from the Father" and to do so with salutary power to the end that, being "launched into history," the church is built up and believers advanced in assurance and sanctity until the time when the glory of the Kingdom will be manifest.[10]

As Calvin summarizes, Christ "rules—inwardly and outwardly—more for our own sake, than for his."[11] Here, in other words, Christ's kingship is spiritual because the power by which he reigns is heavenly and not "of this world"; it is spiritual because his dominion is accomplished not by worldly means but rather by virtue of his own priestly and prophetic work;[12] and it is spiritual because he is "armed with eternal power" such that "the devil, with all the resources of the world, can never destroy the church."[13] We do well to recognize in all of this the public, gracious, agonistic, and eschatological force of Christ's spiritual rule as Calvin sets it forth. Calvin's exposition of the spiritual nature of Christ's lordship bears the imprint of the witness and language of the concluding verses of Romans 8, and it shares something of their eschatological and apocalyptic tone.

We find something similar in Martin Luther's influential treatment of this same motif. Like Calvin, Luther too is at pains to emphasize the *spiritual* character of Christ's kingship. Citing John 18:36 ("My kingdom is not from this world"), Luther considers that Christ is a true king, "but not after the fashion of the flesh and the world, for . . . He reigns in heavenly and spiritual things and consecrates them—things such as righteousness, truth, wisdom, peace, salvation, etc."[14]

In his work "The Freedom of a Christian," however, Luther also shows himself to be concerned that firm stress on the spiritual character not be taken to imply the impotence of Christ in the world: quite the opposite is true. In a cardinal passage that amounts to a sustained gloss on Romans 8:28–39 and its Pauline parallels, he speaks of the decisive effectiveness of Christ's reign in the world. To speak of Christ's kingship as spiritual "does not mean that all things on earth and in hell are not also subject to him— otherwise how could he protect and save us from them?—but his kingdom

---

10. "Launched into history, [the church] grows and increases until the advent of Christ," declares T. F. Torrance, who identifies these two motifs of *aedificatio ecclesiae* (building up of the church) and *profectus fidelium* (perfecting of the faithful) as hallmarks of Calvin's understanding of the reign of God in and through Christ; see Torrance, *Kingdom and Church*, 96, 116; cf. 113–21.

11. Calvin, *Institutes* 2.15.4.

12. Torrance, *Kingdom and Church*, 123.

13. Calvin, *Institutes* 2.15.3.

14. Luther, "Freedom of a Christian," 62.

consists neither in them nor of them."[15] When we speak of Christ's kingship, we speak of his *power*, a power by means of which the Christian is secured and made radically free within the world; indeed, it is an "inestimable" power that reigns "in the midst of enemies and is powerful in the midst of oppression."[16]

Saying that this power is spiritual, as Luther consistently stresses, does not mitigate or delimit it but rather specifies its form and aim. The purpose of Christ's royal power is ever to secure human salvation, and its form is the communication of a radical liberty for human service, which is grasped by confident faith in the evangelical promises of God even—and especially—amid weakness, suffering, and persecution in the world.[17] Importantly, Luther here elects to interpret Romans 8:28—a *locus classicus* for reflection on general divine providence—by referring it specifically to Christ's exercise of his royal office. It is also notable that Luther's discourse on this motif, like Calvin's, echoes the agonistic and apocalyptic tenor of Paul's discourse in the eighth chapter of Romans.

It must be said, however, that the subsequent career of this Reformation emphasis on the spiritual character of Christ's royal office leads in a quite different direction from that seemingly pursued by Calvin and Luther themselves. In later debates concerning the nature of Christ's kingship, an ambiguity comes to attend the meaning of "spiritual": with what is it rightly contrasted? As "soul" with "body"? As "inner" with "outer"? As "church" with "world"? As "future" with "present"?[18] When the "spiritual" question arises, the leading resolution of these ambiguities in modern Protestant theology is decisive and of lasting influence. Schleiermacher's important and influential account of the *munus regnum* conceives that "nothing remains as the immediate sphere of His kingship but the inner life of men individually, and in their relation to each other"; this reign being exercised entirely in virtue of "the inner vital relationship in which each individual stands to Christ."[19] Amplifying and sharpening distinctions long made in Protestant orthodoxy between Christ's economic or donative rule and his natural or essential rule, Schleiermacher firmly demarcates Christ's kingship from the divine sovereignty of the Father, concentrates its form and scope exclusively in the church, and furthermore

15. Ibid., 62.

16. Ibid., 63–64.

17. For insightful commentary on this vital passage in Luther's tract, see Jüngel, *Freedom of a Christian*, 70–76.

18. For recent discussion of these debates see VanDrunen, *Natural Law and the Two Kingdoms*, esp. 432 for summary remarks.

19. Schleiermacher, *Christian Faith* §105, here 467, 473.

within the church, in the souls of individuals who experience "the purely spiritual lordship of His God-consciousness."[20]

It is fair to say that the end point of this trajectory is honestly and elegantly set out in a famous passage from Adolf von Harnack's *The Essence of Christianity*:

> The kingdom of God comes by coming to the individual, by entering into his soul and laying hold of it. True, the kingdom of God is the rule of God; but it is the rule of the holy God in the hearts of individuals; it is God himself in his power. From this point of view everything that is dramatic in the external and historical sense has vanished; and gone, too, are all the external hopes for the future. . . . It is not a question of angels and devils, thrones and principalities, but of God and the soul, the soul and its God.[21]

Shorn now of any dramatic and historical "husk," the kernel of Jesus's message regarding the reign of the God of the gospel in and by him remains as "a still and mighty power in the hearts of men."[22] In fact, to speak of Christ himself actively "reigning" is still a step too far into antique mythical discourse for the properly modern mind. In this line, to affirm that the kingdom which Christ teaches is "spiritual" demands that it be conceived as something wholly inward, wholly personal, wholly immaterial, and wholly actualized by the personal moral actions of women and men. The historical, external, public, and political are, as it were, largely left to themselves. These developments, it must be said, inadvertently fertilized the soil in which were to grow up dangerously distorted accounts of the doctrine of the two kingdoms in subsequent decades.[23]

The modest ambition of this chapter is to reflect on what a fresh hearing of the witness of Romans 8—and in particular of its closing section—offers for theology anxious to revisit the question of the "spiritual" character of the *munus regnum* of Jesus Christ. I do so cognizant of the evident influence of this text and its themes in the formative accounts of Christ's royal office found already in Calvin and Luther as noted above. If Romans 8:31–39 offers

---

20. Ibid., here 473. On these distinctions in Reformed theology of the seventeenth and eighteenth centuries, see Heppe, *Reformed Dogmatics*, 481–82. For the parallel materials from Lutheran theologians, see Schmid, *Doctrinal Theology*, 370–71, esp. the distinctions drawn between the Christ's *regnum potentiae*, *regnum gratiae*, and *regnum gloriae* (reign of power, reign of grace, and reign of glory).

21. Harnack, *What Is Christianity?*, 56.

22. Ibid., 54.

23. For survey and analysis of leading nineteenth- and twentieth-century interpretations, see W. Wright, *Martin Luther's Doctrine of God's Two Kingdoms*, 17–44.

not only a summary of chapter 8, or even of the argument of chapters 5–8, but in fact presents us with "the sum of Paul's theology," as might be claimed, then we have good reason to inquire as to its bearing on this matter.[24] More particularly, I am provoked to revisit this theme in relation to this text by two observations made by Reformed theologian Otto Weber in his own discussion of the *munus regnum*.

First, Weber remarks that Calvin's rendering of the doctrine reflects the deep logic of evangelical *promeity*, that is, that the God of the gospel is fundamentally "for me" or "for us" in love and grace. He argues that "the emphasis on 'for us' is the central theme of all that Calvin has to say about the 'office' of Christ. Nothing happens here 'for itself,' but everything is 'for us.' Soteriology is nothing other than Christology properly understood and accepted."[25] Celebration and elucidation of the theme of "God for us" is undoubtedly at the heart of the climax of Romans 8, and deepening our appreciation of these promises will help us win through to a proper understanding of Christ's kingship. Second and in strong reaction to the position represented by Harnack, Weber argues for a markedly different understanding of the spiritual nature of Christ's dominion. Over against a construal of Christ's spiritual rule—here in Albrecht Ritschl's formulation—as the "divinely vouched for highest good of the community" and an "ethical idea" for the sake of whose realization Christians "bind themselves together through their definite reciprocal action," Weber contends that Christ's dominion is spiritual precisely as it is *eschatological*.[26] As he writes:

> "Spiritual rule," a traditional term, does not mean that the kingly rule of Christ is intellectual [*geistliche*] or ethical in nature. We do not understand the Kingdom as a "religious idea" . . . but rather as the Eschaton, which we do not bring about but which we are called to accept and to expect. . . . The "reign" is "spiritual" properly understood as an eschatological reality, breaking into our world pneumatically . . . [i.e.,] that which is presently active in the Spirit, which is already being introduced . . . [but] cannot be calculated in terms of what is going on within the "history of death."[27]

Such a firmly eschatological account of the royal office comports very well with a wider hearing of Paul's own apocalyptic gospel, a gospel whose primary

---

24. So Käsemann, *Commentary on Romans*, 252.
25. O. Weber, *Foundations of Dogmatics*, 2:174.
26. The citation from Albrecht Ritschl comes from his *Instruction in the Christian Religion* as found in *Three Essays*, 174–75.
27. O. Weber, *Foundations of Dogmatics*, 2:253–54, translation altered.

concern is with "the assault of grace on the world and the sphere of corpo-reality" and the seizure of power in and over us by the determinative onset of the Spirit of Christ, the crucified and risen Lord.[28] Paul's witness in Romans 8 serves to remind us that the royal office of Jesus Christ is not an abstract idea to be implemented by us but rather our acknowledgment of "the presence of the Lord who acts."[29] The point is that in discharging his royal office, Jesus Christ really "*makes history* for all of humankind" in virtue of his being the sovereign power and claim of the very God of love.[30]

The Witness of Romans 8:31–39—The Dominion of the Lord of Love

The following theological observations on the form and substance of the final verses of Romans 8 aim to elucidate Weber's suggestive assertion that Christ's spiritual lordship is eschatological in nature. Alert in particular to the apocalyptic character of Paul's climactic conclusion to the so-called second proof of his letter in chapters 5–8, I will remark briefly on three salient aspects of this witness: first, the depiction of the *agōn* (struggle) of the church militant; second, Christ's possession of the saints and his status as cosmocrator; third and finally, the mutually defining relation of divine love and divine lordship.

"We Are Reckoned as Sheep for the Slaughter": A Church Militant

The community that acknowledges the revelation of Christ's lordship is beset in this world. These verses represent the church as a community under assault. Indeed, much of the passage (Rom. 8:31–39) is devoted to enumerat-ing the manifold threats that conspire against those Christ claims as his own. Paul distills the threats into the series of rhetorical questions that animate the passage. The Christians to whom he writes are afraid of that which stands *against* them (v. 31), which threatens to *impeach* and *condemn* them (v. 33) and so also to *separate* them from their God and Christ (vv. 35, 39). The present is a time of suffering for the community, as Paul has already said (v. 18): faith knows that the Pax Romana—and all its successors, which purportedly govern our own day and age—deliver no real peace at all.[31] The trials of affliction, distress, persecution, hunger, nakedness, peril, and the sword—a list perhaps reflecting Paul's own experiences, perhaps recalling those of Christ himself,

---

28. Käsemann, *Commentary on Romans*, 213, 222.
29. Bosc, *Kingly Office of the Lord Jesus Christ*, 44.
30. Jüngel, "Der königliche Mensch," 240, my translation.
31. See Jewett, *Romans: A Commentary*, 508–9.

or else reiterating a stereotyped antique catalogue of tribulations[32]—are all too well known to the churches in Rome, for they are a consequence of the violent reflexes of the age that is passing away. Whatever Christ's kingship entails, it does not insulate the Christian community from the agony of the clash of the ages; neither is the existence of such distress a mark of divine disfavor, as might perhaps anxiously be thought. Rather, Paul stresses that such sufferings are truly for the sake of the God of the gospel (v. 36); they are the mark of a faith conformed to Christ, who was himself delivered over to death (vv. 32–33). As Karl Barth comments, "Even this tumult can only bind Christians more closely to him against whom that tumult is really aimed."[33]

Although the threat has a variety of specified aims and forms, here it has no single clear source or definite identity. The origin of this assault, whatever it is that brings about "all these things" (v. 37), would seem to be the "no one" that is the implied answer to Paul's driving questions: "Who is against us?" "Who shall impeach us?" "Who will condemn?" "Who will separate?"[34] The juxtaposition of this "no one" with frank and open admission of the painful reality of the assault is jarring. Perhaps like those "gods that are no gods" yet still previously enslaved the gentiles (cf. Gal. 4:8), so here the powers of the dying age exercise themselves impotently yet still actually on the church, even as they once did on its Lord. "Paul has," Barth writes, "visualized a whole upsurge of spiritual realities, a whole agitated sea of hidden rebellion of which the persecution of the Christians is merely a symptom."[35] Perhaps this reality is also reflected in the *hapax legomenon* "supervictors" or "more than conquerors [ὑπερνικῶμεν, *hypernikōmen*]" in verse 37: Christians do not simply prevail against such assaults because the struggle here is not being fought by opponents of the same kind. Rather, Christians are themselves a stake in the contest between the powers of the fallen creation animated by the *nihil*—the annihilating nothingness—of the passing age and Jesus Christ, "the unresting arm of God."[36] Theirs is a "triumph of the assaulted" that is owed entirely to the work of another.[37] George Fox, the early Quaker leader, memorably expresses this salutary asymmetry when he comments on this passage: "Such as are more than conquerors see the end of wars, and that which causeth wars. He that is a conqueror may be in the war; but he that is

---

32. Ibid., 544–45; cf. Witherington, *Paul's Letter to the Romans*, 233.

33. K. Barth, *Romans: A Shorter Commentary*, 108.

34. Beverly Gaventa observes that in the first instance Paul implies only that "some agent" (τις) does in fact attempt—impossibly but really—to stand against those whom God is for ("Neither Height nor Depth: Discerning," 273).

35. K. Barth, *Romans: A Shorter Commentary*, 108.

36. K. Barth, *Epistle to the Romans*, 327, translation altered.

37. Käsemann, *Commentary on Romans*, 251.

more than a conqueror, is in that which takes away the occasion of wars, and is come to that which was before wars were."[38]

The painful struggle in which Christians are caught up is not merely with "blood and flesh" (Eph. 6:12) but with conspiring powers that beset the people of God: these powers of the "old aeon, rebellious, threatening, and perverted,"[39] are themselves being overcome by "the God of peace who," Paul assures, "will shortly crush Satan under [their] feet" (Rom. 16:20). This is what funds the hope that all creatures may yet be drawn into the divine peace that was indeed intended from the first, "before wars were." The belligerence of the passing age has been and is ever outbid by the peaceable sovereignty of the Christ of God exercised on the cross. Paul admits that faith hopes for this peace in the teeth of all appearances (8:24–25) in a Spirit-inspired act of the "most powerful, the most paradoxical, and the most venturing faith."[40]

In sum, Christ's spiritual kingship is eschatological in that it draws the congregation into—and promises ultimately to lead it through—the present struggle between the old and new ages. Life animated by the hope of such a supervictory has already been seized by the congregation on the basis of the reality of Christ's redemption, and so it polemically "represents the earthly rule of the truth" in the present by its faith and discipleship. Käsemann was surely right to claim that "only the apocalyptic worldview can describe reality *thus*."[41]

"None Can Separate Us": Christ's Possession of His Church amid the Cosmos

The second motif to be considered is closely related to the first. The great list of threats to the Christian community that Paul enumerates here is summarily captured in a single concept: *separation*. The term (χωρίζω, *chōrizō*, to separate) is used elsewhere in the New Testament and cognate literature to describe a movement into isolation, a distancing, and the undoing of personal relationships, including the case of divorce.[42] In this context, the separation that threatens is severance from "the love of Christ" (v. 35) or the "love of God in Christ Jesus our Lord" (v. 39). To be removed from the ambit of divine love would entail nothing less than the forfeit of salvation itself.[43] It would be

---

38. Fox, *Great Mystery*, 3:160.
39. Käsemann, *Commentary on Romans*, 247.
40. Tillich, "Meaning of Providence," 106.
41. Käsemann, *Commentary on Romans*, 251.
42. See Danker et al., *Greek-English Lexicon*, s.v. "χωρίζω."
43. See Jewett, *Romans: A Commentary*, 543.

synonymous with the dissolution of our being "in Christ," a soteriological motif at the heart of Paul's gospel.[44] There can surely be no thought of cool mystical ontology in connection with this motif: as we have just observed, this passage makes plain that to be "in Christ" is to be recruited by the sovereign movement of grace and the Spirit's advent for worship and active service in the church militant. To be "in Christ" is to have been seized by divine grace and set within the sphere of his active domain; it is to be incorporated into the lordship of the crucified.[45] Thus, while the peril of separation Paul considers here can be thought to be that of personal defection, it ought more properly and basically to be understood as the threat of being repossessed by other alien powers and lords (cf. Gal. 5:1).

We can improve our purchase on this idea by recalling that basic to Pauline anthropology is the view that to be a human being—to have life in the body as a creature of this world—is to be irrevocably knit into the fabric of "the world" and always and everywhere subject to rule. In his famous essay "On the Subject of Primitive Christian Apocalyptic," Käsemann explains:

> Man, for Paul, is never just on his own. He is always a specific piece of world and therefore becomes what in the last resort he is by determination from outside, i.e., by the power which takes possession of him and the lordship to which he surrenders himself. His life is from the beginning a stake in the confrontation between God and the principalities of this world. In other words, it mirrors the cosmic contention for the lordship of the world and is its concretion. As such, man's life can only be understood apocalyptically.[46]

Romans 5:12–21 portrays the antithesis of Adam and Christ as a global confrontation of "alternative, exclusive, and ultimate" spheres in which the "old world and a new world are at issue. . . . There is no third option."[47] To be at home in the world of Adam is to be claimed, formed, and driven by its constellation of overlapping and mutual contesting sovereignties; it is to be possessed by the "ravishing and enslaving powers" of the rebellious creation.[48] Owned in this way by sin, women and men are bound to serve what Barth calls the "inevitable" and "monstrous" disparities of the rebellious creation,

44. See Campbell, *Quest for Paul's Gospel*, 38–42, 110–11.
45. See Käsemann, *Commentary on Romans*, 219, where he contends that the motif of "union with Christ" must be understood as dynamic incorporation into Christ's lordship by the power of the Spirit.
46. Käsemann, "On the Subject of Primitive Christian Apocalyptic," 136.
47. Käsemann, *Commentary on Romans*, 146.
48. Martyn, Comment 39, in *Galatians*, 370–71; cf. Käsemann, "On Paul's Anthropology," 27–28; Käsemann, "Healing the Possessed," 198.

and to be ground up in their arena.[49] On such a view, salvation must come as *redemption*, a repossession of creaturely life by God out from under the catastrophic dominion of sin and so the consequent surrender and loss of a whole previously determinative world of meaning.[50] As has already been signaled, the concept of lordship proves decisive here. Käsemann again declares: "Redemption means nothing else but a change of lordship—indeed, a return from slavery to supra-earthly and earthly powers to the Father who awaits his children and in promise says to each, 'I am your God because I remain your Creator, and as Creator, I must be and remain for and not against humankind. . . . Transferred into the kingdom of his beloved Son, we belong to a world that likewise has its lord and king.'"[51] Paul can distill the "problem" of Romans 5–8 into a singular fear of separation precisely because the positive reality of salvation is essentially that of being repossessed from the world of sin by the effective reign of the crucified and risen Christ, the Lord who gathers us into the freedom of his service, and by whom we are ever claimed. His people—chosen, called, justified, and glorified—fundamentally *belong* to Jesus Christ, in whom God's primordial purpose is publically realized and displayed.[52] By winning and holding his people "in Christ," God demonstrates a divine faithfulness to creation and covenant that surpasses any and all "human dereliction."[53] The saving action that begins with election cannot ultimately be frustrated: once again we see that present faith and hope rest on an eschatological reality, here that of Jesus Christ as Lord *of lords*, who will not be dispossessed of all he would win for the Kingdom of God. The incarnate Son is recognized to be the strong man of his own parable, "who invades the tyrant's house and by his power subdues him, binds him, and spoils him of all he has unjustly usurped."[54]

Hence, although it is undoubtedly true to affirm that Paul here teaches that "God's power to pursue is greater than our power to escape,"[55] in fact his gospel is more basically concerned to affirm that Christ *must reign* (1 Cor. 15:25)

49. K. Barth, *Epistle to the Romans*, 329.

50. On this, see Martyn, "Apocalyptic Gospel in Galatians," 257–58. One wonders how these pairs of creaturely/cosmic realities (vv. 38–39) might be related to those other cosmic antinomies that Paul knows to have been rendered meaningless by the apocalypse of the gospel in Galatians 3 (esp. 3:23–29). See Martyn, "Apocalyptic Antinomies."

51. Käsemann, "Healing the Possessed," 198. One thinks of passages such as Rom. 5:17, 21; 6:9, 12, 14, where Paul speaks of the displacement of the reign of sin and death by the reign of Christ and grace.

52. See Ziesler, *Paul's Letter to the Romans*, 218.

53. Käsemann, "Righteousness of God in an Unrighteous World," 183.

54. See Torrance, *Incarnation*, 78, 155.

55. Rossow, "Hound of Heaven," 93.

amid and over all the disordered powers of the creation. As I mentioned in the introduction to this book, Beverly Gaventa has rightly reminded us that Paul's theology centrally concerns "the unimaginable size of God's actions on behalf of the entire cosmos, including humanity itself."[56] For Paul, discussion of the fate of the Christian community and its assurance is encircled and bound up with a decidedly *cosmic* discourse: it is the whole creation (not just the Christian congregation) that longs and hopes for the eschatological resolution of God's saving work (Rom. 8:9–25), and as the final verses of chapter 8 indicate, it is the cosmos in all its dimensions that is subjected to God's sovereign love for the sake of realizing that very salvation. The catalogue offered in verses 38–39 is particularly notable on this score. For it signals that all dimensions of creaturely life are effectively superintended by the dominion of Christ's saving love: the biological (life, death), the temporal/historical (present, future), and the metaphysical (angels, powers, and principalities), as well as the physical or possibly astrophysical (height, depth). The inclusion of *all things* in Paul's final flourish—"nor anything else in all creation"!—is not hyperbole but an "all-embracing addendum" expressing faith's conviction that, having been raised to the right hand of the Father, Christ even now exercises his royal office over all things (v. 34).[57] As Edward Adams explains, "The rhetorical effect of closing the catalogue with *tis ktisis hetera* [anything else in creation] is to qualify the preceding items in such a way that these potential threats are now brought within the compass of God's creation and the sphere of his control. . . . All possible menaces to the believer are comprehended within God's creative and providential purposes: even the hostile spiritual powers are placed within the orb of the created order."[58] For present purposes, note in particular the way Paul here closely associates the salutary work of the risen and ascended Christ with divine governance of creation as a whole, perhaps thereby indicating the grounds for his earlier providential claim that "all things work together for good for those who love God" (v. 28). The only world Paul knows is the one in which creaturely powers of all kinds are "being reduced" under "continued pressure from the regnant Christ."[59] In this way Paul identifies the power of Christ as the very power of the Creator, suggesting thereby that the characterization of salvation as "new creation" is no mere rhetorical flourish when understood evangelically. Moreover—and this is a

---

56. Gaventa, *Our Mother Saint Paul*, 84.

57. For discussion of the details of the catalog, see Jewett, *Romans: A Commentary*, 550–54; cf. Gaventa, "Neither Height nor Depth: Discerning," 273–77; E. Adams, *Constructing the World*, 183–86.

58. E. Adams, *Constructing the World*, 185.

59. Caird, *Principalities and Powers*, 82; cf. 16.

theme to which we will return—if it is true that we may discern something of the nature of Christ's lordship from its association with the power of the Creator God here, then surely the reverse must also be the case: the specific character of Christ's reign as it is attested in the gospel speaks decisively of the nature of divine creative and providential rule per se.

In these ways we learn that to characterize Christ's kingship as *spiritual* means acknowledging that Christ exercises a *divine* office marked by the power to redeem his beloved creatures from their captivity to false gods and lords, an act whose nature, scope, and effectiveness bespeak nothing less than the creative power of God. This kingship is *eschatological* inasmuch as it stakes a full and indissolubly *final* claim on our lives, our service, and our destiny. This it can and may do because there is nothing within the sphere of the creation—heaven and earth, invisible and visible—that falls beyond the present rule of the ascended Christ.[60]

"The Love of God in Christ Jesus Our Lord": A Lordship of Love

We come then, more briefly, to venture a third and final observation on the significance of Romans 8:31–39 for our understanding of the lordship of Christ. It is highly significant that in these verses Paul explicitly testifies that the royal work of Christ is the outpouring of divine *love* itself. The claim that God is "for us" (v. 31) stands as a title over the remainder of the chapter. And the substance and form of this *promeity* are simply the very series of events in which God does not spare his Son but comes low, giving him up unto death, then raises and exalts him to the heavenly session for the sake of his intercession for us (vv. 32–34). The love of God is thus not so much represented here as a divine emotion or disposition as it is identified with a divine *act*: God's gracious saving action on our behalf in Jesus Christ.[61] Paul catches up the essence of this entire narrative when he refers to Christ by the epithet "[he] who loved us" (v. 37). Christ is the one who takes possession of us by a powerful work of love and thereby secures for us a place within the sphere of his own dominion. By identifying the love of Christ (v. 35) with the love of God itself, eternal and omnipotent (v. 39) in this way, Paul specifies just what it means in this life to call this Jesus of Nazareth *our Lord*.[62]

---

60. See Cullmann, "Kingship of Christ," 122. It is perhaps a little misleading, therefore, when Douglas Moo asserts, in relation to this passage, that "it is not with the universe but with Christians, that Paul is concerned here" (*Epistle to the Romans*, 54), for it appears that all such concerns are thoroughly entangled within Paul's apocalyptic gospel.

61. The point is frequently made; see, e.g., Moo, *Epistle to the Romans*, 543.

62. See Meyer, *Word in the World*, 193. T. F. Torrance has argued that among the Reformers it is Martin Bucer who wins through to this "profoundly Pauline and moving understanding

It is the witness of this tract of Romans that in Christ's person and work we are met by the "marriage of God's omnipotence to God's compassion."[63] In him the God of the gospel has come upon the world and made himself known: to claim with Paul that "God is for us" is therefore not to proffer an abstract concept of divine benevolence but rather to fix one's eyes on the saving act centered on the death of Jesus wherein God concretely exegetes his own identity and purpose.[64] And in this marriage of power and agape, power is properly ordered to love: God's saving acts in Jesus Christ disclose that divine power is the power of gracious, divine self-giving. Here revelation is clearly less a matter of drawing back the curtain to afford a glimpse of the otherwise obscure identity and purposes of God than it is of acknowledging, as J. Louis Martyn has put it, that the "One who has been on the other side rips the curtain apart, steps through to our side, altering irrevocably our time and space."[65] A passage such as Romans 8 is bold to characterize this movement, this divine apocalypse, as a movement of love. In the free and sovereign coming of the Son, in his self-giving unto death, and in his resurrection and ascension to the right hand of the Father, God's love has invaded and traversed the landscape of the fallen world concretely and with momentous effect. Christians can be assured that nothing can separate them from God, because the power of God that appeared in his Son is the power of love, by which God has chosen and gathered his people to himself and holds on to them forever.[66] The Kingdom of heaven is a dominion of love because its Lord is the Word of love incarnate, a Word we can and must "hear and which we have to trust and obey in life and in death," as the Barmen Theological Declaration puts it. Christ's kingship is not an austere and distant sovereignty demanding our obedience alone: it rather is an eschatological gift of love that redeems women and men from the world of unlove by an irresistible divine self-giving, thereby conscripting them into his service as creaturely agents of his love and its purposes.[67]

---

of love as the eschatological reality that abides" and by which he is able to conceive of the *regnum Christi* extending beyond the church per se and pressing "externally upon the state" (*Kingdom and Church*, 89).

63. Rossow, "Hound of Heaven," 91.

64. See Käsemann, *Commentary on Romans*, 247; cf. Witherington, *Paul's Letter to the Romans*, 232: "Not an abstract concept of God, but rather God with flesh on, God in Christ reconciling the world to himself, characterizes Paul's understanding of deity. Paul speaks of God only as the God who reveals himself."

65. Martyn, "From Paul to Flannery O'Connor," 282.

66. See Stuhlmacher, *Paul's Letter to the Romans*, 141.

67. Emil Brunner argues down this line particularly clearly in his treatment of the royal office of Christ in his *Christian Doctrine of Creation and Redemption*, 298–300.

In *Cur Deus Homo*, Anselm famously informed his interlocutor, Boso, and thereby also his readers, that they had "not yet duly estimated the gravity of sin."[68] That may well be true, then as now. Paul, however, calls Christians to put their store in the even greater truth that nothing in all of creation is of sufficient gravity to dislodge us from the orbit of Christ's sovereign love. So it is that "in His love our love celebrates its victory."[69]

The Sovereign Love of God: Four Propositions

What christological and soteriological insights are to be taken away from reflections such as these ventured here on the aspects of Paul's apocalyptic gospel? The following brief summary statements attempt to summarize something of what might be learned of Christ's royal office from a fresh hearing of Romans 8:31–39.

First, the royal office of Christ is exercised not only in and as a consequence of the *status exaltationis* (state of exaltation; cf. Phil. 2:10, Vulgate) but also and importantly in and as a consequence of the *status exinanitionis* (state of humiliation; cf. Phil. 2:7, Vulgate). Only when this is so can we grasp the contours of his dominion as a lordship of divine love and recognize that Christ's royal office consists in "the continuous work of the Crucified One."[70] For it is from under the cross and in the power of the Spirit that "full of joy and peace, Christians confess: Lord, our God, other lords indeed rule over us besides you, but we call on you alone and on your name."[71]

Second, Christ's kingship is spiritual in and because it is an eschatological reality that even now invades the world pneumatically, repossessing, sustaining, and directing his people in their corporate faith and life amid the yet unruly powers of the old age. Thus the love of God enacted in Jesus Christ is "the content of the activity of the exalted Lord, who rules the world by the word of the gospel and the power of the Spirit, creating faith in the gospel, putting all opposition to it to shame, assembling believers and in this way preparing the way for the kingdom of the Father in the world."[72]

Third, acknowledgment of the cosmic scope of Christ's lordship requires that theology draw together its understanding of the *munus regnum Christi*

68. Anselm, *Cur Deus Homo*, 21.
69. K. Barth, *Epistle to the Romans*, 327.
70. Stuhlmacher, *Paul's Letter to the Romans*, 140; cf. Thielicke, *Evangelical Faith*, 2:421: "as the exalted one he is still he whose love impelled him to become man to enter into the solidarity of the most profound humiliation."
71. Käsemann, "One Lord Alone," 251.
72. Pannenberg, *Systematic Theology*, 2:448.

and its account of divine providence generally. As a result, we ought also to resist any strong separation between the "essential" and "economic" modes of Christ's royal office.[73] An evangelical doctrine of providence will look to conceive of God's *conservatio* (continuing preservation), *concursus* (cooperation), and *gubernatio* (governance) by reflecting on the entailments of Christ's lordship over church *and* world.[74] This raises interesting questions for political theology, where accounts of church, state, and politics have often been framed precisely in accordance with a sharp demarcation of these doctrines. But when the gospel acclaims that Christ is for us the true Lord of the world, it acknowledges his lordship "over body and soul, heart and mind, disciples and demons, this world and the world to come, [as] a *political fact.*"[75]

Fourth and finally, faith in Christ's exercise of his royal office shapes lives of Christian freedom marked by joyful assurance in the midst of adversity and the perplexities of life in the not-yet-redeemed world. Such was Luther's insight: as those who have a share in Christ's priestly reign, Christians are free to love and serve God and neighbor without fear or moral calculation, thereby giving faithful witness to the victory that Christ has won for us over the powers of the age.[76] Even when conflagration threatens Christians on all sides, Käsemann argued, they are "marked by the Lord, who is present for [them]" such that, being established in παρρησία (*parrēsia*, courageous forthrightness), they will refuse to let their discipleship be hindered.[77] By their very freedom and their cruciformity, Christian lives may testify to the truth of Christ's eschatological lordship in the world, a world of which he can and will not be dispossessed.

---

73. Helmut Thielicke asked the pertinent question when he noted that key to any account of the *munus regnum* is "understanding how the kingdom of power and the kingdom of grace are related to one another in the lordship of Christ. What is meant by the personal union between the Lord of the world and the Lord of the community?" (*Evangelical Faith*, 2:422–23). He did not answer his own question here, though he does refer his readers to related discussions of the relevance of Christ's lordship for social and political ethics in his *Theological Ethics*, 1:359–82 and 2:565–613.

74. See Dantine, "Creation and Redemption," 139; cf. also his essay "*Regnum Christi—Gubernatio Dei.*"

75. Käsemann, "What I Have Unlearned," 334–35.

76. Caird, *Principalities and Powers*, 95.

77. Käsemann, *Commentary on Romans*, 251; cf. Bosc, *Kingly Office of the Lord Jesus Christ*, 147: The church "knows that all fatalism, whether of sin, or falsehood, or of slavery in its many forms, is conquered and that it can confront *royally*, that is, without fear and in the integrity of its being, all the powers opposing it. But it is a place of liberty *in the world* and *in history*, which it knows to be in the hands of its Lord. . . . It is thus free for [the world] in being a sign that this freedom is already present, as a gift, but as a gift already given."

4

Christ Must Reign

The Priority of Redemption

The first thing necessary for you is to be conquered by God; only
as God's vanquished captive can you share in God's victory.

—Heinrich Vogel, "Shortened Course
of Instructions for a Soldier of Jesus Christ"

In a valuable contribution to current debates about soteriology, Alan
Spence weighs the merits of the so-called victory model and asks whether
it can provide an adequate paradigm for exposition of the Christian doctrine
of salvation generally, and of Paul's account of salvation in particular.[1]
N. T. Wright and Gustaf Aulén are called on as advocates of the *Christus
Victor* (Christ as victor) doctrine of the atonement. In Spence's judgment,
Wright's recourse to the doctrine in his exposition of Paul's theology simply "does not do justice to the material before it," actively requiring him to
neglect a whole range of crucial concepts such as forgiveness, mercy, guilt,
and reconciliation.[2] Spence is also unpersuaded by Aulén's claim for the
primacy and sufficiency of the "dramatic" model of salvation; once again,
the inability of this discourse to capture the realities of enmity, forgiveness,

1. Spence, "Unified Theory."
2. Ibid., 416. Spence concentrates almost exclusively on N. T. Wright's presentation of the
case in *What St. Paul Really Said*.

reconciliation, and finally also grace itself tells decisively against it. As he explains, "Aulén never goes on to help us understand how the battle motif, so helpful in explaining the experience of human freedom and liberation, is able to shed light on the problems of guilt, judgment and animosity."[3] Spence's chief worry is that by construing salvation as rescue, victory models inadequately express the personal transformation of the individual sinner required when human beings are acknowledged to be agents of sin rather than merely the victims of sin.

There are any number of ways in which one might press further into this matter and engage Spence's critical judgments concerning the limitations of the "victory model." One could augment and complicate the assessment of N. T. Wright's exegetical project by drawing on his much wider corpus.[4] Similarly, one could engage more fully with Aulén's theology and its sources in an effort to display its wider explanatory power and adequacy.[5] Alternatively, one could look to more recent iterations of the *Christus Victor* model that may do better justice to those "mediatorial concepts" that are at the heart of Spence's critical concern: J. Denny Weaver's much-discussed work might recommend itself here.[6] Leaving such lines of inquiry to others, however, in this chapter I pursue another angle. What I want to do here is to reconsider aspects of the theological legacy of Ernst Käsemann as a basis on which to argue for the adequacy of a Christian doctrine of salvation whose central motif is the eschatological struggle and victory of God over Sin for the sake of his beleaguered creatures. My aim is to gesture toward an account of redemption that is christologically concentrated and apocalyptically charged, and then to begin to intimate something of the kind of Christian life that would be concomitant with it. Because apocalyptic conspires materially with Christology in a particular way in his work, Käsemann's soteriology can be shown to do justice to the concerns that motivate Spence's criticism of the "victory model" and to do so not by diffusing but in fact by radicalizing its insights. Working out

---

3. Spence, "Unified Theory," 417; cf. 405, 416.

4. N. T. Wright's contributions to recent exchanges surrounding the doctrine of justification, for instance, would provide much directly relevant material. For a concentrated presentation, see his *Justification*.

5. Assessing the role of the *Christus Victor* motif in Aulén's theology as a whole would involve careful analysis of his *Faith of the Christian Church* and careful exploration of his reception of Luther himself on this score. For a recent reassessment of Aulén's own proposal from an evangelical perspective, see Ovey, "Appropriating Aulén?" For a detailed analysis study of the "salvation as battle" motif in Luther, see Rieske-Braun, *Duellem mirabile*.

6. See Weaver, "Atonement for the Nonconstantinian Church," and more fully his *Nonviolent Atonement*, esp. chaps. 2 and 3 on "Narrative Christus Victor."

just such a soteriological vision is, I think, a crucial part of the ongoing "recovery of apocalyptic imagination" in the present.[7]

J. Louis Martyn, whose work is a fundamental provocation for this project as a whole, happily acknowledges the influence of Ernst Käsemann on his own understanding of Paul's apocalyptic gospel of the invading grace of God in Christ, remarking that his account is "indebted above all to the works" of the great twentieth-century German pastor, exegete, and theologian.[8] Käsemann, for his part, also saw Martyn as one of the few in the English-speaking world who could be relied on to "step up for [him] from the trenches."[9] Käsemann's work elucidates the formative categories and patterns of reasoning of an understanding of salvation that takes with utmost seriousness the New Testament's witness to the apocalyptic nature of the outworking of divine mercy. Käsemann was led to characterize the righteousness of God as "God's sovereignty over the world revealing itself eschatologically in Jesus,"[10] and he took as his watchword Paul's declaration that Christ must reign until all his enemies have been put underfoot (1 Cor. 15:25).[11] While vigorously defending the central place of justification in Christian theology, he fundamentally reconceives that doctrine by shifting the locus of divine salvation away from anthropology and into cosmology, as the advent of God's righteousness means that "God's power reaches out for the world, and the world's salvation lies in its being recaptured for the sovereignty of God."[12] The categories of traditional "mediatorial" soteriology—such as grace, faith, forgiveness, repentance, and so on—are heavily inflected by this eschatological reframing. So too are the understanding of the life of faith and the fundaments of ethics and politics Christianly conceived (about which more in later chapters). Theology, he argues, takes its essential bearings in the present time of faith and obedience from the coming of the Kingdom. This is a supremely practical, not theoretical,

---

7. See Braaten, "Recovery of Apocalyptic Imagination." There is no question that Käsemann's own interest in "apocalyptic" had both exegetical and substantive contemporary *theological* concerns motivating it. See Way, *Lordship of Christ*, 173.

8. Martyn, *Theological Issues*, 65n36. Never in fact a student of Käsemann's, in the preface to the 1967 first edition of his *History and Theology in the Fourth Gospel*, Martyn simply calls Käsemann his "friend" (12). Writing in 1985, Robin Scroggs remarked that Käsemann's lasting importance would perhaps be as a *theologian* rather than as an exegete ("Ernst Käsemann: The Divine Agent Provocateur," 260). For a valuable recent survey and analysis of Käsemann's legacy, see Adams, Eckstein, and Lichtenberger, *Dienst in Freiheit*.

9. In a 1995 letter from Käsemann to Paul Zahl; see Zahl, "Tribute to Ernst Käsemann."

10. Käsemann, "Righteousness of God in Paul," 180.

11. Curiously, despite his regular invocations of 1 Cor. 15:25–28, Käsemann never published a detailed exegesis of the passage itself; see Way, *Lordship of Christ*, 138. Cf. Käsemann, "On the Subject of Primitive Christian Apocalyptic," 133.

12. Käsemann, *New Testament Questions*, 182.

claim, since its truth is acknowledged and attested by ways of living as well as by discrete human actions that make manifest that "Jesus of Nazareth is in fact our Lord and the Lord of the world."[13]

Here the stakes for Christian theology are high. By virtue of its decisiveness for Christian faith, life, and thought, Käsemann himself thought the matter of the apocalyptic gospel to be "at least as important as that of the historical Jesus, and ought perhaps even to take precedence over it."[14] In a notable understatement, Martyn once observed that if Käsemann's thesis concerning the eschatological character of divine rectification is correct, then "not a little of the discussion among systematicians will have to be changed."[15] And so we ask: what follows for an account of salvation when the *duellum mirabile*—the miraculous contest between Christ and the antithetical powers of sin, death, and the devil—is allowed to frame the doctrine as a whole? What soteriological imagination is opened up when the apocalyptic struggle that God fights against the whole inimical dominion that holds humankind in bondage—a struggle whose turning point is the cross of Christ—provides its center of gravity?[16] Amid lively contemporary debates about the interpretation of Paul, the doctrine of the atonement, and the scope of salvation and its relation to Jesus Christ, I suggest that Käsemann's clear hearing of the apocalyptic gospel of salvation has much to teach us yet. Not least he can remind us that the essential task and promise of such Christian theological labor is that the Spirit "so binds the interpreter to the hearing of the Scripture that he cannot attempt translation into the world's different languages without returning to its substance, finding its heart in the midst of its variations, and thus acquiring criteria for discerning the spirits."[17]

Saved by the Apocalypse of Sovereign Divine Love

For present purposes, the account of human existence that Käsemann discerns to be ingredient in the eschatological announcement of the gospel of God is of great importance. This distinctive theological anthropology ensures that the full range of soteriological concepts finally find a place within an apocalyptic description of the outworking of salvation. Yet, in keeping with the nature of the eschatological gospel itself, anthropology is subsequent to other more

13. Käsemann, *Kirchliche Konflikte*, 1:216.
14. Käsemann, "Righteousness of God in an Unrighteous World," 182.
15. Martyn, review of *New Testament Questions*, 557.
16. Aulén uses the Latin phrase in his "Chaos and Cosmos," 157.
17. Käsemann, "Some Thoughts on the Theme 'Doctrine of Reconciliation,'" 62.

basic and determinative realities: the realities of God in Christ and of the fallen world. As Käsemann has it, the anthropology ingredient in the apocalyptic gospel must be grasped as but "the projection of cosmology."[18] In order to understand this claim, we begin with one of Käsemann's programmatic statements on the matter. As we observed in chapter 3, Käsemann understands human existence to be fully embedded in the contested world; thus it has a "stake in the confrontation between God and the principality of this world," just so to "mirror the cosmic contention for the lordship of the world."[19]

Several key claims are made here. To be a human being, to have life in the body as a creature, is to be irrevocably knit into the fabric of a larger reality: "the world." This at first seemingly banal claim proves to be anything but. For, in the first place, it signals a polemical repudiation of modern characterizations of human beings whose chief currency is talk of individual autonomy and "self-reflexivity."[20] Such visions of autonomy are recognized to be illusory when we acknowledge, as Paul does, that the human "body" is "that piece of world which we ourselves are and for which we bear responsibility because it was the earliest gift of our Creator to us."[21] To be a human being is to live in and to be "of a piece with" a world that is constitutive of our individual existence. All humanity is always already *claimed* humanity.

Now, envisaged evangelically, human existence is held firmly within a specific understanding of the world as a field of struggle between competing powers, and indeed finally as the site of a single contest between God and the anti-God powers of the fallen creation. It is precisely the force of Paul's witness in Romans 5:12–21 to make plain that the antithesis of Adam and Christ represents a global confrontation of "alternative, exclusive and ultimate" spheres.[22] For Käsemann, Adam and Christ stand in an antithetical, if asymmetrical, correspondence in which "both are bearers of destiny for the world. . . . These two—and basically these two alone—have determined the

18. Käsemann, *Commentary on Romans*, 150. For more expansive discussions of Käsemann's anthropology, see Zahl, *Rechtfertigungslehre Ernst Käsemanns*, 148–68; and Way, *Lordship of Christ*, 54–61, 154–63.

19. Käsemann, "On the Subject of Primitive Christian Apocalyptic," 136.

20. Käsemann uses the term "idealism" as a collective epithet for such anthropologies, signaling thereby both their indebtedness to discretely modern European philosophical tradition and their contrast with other, "realistic" accounts of human existence—the latter a moniker he certainly claims for Paul's apocalyptic account of humanity embodied in and indeed by the world. This issue is central to his break with Bultmann's exegetical program; see Käsemann, "What I Have Unlearned," 329–31.

21. Käsemann, "On the Subject of Primitive Christian Apocalyptic," 135. Cf. Käsemann, "On Paul's Anthropology," 28: "We ourselves do not determine what we are. It is delusion to imagine that this is the case and presumption to rely on it."

22. Käsemann, *Commentary on Romans*, 146.

world as a whole."[23] So, as "specific pieces" of *this* world, human beings stand under one of two signs, that of the Christ of God or that of the Sin that owns Adam: one has either Christ or anti-Christ as a lord. In such an apocalyptic vision of things, there is no thought that human existence as such is or could ever be neutral vis-à-vis the eschatological either-or that exists between the claim of God and his Christ and the sphere of Adam.[24] In working out the soteriological significance of such a view, just what it means to "have a lord" here proves decisive.

If, as Käsemann contends, the basic idea of Paul's anthropology is that "a person is defined by his particular lord," this is because the world as a "sphere of sovereignty" is simply the place wherein and from which human life is determinately claimed, formed, and animated.[25] The world of Adam—as a constellation of overlapping, fluctuating, and mutually contesting sovereignties that are variously and together in rebellion against God—in this way defines humanity in Sin.[26] To be lorded over by these powers is not simply to suffer their oppression externally, though it certainly involves that. More than that, it means having been conscripted into their service. So Käsemann can describe death as "a force which shapes the *cosmos*" and as "a curse in the texture of earthly life which ineluctably affects every individual." The upshot is that one is less the subject than the "object and projection" of one's history, a person firmly "in the grip of forces which seize his existence and determine his will and responsibility at least to the extent that he cannot choose freely but can only grasp what is already there."[27] Moreover, the lordship one suffers works itself inside the self, establishing a specific orientation within which life is lived, making us "of a piece with" that world of which we are a part. One is thus never properly only an individual but is always "oneself *and* the world at any given time."[28] For the human creature is one who, "radically and representatively for all others, submits to his lord"—in this case to the distorting and ruinous power of Sin—"becoming the instrument which manifests [its]

23. Ibid., 153. On the development of Käsemann's use of the concept of Christ as a "bearer of destiny," see Way, *Lordship of Christ*, 167–68.

24. "Man can never be 'neutral in himself' and is certainly not so in his corporeality, which is always already modified. An ontology that deprives him of this already existing modification in order to observe him *per se* falls victim to an abstraction and no longer allows him the humanity of creatureliness" (Käsemann, "On Paul's Anthropology," 20). Or again, "Whoever abrogates obedience to the Creator from then on lives for idols" (Käsemann, "God's Image and Sinners," 114).

25. Käsemann, *Commentary on Romans*, 250.

26. Käsemann, "On Paul's Anthropology," 27–28. Cf. Martyn, Comment 39, *Galatians*, 370–77.

27. Käsemann, *Commentary on Romans*, 141, 147.

28. Käsemann, "God's Image," 115.

power and [its] universal claim."[29] Thus women and men subjected to Sin
are not merely its passive victims; they also become its active servants. To be
lorded over by Sin is to have been recruited and deployed as its representative,
a "member, part and tool."[30] This point is crucial. For this apocalyptic vision
does not conceive of our subjection within the sphere of Adam as a purely
extrinsic affair and so fatalistically construe human existence as tragic. Since
women and men are active sinners even under (and as a result of) the curse of
Sin, "personal accountability can neither be eliminated nor isolated." This is
because in our very existence "we are *exponents* of a power which transforms
the cosmos into chaos," our lives actually "making a case" for the power that
possesses us and in whose service we are enrolled.[31] This is why Paul characterized the guilt of sin not in terms of ignorance but rather in terms of active
"revolt against the known Lord."[32]

Now all this—which might be taken as a sketch of the architecture of an
apocalyptic doctrine of original sin[33]—bears directly on the description of
salvation at the heart of the gospel of God. As mentioned above, Käsemann
essentially construes the matter thus: "God's power reaches out for the world,
and the world's salvation lies in its being recaptured for the sovereignty of
God."[34] Deliverance involves the "assault of grace upon the world of the
body"[35] in order to effect a change of lordship, effectively translating the
human being out from the sphere of Sin and idolatry and into the sphere of
Christ.[36] Exercising divine right as Creator, God comes on the scene in Christ
to wrest his captive and complicit creatures from their servitude and plight
under the false yet all too actual reign of Sin. To talk of an exchange of lordships or transfer of spheres in this way is to evoke nothing less than the advent
of the new creation, the gift of a new world whose only presupposition is the
invading power of divine grace itself.[37]

29. Käsemann, "On Paul's Anthropology," 28. Cf. Käsemann, *Commentary on Romans*,
150: Paul speaks of "ruling powers which implicate all people individually and everywhere
determine reality as destiny."
30. Käsemann, "God's Image," 115. Cf. Käsemann, *Commentary on Romans*, 220.
31. Käsemann, *Commentary on Romans*, 154, emphasis added; Käsemann, "God's Image," 115.
32. Käsemann, *Commentary on Romans*, 41, 42.
33. So Käsemann writes, "Christianity has unjustly forgotten or at least diminished the
theologically non-rescindable, though haplessly described doctrine of original sin" ("Justice
for the Unjust," 232).
34. Käsemann, "Righteousness of God in an Unrighteous World," 182.
35. Käsemann, *Commentary on Romans*, 213.
36. Ibid., 155: "The plus of grace consists in transfer from the sphere of death to that of life
as resurrection power." Cf. also Käsemann, "On Paul's Anthropology," 28–29, where we read
that hope lies in a "change of lordship and life in another world."
37. Käsemann, *Commentary on Romans*, 154.

In Käsemann's account, the concepts of grace and righteousness overlap and are inseparable, as they each denote "under different aspects the same thing, namely the *basileia* [kingdom] of Christ."[38] Righteousness, for Käsemann, names "the rightful power with which God makes his cause to triumph in the world which has fallen away from him and which yet, as creation, is his inviolable possession."[39] By "grace" we indicate not a disposition or attitude of God toward humanity—perhaps a "merely inscrutable or arbitrary love"—but rather name the effective form of God's saving power.[40] As modalities of his reign, these gifts of God are the very means by which he "subordinates us to his lordship and makes us responsible beings"; as gifts *of God*, they remain in his possession even as God gives them fully and freely to us.[41] By the concrete exercise of his reign of righteousness and grace in Christ, God rectifies the world, setting things to rights in accordance with his own merciful deity.

Eberhard Jüngel expressly affirms the importance of Käsemann's insights by asserting that contemporary theology must lay distinctive stress on the fact that "God's righteousness is a power that penetrates into the fallen world in order to make over anew the world's unrighteous relationships."[42] Theology must credit the creative—or rather, re-creative—reality of God's simultaneous exercise of his right as God and the eschatological gift of his Son in a single act of salvation. In this single act of sovereign self-disclosure and gracious self-giving, both the true deity of God and the true humanity of women and men are revealed with saving effect: God's righteous mercy conquers and expels the false gods of the age, thereby securing for his beloved, threatened creatures that "other world," that new creation constituted by the effective lordship of the Crucified One. Thus the justification of the ungodly, Käsemann concludes, simply means "God's victory over the world that strives against him."[43] Salvation is obtained in Christ because in him the victory of God over the contentious world for its own sake is accomplished.

---

38. Ibid., 154, 158. Cf. Käsemann, "Righteousness of God in Paul," 174, where he writes that there is an "indissoluble connection of power and gift within the conception of divine righteousness." Cf. K. Barth, *Römerbrief*, 196: "Grace is the kingdom, the lordship, the power and the rule of God over humanity" (as translated and cited by Way, *Lordship of Christ*, 42n112).

39. Käsemann, "'Righteousness of God in Paul," 180.

40. Käsemann, "Justice for the Unjust," 230.

41. Käsemann, "Righteousness of God in Paul," 174.

42. Jüngel, *Justification*, 64–65. Although certainly admitting that justification involves the gift of righteousness to sinners, Käsemann insisted vehemently that Paul primarily has in view, as the basis of this gift, God's own righteousness, which rectifies the world. As Leander Keck wagers, "Käsemann's reconstruction of the morphology of this meaning has been criticized; nonetheless, when the dust settles he will be more 'justified' than not" (*Paul and His Letters*, 113).

43. Käsemann, *Commentary on Romans*, 82.

When salvation is understood along such lines as these—when it amounts to the lordly gift of "the God who brings back the fallen world into the sphere of his legitimate claim, . . . whether in promise or demand, in new creation or forgiveness, or in the making possible of our service"[44]—then, in a structural analogy with the reality of human captivity *and* active complicity with the aeonic power of Sin, human beings are at one and the same time those whom God rescues and, precisely as such, those made new in and by his rescue. The victory that God wins when Christ takes power over us is won *for us* even as it is won *against us* insofar as we are exponents and instruments of that other false lord, insofar as we ourselves are "a piece" of the world now vanquished and overturned. Our redemption out from under the power of Sin is therefore a liberation whose form is precisely that of judgment and forgiveness: it involves the overcoming of enmity and the reconciliation of renewed creatures with God. As liberation, salvation includes rather than bypasses personal sin: the gospel promises that God wills to wrest the earth out from "our egoism and our deep-seated indolence and hypocrisy," and that God does so by freeing us from the tyrannical powers that enslave us.[45] These are two aspects of the one rectifying movement of God's sovereign grace.

The world from which Christ sets us free is our world—a world for which we are responsible—in the radical sense that it has been constitutive of our very identities. We have been agents of its enmity toward God. It is for this reason that to be severed from that world is to have to die so as to be made alive; it is to have had the world "crucified" and to have been crucified to the world (Gal. 6:14). To be translated out of that world is a profound act of salutary alienation, one for which the concepts of defeat, judgment, and death are not exaggerations. The exercise of divine righteousness "establishes his justice by being gracious," Käsemann argues, because God is ever putting an end to our illusions, for "God's truth is his lordship over the creature. It shatters as such our self-assertion and when accepted sets us in the power of grace. Grace is granted only from the Judge's hand."[46]

We can perhaps begin to see the importance of this apocalyptic anthropology: to see that a person's reality is decisively determined by that person's lord, such that "the servant becomes like his master and shows this by his behaviour," has thoroughgoing consequences in soteriology.[47] It authorizes and makes sense of the strongest possible version of the victory model, in

44. Ibid., 29.
45. Käsemann, "What I Have Unlearned," 334.
46. Käsemann, *Commentary on Romans*, 83. "The apocalyptic future brings new reality in the present through creative negation" (Braaten, "Significance of Apocalypticism," 491).
47. Käsemann, *Commentary on Romans*, 43.

which salvation is strictly identified with having the lordship of Christ exercised over oneself, for one's own sake, as a consequence of God's eschatological revelation of divine sovereignty in him. At the same time, because sinners are understood to be not merely insulated victims of the "world of Sin" but rather also its settled inhabitants, actively habituated to its ways and means as subjects of its false gods and in their service, the soteriological motifs of enmity, guilt, judgment, forgiveness, and reconciliation all find a proper place within this account of salvation as divine victory, rather than simply falling outside as alternate and possibly parallel "metaphors" for salvation. Käsemann himself argues that while the juridical and cultic aspects of the reality of salvation are necessary implicates of its cosmological understanding, the converse cannot be said. Reconciliation—a motif particularly prominent in modern soteriologies—is itself best understood within an apocalyptic framework, Käsemann suggests.[48] Summarizing the point at some length, he writes that the eschatological Christian gospel

> is characterised by the open proclamation of the seizure of power by God and his appointed Saviour and by the verification of that proclamation in the union of both Jews and Gentiles in the Christian church. Heaven is no longer a closed realm hovering above the earth, and the world is no more the battlefield of every man against his neighbour and the arena of mutually exclusive sovereignties. The principalities and powers have been dethroned. If this picture is correct, reconciliation in this instance implies an eschatological, even an apocalyptic, phenomenon which is not primarily connected with, and cannot be appropriately conceived by the use of, either juridical or cultic categories. The eschatological and worldwide *regnum Christi* [reign of Christ] necessarily breaks the bounds of a community understood along merely juridical or cultic lines.[49]

Held firmly within this context, talk of reconciliation (Spence's "mediatorial" motifs) serves to proclaim "God's solidarity" with humanity in Christ "as the basis for human solidarity" as well as to indicate the fact that "God aids and purposes to aid *his enemies* (and thus the whole world)."[50]

The capacity of Käsemann's apocalyptic soteriology to incorporate the breadth of scriptural "models" and concerns is further confirmed when we attend

48. Käsemann, "Some Thoughts on the Theme 'Doctrine of Reconciliation,'" 53–56. Spence makes a contrary case for the sole adequacy of the mediatorial model to encompass and explain the main lines of the others; see Spence, "Unified Theory," 417–20. On this see my "Very Short Theology of Reconciliation."

49. Käsemann, "Some Thoughts on the Theme 'Doctrine of Reconciliation,'" 55.

50. Ibid., 64, 63, emphasis added. Cf. Martyn, *Galatians*, 336: "Before the advent of Christ humanity was an enslaved monolith; in Christ humanity is becoming a liberated unity."

to the description of the Christian life that follows on from such an account. Once again, what proves decisive is Käsemann's insight that "the ontological structure of anthropology remains determined by lordship as in the old aeon," though now in keeping with the truth of God's deity enacted in Christ.[51] What does it mean for us as "pieces of the world" that we should have *this God* as our Lord? What kind of existence arises when Christ takes possession of us, when he bears to us our destiny as the children of God? What does it look like for human beings to be crafted into representatives and exponents of the Lord of love? These are the questions to which the doctrines of sanctification and ecclesiology (among others) must provide serviceable answers. We begin to explore and develop some of these themes in later chapters of this book. But it is not out of place even here to give some brief indication of the direction in which Käsemann himself takes theological exposition of the Christian life if only to secure one point of decisive importance: namely, that his apocalyptic rendering of the *Christus Victor* can do justice to the full range of soteriological motifs for which the New Testament makes Christian theology responsible in its service of the coherence and clarity of the proclamation of the gospel.

First, Käsemann insists that the apocalyptic inflection of Paul's doctrine of salvation takes it in a more, rather than less, realistic direction.[52] Rather than making the message of reconciliation into a utopian myth, understanding it apocalyptically ensures that attention is riveted to the historical sphere of "concrete daily life and corporal community," where the gift and aim of salvation are in fact actualized. In this vein, Käsemann observes that talk of reconciliation keeps such close company in the New Testament with paraenesis precisely because "cosmic peace does not settle over the world, as in a fairy tale. It takes root only so far as men in the service of reconciliation confirm that they have themselves found peace with God. The message of the reconciled world demonstrates its truth in the reconciled man, not apart from him or beyond him."[53] The same realism is echoed when Käsemann claims that "the earth is only liberated from enmity and chaos and made a new creation in so far as the service of Christ is carried on in her," not because our striving achieves it but rather because faith knows that, beyond all human striving, we by grace receive and are made to bear "the divine work to a world which God has not forsaken."[54] Hence, though the gospel of salvation certainly "posits

51. Käsemann, *Commentary on Romans*, 155.
52. "The earth is constantly claimed also by false gods, about which only the naïve can say, 'they are invisible': Who is our Lord? And who should finally become our Lord? These are the central questions of existence" (Käsemann, "What I Have Unlearned," 335).
53. Käsemann, "Some Thoughts on the Theme 'Doctrine of Reconciliation,'" 56.
54. Ibid., 64.

reality," the pressing question as to whether this "remains a living reality" and whether Christians are preserved "in obedience" is forever bound up with the actualization of the promise in the lives of forgiven sinners in the church.[55] In short, because Christians most fundamentally *belong* to their Lord, their very existence is conscripted into the service of making his lordship manifest. This line of thinking makes *discipleship* a crucial category by which to understand the Christian life, as the only self-understanding available to those redeemed by the Crucified One "arises from the act of following" itself and not from any abstract idea.[56]

Approached in this way, biblical concepts of participation "in Christ" and of "union" with him are liable to distinctive interpretation. They now are heard less as mystagogical descriptions of ontological ascent and more as realistic descriptions of our effective recruitment into Christ's cause and thus to his active service here and now. As Käsemann argues, it is the work of such concepts in theology to give powerful expression to our incorporation under the lordship of the Crucified. These concepts denote the position of the justified, where "justification" names the act by which Christ assumes his rightful claim and exercises his power over our lives, thereby binding us to him, securing our allegiance, and enabling our witness and service by his grace. To be "in Christ" is therefore to "abide in the gift which we have received, and it can abide, living and powerful, in us" by the powerful activity of his Spirit.[57] Here an essential dynamism is injected into what can otherwise be taken to be static descriptions of a human state: our being in Christ is a matter of movement because "the new Lord cuts us off from what we were before and never allows us to remain what we are at any given time, for otherwise he might be the First Cause but he would not be our Lord in the true sense."[58]

---

55. Käsemann, "Righteousness of God in Paul," 177.

56. Käsemann, "What I Have Unlearned," 330; Käsemann, *Commentary on Romans*, 224. Cf. Käsemann, "On the Subject of Primitive Christian Apocalyptic," 134: "In the bodily obedience of the Christian, carried out as the service of God in the world of everyday, the lordship of Christ finds visible expression and only when this visible expression takes provisional shape in us does the whole thing become credible as Gospel message." Or again, "What is really at stake is this: we ourselves must become alert and, indeed, so must all who want to remain Christians. . . . We have to remember that it is discipleship which is laid upon us all and nothing else. But in the same measure as discipleship takes hold, everything else follows of its own accord" (Käsemann, "Theologians and the Laity," 289–90).

57. Käsemann, "Righteousness of God in Paul," 175. Here and elsewhere Käsemann lays great emphasis on the present work of the Spirit in the present outworking of Christ's lordship in the Christian life. The concepts of being drawn into the body of Christ and the effective exercise of Christ's lordship are mutually interpretative, and indeed finally identical, so that Käsemann can say, "By the Spirit Christ seizes power in us, just as conversely by the Spirit we are incorporated into Christ" (*Commentary on Romans*, 222).

58. Käsemann, "Righteousness of God in Paul," 176.

As Zwingli once put it, participation "in Christ" occurs precisely in the faithful acknowledgment of him as the "Captain" of our present existence in this world.[59] All of this is in keeping with the construal of the Christian life as a gracious conscription to discipleship brought about by the fact that Christ has acted to take "total possession" of our lives such that we now stand in the "field of force" that is his effective reign.[60]

An apocalyptic account of salvation in Christ such as this stresses the radical objectivity and exteriority of God's saving acts: salvation is always something that happens to us; it is something that befalls us *ab extra* (from the outside) despite ourselves. And yet, what is equally clear is that Käsemann's no less vigorous insistence on the sovereign agency of Christ and the Spirit in the actualization of salvation ensures that it is inescapably actual *for us* and that it catches us up in its outworking. If we ask about the contours of our discipleship, if we inquire into the form and direction of human existence held by the Spirit in the sphere of the crucified Lord's power, we hear from Käsemann chiefly talk of freedom, witness, struggle, and resistance.[61] If the first two of these motifs reflect the present eschatological force of the exchange of lordships, the second two signal the patient dedication of Christian faith and life to the future when Christ's lordship will be fully apocalypsed, which is to say revealed and realized. At present, during the time of Christ's own militant lordship—in the era during which he "must reign until he has put all his enemies under his feet" (1 Cor. 15:25)—faith is exercised precisely in trusting "in the love of Christ against all appearances"; its modes are often best captured in negative descriptions as refusals "to let discipleship be hindered" or to be abandoned under pressure from the rearguard action of the defeated power of Sin (Gal. 5:1).[62] Our reconciliation with God engenders a new sort of enmity with the world "according to the law of apocalyptic,"

59. "For Jesus Christ is the leader and captain whom God has promised and given to the whole human race" (Zwingli, *Sixty-Seven Articles of 1523*, 36, art. 6). I return to this idea in chap. 13 below.

60. Käsemann, *Commentary on Romans*, 219, 223. Cf. Käsemann, "What I Have Unlearned," 331, where he writes, "What is proclaimed and should be taken with utmost seriousness is the Nazarene's path to world lordship, which becomes concrete and observable in the individual believer."

61. Käsemann, "What I Have Unlearned," 334: "Along with its preaching and ministering in our time, the church has to be the resistance movement of the exalted Christ in a world claimed by him and invited into his freedom." Cf. the concluding words of his autobiographical "Theological Review": "As a last word and as my bequest, Let me call to you in Huguenot style: 'Resistez!' Discipleship of the Crucified leads necessarily to resistance to idolatry on every front. This resistance is and must be the most important mark of Christian freedom" (*On Being a Disciple of the Crucified Nazarene*, xxi).

62. Käsemann, *Commentary on Romans*, 251.

because, as Käsemann writes, "received blessing brands us, but it also sets us in conflict and contradiction. It places us before the need to persevere and in the possibility of relapse. It is not an irrevocable destiny which puts an end to the history of existence and the world. It gives free play to real history by making it the place, not of fallenness and doom, but of the assaulted freedom of faith and of the grace which is to be seized unceasingly in renunciation of the old aeon."[63]

In keeping with the logic of the *Christus Victor*, the overarching conceptuality of the Christian life here receives a decidedly *political* cast. Given the realism of Käsemann's apocalyptic hearing of the gospel, this once again is no mere trope. As Käsemann writes, Christ's "lordship over body and soul, heart and mind, disciples and demons, this world and the world to come, is a political fact."[64] Politics, in the normal course of things in the yet-unredeemed world, seems to involve something like an all-too-human struggle to cast out demons by the power of other demons, the effort to check the exercise of power by the deployment of other countervailing powers.[65] But cleaved to the body of Jesus Christ as people who, in the power of Spirit, acknowledge that they have been set under his sovereign liberation and claim, Christians now serve the extension of his reign. It is a reign different in kind from that of political powers (John 18:36), and it is all the more real for being so. Jesus resists assimilation of his lordship to the patterns of this age, saying, "If it is by the Spirit of God that I cast out demons, then the kingdom of God has come to you" (Matt. 12:28). Accordingly, the Christian's political service to Christ's reign can and must be politics *by other means*, a politics of the third pneumatological article of the church's ancient creeds, we might say. In several occasional works from later in his life, Käsemann rather provocatively in this vein proposed that Christian service in the world should be thought of as a form of *exorcism*.[66] This suggestion trades heavily on the apocalyptic grammar of New Testament narratives within which concepts such as freedom, liberation, and resistance represent important theological terms of art. To see the Christian life in terms of possession and exorcism, idolatry

---

63. Ibid., 249, 156; cf. also 247: "The old aeon, rebellious, threatening, and perverted is still present, so that Christians are under attack," and yet "in the Spirit God does not merely maintain his right. He also graciously brings [those he upholds] home and preserves them. In this way he manifests his love as Creator. This is the triumph of the assaulted."

64. Käsemann, "What I Have Unlearned," 334–35.

65. Perhaps the Niebuhrian account of justice as the achievable balance of competing human egoisms being matched under the conditions of sin may be open to such an exousiological redescription; see Niebuhr, *Nature and Destiny*, 2:252, 254.

66. See esp. Käsemann's two essays "Righteousness of God in an Unrighteous World" and "Healing the Possessed."

and iconoclasm, is to tether our theopolitical rhetoric of the Christian life not only to the New Testament but also crucially to the honoring of the First Commandment. Further, it rightly emphasizes that the struggle to tell the evangelical truth in and about the human situation is a struggle not just with error and ignorance but finally also with powerful, enrapturing superstitions and hegemonic falsifications (Eph. 6:12).[67] Understood in this way, Christian freedom is the name for the power that animates a life of joyful, bold, and costly witness, the hope of which is to serve Christ as the Lord of grace and to "bring him as such to others."[68]

A Brief Excursus on Gustav Aulén

Some twenty years after the 1931 publication of *Christus Victor*, Gustaf Aulén reprised and expanded the constructive element of that study in a concise essay titled "Chaos and Cosmos: The Drama of the Atonement."[69] Though the term "apocalyptic" itself never appears in that text, the proposal is in close keeping with the hearings of Paul's apocalyptic gospel set forth by Käsemann, Martyn, and others in later decades and may readily be supplemented and expanded by tapping this vein of New Testament theology. Aulén stresses that a properly evangelical soteriology can and must understand "atonement" firmly within that "cosmos-encompassing dramatical perspective" that is "fundamental for all Christian thought."[70] The central motif of the biblical drama is the story of God's love, mercifully rampant against the "hostile powers" that bind and oppress humanity. In the New Testament these powers bear the particular names of Sin, Death, and the Devil, together with the Law and other creaturely powers themselves rendered inimical to God by the oppressive power of the same. The drama thus comprises a clash of antagonistic dominions the catastrophic culmination of which is the confrontation in Christ between the loving lordship of God and the inhuman sphere of "all the inimical domination." Such fearsome rhetoric as this is required, Aulén says, in order to "set forth in a concrete and active manner

67. See Käsemann, "Healing the Possessed," 199–201.
68. Ibid., 204. Moreover, "it must be shown and proved that the gospel rids of demons, that it deserves to be called mother of Enlightenment and, in league with the Enlightenment, unmasks idols" (203). Cf. also Käsemann, *Commentary on Romans*, 251: Christian freedom—"as an anticipation of the resurrection and the joy of conquerers"—is such that "even when inferno threatens on all sides, the Christian is stigmatized by the Lord who is present for him, and is set in *parrēsia* [courageous confidence]."
69. Aulén, "Chaos and Cosmos." Cf. also §26 of his *Faith of the Christian Church*.
70. Aulén, "Chaos and Cosmos," 157, 156.

the constant, radical, and spontaneous opposition of the divine will of love to all that is opposed to it and therefore destructive."[71] Thus, as with Käsemann, the idiom of apocalyptic is acknowledged to give uniquely fitting expression to the dynamism, radicality, and effective scope of the outworking of God's loving will, which is at the heart of the gospel.

In keeping with this emphasis, Aulén goes on to stress that the primary agent of salvation is ever *God*: it is God who comes low in the person of his Son to win the victory and reconciliation for beleaguered creatures. Indeed, to compromise the activity of God at this juncture would at once "deny the reality of the Incarnation" and "destroy" the gospel truth. As Luther puts it, "To abolish sin, to destroy death, to take away the curse in himself, and again, to give righteousness, to bring life to light, and to give the blessing, *are the works of the divine power only and alone*."[72] This is true of the accomplished work of Christ; it is also true of the ongoing reality of the Christian life. For just as with Käsemann, here too the Christian life is firmly set under the effective promise of the present and future activity of both Christ and his Spirit. In *Christus Victor*, Aulén argues that because Christ's victory over all creaturely enmity to God was an eternal triumph, it is a present reality as much as it is a past reality.[73] In later work he speaks in more dramatic terms of the present time being one that is superintended by the "permanent work of the victorious Christ in his church" in and through the word of the gospel, a work "continuously realized in the present," whose character is ever that of "self-giving, victorious and sovereign love."[74] On the other side of the turning point of the cross and resurrection, "the Spirit of God has the same hard work to do with every new generation and every new man."[75]

Aulén again, much like Käsemann, recommends the apocalyptic discourse of *Christus Victor* in part because of its power to demythologize our all-too-human common sense that thinks of us, wrongly and desperately, as the only agents on the field of history. For in the "classical" account of salvation, he says, we hear afresh "*the old realistic message* of the conflict of God with the dark, hostile forces of evil and His victory over them by the Divine self-sacrifice."[76] Writing in the wake of the Second World War, he contends that "it would be rather striking if the thought of demoniacal powers, devastating in

71. Ibid., 160, 163.
72. Ibid., 158–59. The citation is from Luther, *Paul's Epistle to the Galatians*, 277, Aulén's emphasis.
73. Aulén, *Christus Victor*, 150.
74. Aulén, "Chaos and Cosmos," 166; *Faith of the Christian Church*, 216, 215.
75. Aulén, "Chaos and Cosmos," 167.
76. Aulén, *Christus Victor*, 159, emphasis added.

our world, would be unfamiliar to men in the present age," since his generation had "experienced beyond measure how such powers have swept over us
like a pestilential infection; we know very well their might to poison and lay
waste."[77] The apocalyptic "atmosphere" proper to the announcement of the
gospel has an uncanny traction in our own day: it offers an ancient and timely
realism and provides us with *the metaphorical characterization of moral
and cosmic realities which would otherwise defy expression.*"[78] Apocalyptic
concepts and categories are able to describe reality as we find it in the world
of struggle at the front line of the incursion of the Kingdom; so too are they
able to help us discern and to raise up "the cry of an enslaved creation and
see the messianic woes taking place therein."[79] As Carl Braaten once observed,
while other theological idioms are not incapable of giving voice to such truths,
apart from an apocalyptic perspective their expression is readily and all too
often obstructed and rendered "sterile or inactive."[80]

Conclusion

In this chapter I have examined some of the central features of Käsemann's
apocalyptic soteriology, as well as something of Aulén's related writing, in
order to set forth and to recommend the power of such a reading of the biblical
witness to salvation. As the basic idiom of soteriology, an eschatological account of *Christus Victor* is capable of articulating Sin's vast power and scope,
but also the ever-so-much-greater power and scope of divine grace rampant
in Jesus Christ. By embedding its theological anthropology firmly within an
apocalyptic cosmology, it does justice to both the bondage and complicity of
humans in Sin, and so it also includes—rather than bypasses—the reality of
human enmity and guilt. Salvation comes on us as liberation that, precisely
because it translates the sinner from one sphere of lordship to another, gives
radical evangelical substance to notions of forgiveness, justification, and new
life. From this follows a compelling orientation toward understanding the
Christian life as the politics of discipleship that honors the living, militant
grace of Christ now come on the church in the power of the Spirit.

Schooled in this apocalyptic gospel of radical and militant divine grace,
Christian theology is led to recognize how Paul's claim that "Christ *must*
reign" is, as Käsemann puts it, "the nerve centre of the design and the firm

77. Aulén, "Chaos and Cosmos," 159.
78. Gunton, *Actuality of Atonement*, 66, emphasis original; cf. 69, 80.
79. Käsemann, *Commentary on Romans*, 251; cf. 250.
80. Braaten, "Significance of Apocalypticism," 499.

ground which gives us confidence concerning our own destiny."[81] This is the confidence of the "wandering people of God,"[82] the church that testifies, as has been confessed in our age, that "in the midst of a sinful world, with its faith as with its obedience, with its message as with its order, that it is solely [Christ's] property, and that it lives and wants to live solely from his comfort and from his direction in the expectation of his appearance."[83] Liberation by Christ's lordship constitutes the church as the company of forgiven sinners who, in their creaturely obedience, deliver over to Christ "the piece of the world which they themselves are," in the firm hope that the day is coming when his reign will be manifest and "untrammelled."[84] In this hope, the apocalyptic imagination of Christian faith maintains and confesses that despite all appearances to the contrary the crucified Nazarene is Lord even now. In so doing, as we will go on to argue below, it wins space for a genuinely human life whose very purpose and promise is the justification of God.

---

81. Käsemann, "On the Subject of Primitive Christian Apocalyptic," 135.

82. This is the central theme of Käsemann's early study of the theology of the Letter to the Hebrews, *Wandering People of God.*

83. Barmen Theological Declaration, art. 3, in Presbyterian Church, *Book of Confessions,* 311.

84. Käsemann, "On the Subject of Primitive Christian Apocalyptic," 135.

5

Not without the Spirit

The Eschatological Spirit at the Origin of Faith

Protestant theology variously connects the advent of faith in Jesus Christ to the reality of divine election, to the proclamation of the gospel and witness of the sacraments, and to the "inner testimony of the Spirit." Within the main lines of the Reformed tradition, the work of the Spirit is typically schematized as bringing to subjective efficacy the objective reality of the word: to the external call of the gospel there corresponds, in the elect, the internal and effectual call of the Spirit. Within such a scheme, questions of human freedom and volition, as well as the issue of the degree of correlation between the external call and the internal call, become particularly neuralgic preoccupations. Without entirely dispensing with such emphases, in this concise chapter I want to undertake to draw the matter of the Spirit's work in the advent of faith back into the eschatological framework in which it stands in the New Testament generally and in Paul's witness in particular.

To confess faith in the lordship of Jesus Christ may be considered the originary practice of the Christian life. As such it recommends itself as a primary site at which to investigate the relation between the agency of the Holy Spirit and human activity. We begin with reflections on 1 Corinthians 12:1–3, where Paul identifies the act of the Spirit as the sine qua non of the confession of faith. Attending to this passage as a piece of Paul's apocalyptic gospel, we hope to shed somewhat different light on inherited teaching concerning the nature of faith and "effectual calling." This doctrine has always understood the confession of faith to be a charismatic practice, a direct fruit of the Spirit's working. I suggest that proper appreciation of what is at stake in such a claim turns on a forthright recognition of the Spirit as the present power of God's eschatological reign, militant to determine our reality, and thereby to secure us in faith by entrusting us without reserve to a life "in Christ."[1]

An Exegetical Entrée into the Matter: 1 Corinthians 12:1–3

> Now concerning spiritual gifts, brothers and sisters, I do not want you to be uninformed. You know that when you were pagans, you were enticed and led astray to idols that could not speak. Therefore I want you to understand that no one speaking by the Spirit of God ever says "Let Jesus be cursed!" and no one can say "Jesus is Lord" except by the Holy Spirit.
>
> —1 Corinthians 12:1–3

Two issues commonly preoccupy commentary on these verses. The first concerns Paul's provision of the confession "Jesus is Lord" as a fundamental criterion for the discernment of spiritual gifts within the life of the Christian congregation. The second is the meaning and origin of the arresting phrase *anathēma Iēsous* (Let Jesus be cursed)![2] Our interest here moves in the opposite direction from these typical exegetical priorities. I am concerned not with the christological testing of pneumatological claims but with the pneumatological grounding of christological acclamations. And I am less puzzled by what it might have meant to curse the name of Jesus than curious to discern clearly the origin and nature of faith's open declaration of Jesus as Lord. Three features of this passage seem most salient to these concerns: the agonistic spiritual situation out of which faith arises, the nature of the Spirit's agency at the origin of faith's eruption into confession, and finally the character of confessing faith itself.

First, the confession of faith in Jesus as Lord arises in an ambivalently religious world marked by willful ignorance, idolatry, and pervasive captivity to sin. Paul characterizes the situation out of which the Corinthians came to faith as one in which they were "enticed and led astray to idols." Paul may be alluding to the ecstatic experiences of pagan worship or evoking the image of being swept up in the surging tide of religious festival parades en route to

---

1. See Kraus, *Systematische Theologie*, §§180–87, 451–69.
2. For representative discussion of these matters, see Hays, *First Corinthians*, 209.

the Corinthian temples.[3] However this may be, Paul's tropes are clear and his verbs forceful, even violent. It is not simply that folks have been misguided by muddled "human impulses."[4] Rather, Paul's words bespeak a situation in which people are "not their own masters" but are surrendered to, and dominated by, captivating powers; elsewhere in the letter Paul openly identifies these powers as demonic.[5] The "idols that could not speak" are no gods, to be sure; their very silence betrays them.[6] Yet they assert their claim and exercise their sway. Just as in Galatia, here in Corinth these Christians, in ignorance of God, have previously been "enslaved to beings that by nature are not gods" (Gal. 4:8). To be saved from this is to be redeemed, delivered from dominating powers arrayed against God whose common spirit finds voice in the anti-confession "Jesus be cursed."[7]

Second, on this scenario faith is evidently not a natural or Adamic possibility. Paul makes the point explicitly: "No one can say 'Jesus is Lord' except by the Holy Spirit." The believer is a spoil in the contest between the Spirit of God and the spirit of this world (1 Cor. 2:12), and the victory of the Spirit of God in this contest is the sole possibility for the advent of faith. We should conceive of the Spirit's work as one of repossession, a second and salutary overpowering that translates one out of the thrall of idols and into the sphere of Christ's lordship. Faith follows freely from the event of this repossession by the Spirit. Anyone who utters the confession "Jesus is Lord" "is *ipso facto* living in the sphere of the Holy Spirit's power," as all those who are "in Christ have entered the realm of the Spirit."[8] The Spirit wrests women and men free from their captivity so as to place and hold them knowingly "in Christ." That

3. The argument is made by Paige, "1 Corinthians 12:2—A Pagan *Pompe?*" Thiselton, *First Epistle to the Corinthians*, 911–13, assesses the proposal generously.

4. This is how the situation is characterized by Orr and Walther, *1 Corinthians*, 278. Cf. Thiselton, *First Epistle to the Corinthians*, 914, where he remarks that Paul's target here is finally "all humanly constructed religious 'spiritualities.'"

5. Conzelmann, *1 Corinthians*, 205–6. Robertson and Plummer, *First Epistle of St. Paul to the Corinthians*, 259–60, also stress the violent *compulsion* signaled by the semantics of 1 Cor. 12:2. Cf. Schnabel, *Der erste Brief des Paulus an die Korinther*, 682–83; Barrett, *Commentary on the First Epistle to the Corinthians*, 278–79; Schrage, *Der erste Brief an die Korinther*, 199–20; Fitzmyer, *First Corinthians*, 457–60, who variously rehearses the relevant arguments and textual parallels in antique literature—e.g., a dialogue of Lucian in which we read that love as "a sort of god [*daimōn*] carries us away [*agei*] wherever he wills, and it is impossible to resist him" (Lucian, *Dialogues of the Dead* 8, in *Lucian's Dialogues and Other Greek Extracts* [Albany, NY: D. & S. A. Abbey, 1816], 16). For Paul's later characterization of the powers at work in pagan worship, see 1 Cor. 8:1–6; 10:20.

6. In the Old Testament the muteness of idols is regularly contrasted to the "[God] who comes and does not keep silence" (Ps. 50:3).

7. See Unnik, "Jesus: Anathema or Kyrios (1 Cor. 12:3)," 123–25.

8. Hays, *First Corinthians*, 208.

Paul thinks this to be no small thing is evident; as he says, "If anyone is in Christ, there is a new creation" (2 Cor. 5:17). Invocation of the work of the Spirit is, as it were, a discursive flare fired to signal the radicality, dynamism, and sovereignty of saving divine grace. However else we may characterize faith, it is first and foremost a new creature of the Spirit of Christ.[9]

Third, what of the character and content of faith itself here? The *homologia* (confession) "Jesus is Lord" is one of earliest and most originary acclamations of Christian faith. In the first instance, in the mouth of the Christian it declares an *eschatological* reality, the saving advent of God in Jesus Christ. To utter this confession is to acknowledge Jesus's reign as the sphere in which one now properly lives and acts. Faith in Jesus as Lord is, for this reason, not merely a subjective expression of the significant value Christ might now have for one's life. It is always also an objective declaration that the active presence of Christ constitutes the very environment of life itself: faith is given to know and to confess that the new life is lived "*in* Christ," "*in* the Lord," "*in* the Spirit who is Lord."[10] The confession of faith is a statement of *belonging*, an acknowledgment and invocation of our eschatological *setting*. As such, faith is also a declaration of *allegiance*. Cursing and confessing Jesus are not merely verbal gestures. They are, rather, something performative, "commitments of the whole life."[11] Faith owns the saving relationship with Christ for which the Spirit has repossessed us. To confess Jesus as Lord is therefore an act of practical recognition, in which one entrusts oneself actively and obediently to his disposition and service.[12] Created and propelled by the Spirit, faith in the lordship of Jesus is not only an *assertive* declaration but always at the same time an *expressive* and *commissive* illocution.[13] It has its home in worship, yet also in witness, and therefore also amid controversy and "despite the presence of opponents."[14] Christian faith is, for this reason, always a matter of polemical doxology.

To summarize: in keeping with the contours of his apocalyptic gospel, Paul tightly associates the advent of faith in Jesus Christ with liberation

9. Commenting on this passage, Paul Tillich concludes that the Spirit is the "depth and power which create a new Being in the world, in history, and in man" ("Theologian," 123).

10. See Neufeld, *Earliest Christian Confessions*, 53, 60. Cf. Eph. 1:15; Rom. 16; 2 Cor. 3:17–18.

11. Orr and Walther, *1 Corinthians*, 278.

12. The confession of faith that Jesus is Lord "is true not because it is the right or orthodox formula but because it expresses the proper relation with Jesus," namely, a grateful acceptance of his authority and a declaration of committed service (Barrett, *Commentary on the First Epistle to the Corinthians*, 281). Cf. Fitzmyer, *First Corinthians*, 456.

13. See Thiselton, *First Epistle to the Corinthians*, 924, 927.

14. Neufeld, *Earliest Christian Confessions*, 61, 63–64, 68, 146. Cf. Cullmann, *Earliest Christian Confessions*, 22–24.

from, and open repudiation of, captivity to idols: not only is the confession of faith in Jesus not a human possibility; its emergence is actually also actively resisted by anti-God powers. These idols are ascribed a vague but real agency, against which God moves in the accomplishment of salvation. Paul construes salvation as redemption from under the false lordship of such powers. In so doing he displays an understanding of the nature of the Spirit's action as simultaneously *militant*, *eloquent*, and *graciously sovereign*. In view of this, confession of faith in Jesus's lordship represents an astonished human acknowledgment of the sheer gratuity of the divine victory over the gods of the passing age. In correspondence with the nature of the Spirit's agency in this victory, the confession of faith takes shape in a self-involving act that, owning Jesus before the world, declares and praises the free gift of salvation in him.

The Spirit, Effectual Calling, and the Character of Faith

Historic Reformed sources, much to their credit, track these Pauline emphases quite closely. Drawing attention to some features of their common logic may allow us to refresh and sharpen our understanding of the bare claim of the sixteenth- and seventeenth-century confessional materials that faith is a "gift of God."[15] To expound on this claim, let me venture three observations.

First, Reformed theology advances a doctrine of sin whose seriousness is only overreached by the seriousness of its doctrine of salvation, including its account of conversion to faith. In Paul's telling of the gospel of eschatological redemption, as we have seen, faith arises as we experience our rescue from enthrallment to idols and our repossession by the Spirit, as we are delivered out of the environs of Sin and Death and "into" Christ. Time and again, Reformed sources also stress the gracious agency and sovereign efficacy of the Spirit in freeing those "subdued captive[s] of sin."[16] With notable understatement Eberhard Busch writes that intrinsic to the Spirit's work there "belongs a certain negation," the repudiation of the illusion that we, by our own reason or power, can slip the bonds of our captivity to the "gods who are no gods" and enter into relation with God.[17] As the Scots Confession has it, human beings are dead, stupefied, and trapped in disobedience until and

---

15. Second Helvetic Confession, art. 16, in Presbyterian Church, *Book of Confessions*, 121. More generally, see Heppe, *Reformed Dogmatics*, 510–42.

16. Turretin, *Institutes of Elenctic Theology*, 2:525.

17. See Busch, *Drawn to Freedom*, 210.

"unless the Spirit of the Lord Jesus Christ" enlivens, enlightens, and breaks their captivity.[18] And it is specifically in view of the Spirit's operation that the Canons of Dort describe Christian faith as "evidently a supernatural work, most powerful, and at the same time most delightful, astonishing, mysterious, and ineffable; not inferior in efficacy to creation or the resurrection from the dead."[19] That final clause is no hyperbole: people are no more the agents of their coming to faith than they are of their creation or re-creation.[20] Such talk of the Spirit is a crucial element of a proper trinitarian parsing of the monergism of saving grace. When we praise the Spirit in this way as the sufficient cause of the advent of saving faith, we rightly tether "the efficacy of calling" to the very "motion of God."[21]

Second, we do well to avoid truncated understandings of the Spirit's work that too narrowly identify it with the "interior" call to faith in contrast to the "external" call of the gospel. It is, of course, a commonplace of Reformed teaching that faith arises from the interior or inward working of the Spirit, ordinarily accompanying the public proclamation of the Word. Yet such talk can grow ill-disciplined and, overstrained by explanatory pressures, invites translation without remainder into the categories of religious epistemology or psychology. Paradoxically, the proper aim of theological talk of the *interior* call of the Spirit is to display all the more fully that faith comes to us graciously *ab extra*, from outside. For it is by "the *external power* of the same regenerating Spirit" that God "pervades the inmost recesses of the human person"; the point is to stress the full freedom and scope of the work of grace, not to restrict it "locally," as it were. The doctrine looks to signal that the human person *as such* and in toto is the object of the Spirit's "omnipotent, and at the same time fully intimate, wonderful and inexpressible operation."[22]

---

18. Scots Confession, art. 12, in Presbyterian Church, *Book of Confessions*, 37–38. Cf. Second Helvetic Confession, art. 9, in Presbyterian Church, *Book of Confessions*, 104–6; Westminster Confession, art. 6.4, in Presbyterian Church, *Book of Confessions*, 180: "utterly indisposed, disabled and made opposite to all good and wholly inclined to all evil." Turretin decries as absurd any view entailing that God "will not operate more efficaciously in the conversion of men than Satan operates in their seduction" (*Institutes of Elenctic Theology*, 2:554).

19. Canons of the Synod of Dort, arts. 3–4.11 and 12, available at https://www.rca.org/canons.

20. The Scots Confession, art. 12, in Presbyterian Church, *Book of Confessions*, 37–38, puts it thus: "As we willingly disclaim any honour and glory for our own creation and redemption, so do we willingly also for our regeneration and sanctification." Turretin identifies conversion as re-creation (*Institutes of Elenctic Theology*, 2:526). Cf. the early Christian text of 2 *Clement* 1.8: "For He called us, when we were not, and from not being He willed us to be." (2 *Clement* 1:6–8 sets this claim explicitly in the context of liberation from idolatry, thereby echoing 1 Cor. 12:1–3 very closely.)

21. Turretin, *Institutes of Elenctic Theology*, 2:521.

22. Here I am drawing on Bavinck's analytical paraphrase of propositions from the Canons of the Synod of Dort, arts. 3–4, 11–12, available at https://www.rca.org/canons. See his

To be called to faith is to be fully and irresistibly "accosted by the Holy Spirit."[23]

Appeal to the "interior" work of the Spirit is most closely Pauline when it serves this end, rather than being deployed chiefly to rationalize the irresponsiveness of those unmoved by Christian preaching.[24] Paul makes plain that the Spirit is also the agent of the "external" kerygmatic call to faith, which goes forth (as he said of his own witness) "not with plausible words of wisdom, but with a demonstration of the Spirit and of power, so that your faith might not rest on human wisdom but on the power of God" (1 Cor. 2:2–5). And we have seen (above) how the Spirit's work is the ingredient in the objective accomplishment of our liberation out from under stupefying idolatry. Might recovering this scriptural idiom help resist the fracturing of faith into putatively objective and subjective elements by refusing to allow the concept of faith to drift from its origin in and permanent reliance upon the *dynamis* (power) of the Spirit?[25] Given that the whole business, inside *and* out, turns on the victory of the Spirit, we would do well to reassert the eschatological holism with which the Heidelberg Catechism characterizes faith as that "wholehearted trust which the Holy Spirit creates in me through the gospel."[26]

Third and finally, the distinctive Reformed doctrine of *effectual calling* is liable to a similar kind of pneumatological restatement along these same lines. For reasons just canvassed, we ought to prefer "effectual" over "interior" as the controlling adjective in describing the Spirit's summons to faith. As a conceptual gloss on Romans 8:29–30 in the first instance, talk of "effectual calling" forges a powerful heuristic connection between the faith-creating work of the Spirit, its origins in eternal election, and its telos in the rectification and glorification of creatures in Christ.[27] Traditional Reformed accounts

---

Saved by Grace, 21–22. Cf. van Genderen and Velema, *Concise Reformed Dogmatics*, 584: "*Interna* indicates the specific sphere of influence of the Holy Spirit." See also Turretin, *Institutes of Elenctic Theology*, 2:524–25. In the latter (e.g., 557) much is made of the "friendly" and communicative mode of divine suasion involved, such that the Spirit's efficacious work is never "brute" force.

23. Heppe, *Reformed Dogmatics*, 517, citing Johann Heinrich Heidegger.

24. I therefore am not convinced that the "central question" here ought in fact to be "*why the call engenders such a varied response*" (van Genderen and Velema, *Concise Reformed Dogmatics*, 580).

25. See Berkouwer, *Faith and Sanctification*, 42–44. On the problem of this separation, see Berkhof, *Christian Faith*, 441–42. Hermann Witsius speaks of the word being "fecundated by the transcendent power of the Spirit" (Heppe, *Reformed Dogmatics*, 518).

26. Heidelberg Catechism, q. 21, in Presbyterian Church, *Book of Confessions*, 61–62. Cf. Turretin, *Institutes of Elenctic Theology*, 2:540. This is, in part, the animating impulse of the argument of Vanhoozer, "Effectual Call or Causal Effect?"

27. "For those whom he foreknew he also predestined to be conformed to the image of his Son, in order that he might be the firstborn within a large family. And those whom he predestined

largely focus on the protological (originating) valences.[28] But thinking afresh
with Paul, as we are here, demands that we concentrate more intently on
the eschatological associations. Such eschatological notes are not altogether
absent from historic Reformed teaching by any means: by essentially identifying effectual call with *regeneration*—itself a concept meant primarily to
denote the merciful gift and onset of the new life won from the bondage of
the old—the eschatological character of the Spirit's gift of faith is certainly
honored. As is said, "The Holy Spirit by his effective calling implants a [person]
in Christ."[29] This way of speaking is happily redolent of the Pauline grammar
of the exchange of lordships, which we have traced in previous chapters, and
reflects the idea of the overtaking of the old age by the onset of the new. Effectual calling denotes that event in which *even now* the Spirit takes gracious
possession of us as chattels of God's victory on the cross, securing the life,
freedom, love, and trust of his creatures by an act of sovereign deliverance
that despoils the idols of the age. Active and grateful astonishment at all this
is compressed into the first utterance of faith: "Jesus is *Lord*." The reason
"no one can say 'Jesus is Lord' except by the Holy Spirit" is that the Spirit
is *the* present agent and sovereign advocate of the transit of Christ's reign in
the present age. The regenerate who come to confession are, as Otto Weber
writes, literally "ahead" of themselves, living on the basis of the kingdom
that "is coming toward" them yet is already present and effective for them in
the "event of the Spirit."[30] Those who utter this confession before the world
are thus set apart and sanctified in faith on decidedly eschatological grounds,
or not at all.

Conclusion

The confession of faith in Christ's lordship is an utterance that is itself a
victory of the Spirit over the previous tyranny of silent and silencing idols
in the sinner's life. Such public testimony of faith is a first gift of the Spirit,
the freedom openly to acknowledge what is the case *by virtue* of God's free,
eloquent, and militant act for us and for our salvation. Creatures partake in
this divine victory and are given power to share in its publication by the Spirit.
The confession of faith is a public charismatic practice that courageously

---

he also called; and those whom he called he also justified; and those whom he justified he also
glorified" (Rom. 8:29–30).

28. "When calling is thus added to election, the Scripture plainly intimates that nothing is
to be looked for in it but the free mercy of God" (Calvin, *Institutes* 3.24.1).

29. Heppe, *Reformed Dogmatics*, 518–19, citing Witsius.

30. O. Weber, *Foundations of Dogmatics*, 2:357, 356.

echoes, by grace, the Spirit's own effectual testimony to the lordship of Jesus in the midst of the congregation and in the lives of believers. It represents a realistic and hopeful acknowledgment of the truth of where we are and whose we are by virtue of the working of the same Spirit, "without whom we should remain forever enemies of God and ignorant of his Son, Christ Jesus."[31]

Karl Barth once remarked that "the Christian life begins with a change which cannot be understood or described radically enough."[32] The Heidelberg Catechism confirms this judgment in describing faith as a *creation* of the Holy Spirit. It is the task of Protestant theology generally, and of its account of the Christian life in particular, to demonstrate that such a life is "an impossible newness given as an unfitting gift" by the Spirit, so that the "potency of [divine] grace should be made perfect in our weakness."[33] What is true of the beginning holds true till the end: *nisi per Spiritum Sanctum*—nothing, nothing at all, if not by the Holy Spirit of God. An apocalyptic theology of the kind recommended here can and must set the whole of the Christian life under this rubric.

---

31. Scots Confession, art. 12, in Presbyterian Church, *Book of Confessions*, 37–38.
32. K. Barth, *CD* IV/1:9.
33. Barclay, "Under Grace," 73; Heppe, *Reformed Dogmatics*, 526, citing Johann Heinrich Heidegger.

6

Thy Kingdom Come

The Lordship of Christ and the Reign of God

Let grace come and may this world pass away!
—*Didache* 10.6

The Kingdom of God is a cardinal eschatological motif in the New Testament witness and any theological account of the Christian faith rooted therein. Theology confronts and receives this theme first and foremost in the preaching of Jesus. The significance of the Kingdom of God for faith is further amplified by virtue of being the object of private and corporate prayer whenever Christians implore "Thy Kingdom come!" as they regularly do in the Lord's Prayer. This juxtaposition of the human activity of prayer and eschatology is striking. For eschatology is a tract of Christian doctrine in which claims about the absolute agency of God are to the fore. Prayer, by contrast, represents a distinctively human activity that, it is often argued, makes little sense apart from robust affirmations of human free will and effective agency.[1] Thus, to pray for the coming of God's reign is an act positively riven by this tension. For this reason alone, the understanding and interpretation of the petition "Thy Kingdom come" represents an important test case for

1. Far removed from each other in many ways and yet both with paramount concern to defend human freedom in their discussion of petitionary prayer, see Thomas Aquinas, *Summa Theologia* II-II, q. 83, art. 2; Kant, *Religion within the Limits of Reason Alone*, 180–85.

the assumptions, anxieties, and aspirations of any particular theologian or theological program regarding the relation of divine and human agency.[2]

Leaving aside more philosophical questions concerning the logic of petitionary prayer, this chapter concentrates on understanding the meaning and significance of the prayer "Thy Kingdom come" in its more specifically biblical-theological setting. It is of no small theological consequence that the reality of the Kingdom of God should be made a matter of relentless petition and invocation, and thereby also of persistent Christian longing and hope. But this prayer for the coming of the Kingdom is eschatological not only in its substance but also in its form, having as its very condition of possibility the sovereign outworking of the economy of saving divine grace. In this chapter, I offer an account of the meaning of the petition and its theological implications in conversation with the interpretations advanced by John Calvin and Karl Barth. My overarching aims are twofold. The first is to consider what the distinctive form and content of this dominical prayer entails for an evangelical approach to the doctrine of the Kingdom. I will argue that explicit and sustained attention to the eschatological identity and activity of Christ, as the one who commissions and commands this prayer, is of decisive importance. The second is to reflect on the eschatological "placement" of the Christian who prays in this way and consider what this means for our conception of the essential character and disposition of Christian life and witness. On this score, I contend that we fully appreciate the formative power of the petition on the Christian life only when we recognize that those who pray are personally at issue in the ultimate redemptive contest between Christ and the powers of sin, death, and the devil. In short, I suggest that praying "Thy Kingdom Come" faithfully means inhabiting an eschatological field shaped decisively by both christological and apocalyptic coordinates, and that petitioning God in just this way is properly constitutive of the very fundaments of Christian faith.

Praying for the Coming Kingdom of the Coming One

"Thy Kingdom come," ἐλθέτω ἡ βασιλεία σου (elthetō hē basileia sou), is of course the second petition in the text of the Lord's Prayer as attested by the Gospels of Matthew (6:10) and Luke (11:2), as well as in the *Didache* (8.2). It is a stable element in ancient texts of the prayer, appearing without significant variants, save a very weakly attested (but theologically suggestive) substitution of the entire phrase with "May your Holy Spirit come on us and purify us" in

---

2. See, e.g., concisely Stump, "Petitionary Prayer," 81–91; at length Brümmer, *What Are We Doing When We Pray?*

certain manuscripts and early Christian citations of the Lukan version.[3] The Vulgate renders the phrase as *adveniat regnum tuum*, though some old Latin manuscripts foreswear the interpretive compound verb (*ad-venio*) in favor of simply *veniat regnum tuum*.[4] While paralleled by other more elaborate petitions in Jewish prayer formulas from the rabbinic period,[5] in the canonical Gospels the immediate sense and significance of this very concise petition is intimately related to Jesus's own proclamation of the Kingdom of God.[6] Taken together with the eschatological resonances of the other "You-petitions" of the Lord's Prayer—for example, for the sanctification of the divine name and execution of the divine will—this strongly suggests a thoroughly "eschatological scenario" within which the meaning of the second petition is to be discerned, something further supported by lexical and grammatical considerations.[7] As prayer, the second petition is of course not itself a theological proposition. But

3. Matt. 6:9–13; Luke 11:2–4; *Didache* 8.2. The concluding doxology, absent in Luke yet found in some ancient versions of Matthew and integrated into the text in the *Didache*, strongly echoes the text of 1 Chron. 29:11. See Niederwimmer, *Didache*, 134–38. For thorough discussion of the linguistic, textual, and source-critical matters in Matthew and Luke, see Douglas, "Jesus Tradition Prayer"; W. Davies and Allison, *Gospel according to Saint Matthew*, 1:590–99; Luz, *Matthew 1–7*, 367–72; Bovon, *Luke*, 2:79–97. See also Betz, *Sermon on the Mount*, 370–77; and Lohmeyer, *Lord's Prayer*, 13–31.

4. See Lohmeyer, *Lord's Prayer*, 88. Calvin was aware of the variant Latin translations; see Calvin, *Harmony of the Gospels*, 1:207.

5. For comparable texts and discussion, see Charlesworth, "Jewish Prayers at the Time of Jesus"; Petuchowski, "Jewish Prayer Texts of the Rabbinic Period"; Heinemann, "Background of Jesus' Prayer in the Jewish Liturgical Tradition." The most significant parallels are found in the *Qaddish*, "May He establish His Kingdom in your lifetime and in your days, and in the lifetime of the whole household of Israel, speedily and at a near time" (37); in *Berakoth* 11–12 of the *Eighteen Benedictions*, which asks that God might "rule over us" so as to "uproot, crush, cast down and humble the kingdom of arrogance" (32–33); and the *Alenu*, which has the congregation praying that the whole world will "accept the yoke of Your kingdom, so that You will reign over them soon and forevermore. For Yours is the kingdom, and unto all eternity You will reign in glory" (14). Notable also in this regard is a saying of Rabbi Yohannan: "A benediction which does not mention the kingdom of God is not a benediction" (*b. Berakoth* 40b). See Guggenheimer, *Scholars' Haggadah*, 194.

6. Representatively, see Stendahl, "Your Kingdom Come," 261; and Vögtle, "Lord's Prayer," 102, who stresses that its meaning is anchored to "the basic theme of his preaching of God and his Kingdom, his proclamation of the eschatological acts of God indicated by his speech and action." As Luz concludes, "One must put the *entirety* of the Lord's Prayer into the proclamation and activity of Jesus" (*Matthew 1–7*, 387).

7. So Allison, *Sermon on the Mount*, 116–22. Commentators remark that the aorist tense of the verb strongly signals this, as does the fact that this verb "to come" is part of a well-established eschatological lexicon that speaks of the "day" or "hour" that "is coming." See Luz, *Matthew 1–7*, 377–78; W. Davies and Allison, *Gospel according to Saint Matthew*, 604–5; and the important discussion by R. Brown, "Pater Noster as an Eschatological Prayer," 188–91. For an extended discussion of the signal importance of the apocalyptic vision of Daniel to the shape and substance of the second petition as well as of the Lord's Prayer as a whole, see Beyerle, "Von der Löwengrube ins himmlische Jerusalem," 23–34, esp. 26–29.

the performative language of the Lord's Prayer as a whole, and of this petition in particular, is thoroughly theological in nature and invites and even demands dogmatic reflection if its purpose and importance are to be understood aright.[8]

To pray for the coming of the Kingdom is to beg that God would come upon the world *as God*. For God to do so would end its illegitimate and vicious usurpation by the powers of sin and death, making the whole of creation coextensive with the sphere of his rightful, effective, and salutary lordship.[9] Here "to come" is, as Ernst Lohmeyer explains, "a periphrastic expression for an action of God which so to speak [re-]creates the world and all reality from outside" since "the pure and permanent place and the pure and permanent manner of his action is precisely the age to come."[10] The coming of the Kingdom, the advent of the reigning God, is the epitome of eschatological divine action because it visits on the world that proper telos of which it is otherwise sinfully forfeit. In the parabolic idiom of the Gospels, what is in view is the arrival of the bridegroom (Matt. 25:1–13), the return of the master (21:33–44), the coming of the thief in the night (24:42–44), the inescapable final assize (25:31–46), the threshing of creation's harvest (3:12), the apocalypse of the Son of Man (Luke 17:30), and so, in short, the accomplishment of "that destiny toward which the whole of time is directed."[11] The petition calls upon God to "remember" his own righteousness and invites the Lord to do that which only the Lord can do: to justify himself by realizing his promise to reign.[12]

This eschatological vision is enriched and made more complex by other New Testament testimony to the decisive connection between Christ's person, death, and resurrection and the reality and realization of God's Kingdom. Thus the Kingdom for which we pray is already "at hand" and "upon you" in the coming of Jesus himself (Mark 1:15; Luke 17:21). Paul can similarly adapt this idiom of Kingdom to announce the eschatological proximity of Christ himself: he testifies to the Philippians, "The Lord is near" (Phil. 4:5). The widespread appellation of Jesus as Lord (*kyrios*) implies this intimate connection between

8. A point stressed by Betz, *Sermon on the Mount*, 377–78.

9. Confirmed by Betz, who considers that "the arrival of the kingdom 'also on earth,' that is, the complete victory over evil, is thus the content of this petition. This petition is justified because no one but God can make his kingdom come" (ibid., 390–91).

10. Lohmeyer, *Lord's Prayer*, 93, 94 (see also the wider discussion, 90–95). The point is made more briefly by Ladd, *Jesus and the Kingdom*, 132–33: "The coming of the Kingdom is undoubtedly eschatological; but it is a divine act, not a future realm." Cf. Burrows, "Thy Kingdom Come," 5–6, who observes that the "collation of the idea of the kingdom of God and the idea of coming is itself remarkable" against the backdrop of Jewish testimony and prayer.

11. R. Brown, "Pater Noster as an Eschatological Prayer," 190.

12. Betz, *Sermon on the Mount*, 375, 378, emphasizes the obligations of divine righteousness in making sense of the "you-petition" form as a *hypomnēsis*, or "calling to mind," of a divine promise to rule.

Christ's person and the Kingdom; and it is also signaled by synoptic parallels in which appeal to the name of Jesus, to "the gospel," and to "the Kingdom of God" are simply interchanged (Mark 10:29; Matt. 19:29; Luke 18:29).[13]

Indeed, the gospel announces the coming Kingdom as an event that, in and through Christ, is even "now overtaking what is passing away on earth" and establishing itself as the "most inescapable reality now facing us."[14] As Richard Bauckham has argued, "Early Christian interest was primarily in soteriology and eschatology, the concerns of the gospel, and so, in the New Testament, it is primarily as sharing or implementing God's eschatological lordship that Jesus is understood to belong to the identity of God."[15] The fundamental bond forged here between Christology and eschatology—or better, between Christ himself and the reign of God—became even more explicit by the late second and early third centuries, when Tertullian reports the claim that the gospel concerns "the Kingdom of God, Christ himself" (*dei regnum, Christus ipse*), and Origen coins the word *autobasileia* (the kingdom in person) as a term of art by which to express that Christ is not only the "King of Heaven" but is himself the Kingdom.[16] So strong is the link between Christ and the Kingdom in the early Christian imagination that it becomes possible, even necessary, to construe the eschatological advent of the Kingdom of God exclusively in terms of Christ's own apocalyptic parousia.

In just this way, as Jan Milič Lochman observes, the "inner closeness and indeed identity of the subject of the two basic forms of the New Testament petition 'come'—the Kingdom of God and the Lord Jesus—[proves to be] of vital importance" to theological reflection on the substance and direction of the second petition of the Lord's Prayer.[17] The decisive meaning of the petition "Thy Kingdom Come" is to be found in its intimate material proximity to the apocalyptic prayer "Come, Lord Jesus" (1 Cor. 16:22; Rev. 22:20).

Yet a glance at the tradition suggests that many formative interpretations of the second petition of the Lord's Prayer bypass this "eschatological element" and go their "separate ways."[18] This shows itself where eschatology no longer leavens the understanding of Christ's royal presence and action beyond

---

13. For concise discussion, see Schmidt, "Basileia," 1:589.

14. Morse, *Difference Heaven Makes*, 23–24. Eastman, "Lord's Prayer," rightly draws attention to this.

15. Bauckham, "Divinity of Jesus in the Letter to the Hebrews," 235.

16. Origen, *Commentariis in evangelium Matthaei* 14.7.10 and 14.7.17 (Balthasar, *Origen*, 362). Tertullian, *Adversus Marcionem* 4.33.8. It is ambiguous whether this formulation is taken over solely from Marcion or whether it is Tertullian's own.

17. Lochman, *Lord's Prayer*, 51. Betz, *Sermon on the Mount*, 392, makes this same point on more narrowly comparative and lexical grounds.

18. E.g., Luz, *Matthew 1–7*, 378.

domesticating descriptions of the Kingdom as the interior sway of the divine within the human subject, or the expansion and purification of ecclesiastical life as such. In turning now to consider the theological interpretations of the second petition advanced by Calvin and Barth, we must be particularly alert to their negotiation of the crucial interplay of eschatology and Christology, as well as to the ways in which they connect the eschatological content of the second petition to the Christian life.

Theological Glosses on the Second Petition: Calvin and Barth

Calvin

Calvin's own Geneva Catechism (1541) teaches that the Kingdom of God principally consists in the governance of the faithful by the Spirit together with the confutation of the rebellious reprobate in a simultaneous expression of divine mercy and divine power. In praying for its coming, Christians ask for both the progressive expansion and deepening of the church, and the destruction and abolition of "Satan and the powers of darkness . . . and all iniquity" through the public manifestation of divine justice and truth. In short, they pray that God's reign "may continually increase and advance, until it comes to its perfection in the day of Judgement."[19] These brief teaching articles have behind them Calvin's discussion of the matter in the early editions of his *Institutes of the Christian Religion*. There he ascribes to the petition a threefold sense: first, as prayer for the ingathering of believers and their receipt of the Lord's grace, which deepens "their perfect union with himself"; second, as prayer for God's "light and truth" to dispel the "darkness and falsehoods of Satan and his kingdom"; and third, as prayer for the glorious fulfillment of all this "in the revelation of [God's] judgement" and final defeat of all his enemies (citing 1 Cor. 15:28). As in the catechism, so also here Calvin conceives of the Kingdom's coming as having a twofold valence, concerned as it is with the edification of the elect on the one hand and the "destruction" of the reprobate on the other. Throughout, Calvin once again emphasizes the *spiritual* nature of the Kingdom and designates the Spirit and the Word as its effective agents.[20]

The 1559/60 *Institutes* sees Calvin thoroughly rewrite his exposition while maintaining its overarching features.[21] Several new emphases appear. The two

19. Geneva Catechism, qq. 268–70, in Torrance, *School of Faith*, 47: God "casts down and confounds the reprobate who refuse to subject themselves to His rule, and so makes it clear that there is no power which can resist His power."
20. Calvin, *Institutes* (1536), 79; *Institutes* (1541), 483–84.
21. Calvin, *Institutes* (1559), 3.20.42.

"fronts" of the Kingdom's coming are now set *within* the one praying subject, where "obedient thoughts" war with "the desires of the flesh."[22] Correspondingly, Calvin insists that first and foremost the petition demands mortification, humility, and repentance on the part of the one who prays since "in this way . . . God wills to spread his Kingdom." The spiritual edification of the church remains a primary object of the prayer, but Calvin also speaks freely of how "God sets up his Kingdom by humbling the whole world," imposes vital order and—by the ever greater display of his "light and truth"—ultimately "slays Antichrist with the Spirit of his mouth, and destroys all ungodliness by the brightness of his coming."[23] Notably, it is only in the 1559/60 revision that Calvin adds explicit mention of the second coming of Christ in relation to the content of the petition.[24]

This is all in keeping with the glosses Calvin offered on this same petition in his 1555 *Harmony of the Gospels*, where God's reign is raised up against "the complete disorder and confusion" that is "laying waste upon the face of the earth." It is established in two ways: on the one hand, by the government of human beings by Word and Spirit; on the other hand and "in another fashion," by God's overturning his enemies "when he forces them all unwilling—with Satan at their head—to accept his authority, till all become his footstool." Calvin's eschatological vision is, as Elsie McKee says, "typically moderate" inasmuch as he envisages the steady progress of the Kingdom "stage by stage, to the end of the world."[25] The exposition ends, however, with an arresting totalizing remark: "As far as iniquity holds the world in sway, so far is the Kingdom of God absent—for complete righteousness must come in its train."[26]

What is to be said of Calvin's treatment of the second petition? It would be false to charge that the properly eschatological substance of the petition is suppressed by Calvin, for at every stage in his developing understanding he keeps in view the final eschatological horizon, within which are set the extension of the Kingdom over individual lives, the body of the church, and finally the world. Though consistent emphasis falls on the theme of God's effective governance of the individual soul and the congregation, one could

22. Mazaheri, "Calvin's Interpretation," 109, observes that "self-criticism is an essential feature of the new version." This shift is also picked out of the most notable development by Neusner, "*Exercitum Pietatis*," 100.

23. The conclusion is a paraphrase of 2 Thess. 2:8. The new note of interest in ecclesiological *order* is noticed by commentators; see Mazaheri, "Calvin's Interpretation," 109–10; McKee, "John Calvin's Teaching," 98–99.

24. "But its fullness is delayed until the final coming of Christ, when, as Paul teaches, 'God will be all in all'" (Calvin, *Institutes* 3.20.42).

25. See McKee, "John Calvin's Teaching," 99.

26. Calvin, *Harmony of the Gospels*, 207–8.

argue that they appear as microcosms of the whole and as such are construed as provisional aspects of the one matter of the Kingdom's final advent.[27] The result of this is to forge a meaningful connection between the effective work of grace and the understanding of final divine judgment associated with the establishment of the Kingdom. Yes, Calvin does speak of the Kingdom's coming upon the world in a way that seems to cast it as different in kind—for example, "forces them all unwilling"—from the liberating and transforming work of Spirit and Word.[28] Yet in the end Calvin's ultimate decision to introduce explicit reference to the coming again *of Christ* in association with final judgment, as well as to seal his interpretation of the petition with 2 Thessalonians 2:8 (emphasis added)—"*The Lord Jesus* will destroy [the lawless one] with the breath of his mouth, annihilating him by the manifestation of his coming"—suggests his discernment that the identity of the Coming One leads us to believe that the saving instruments of Word and Spirit will be precisely those by which the final victory of divine right in and over the world is also to be won.

The interpretation as a whole suggests that Calvin himself took the second petition to be a *hypomnēsis* (remembrance), a plea for God to remember his divine righteousness and to make good on the promise of its realization among creatures. These aspects of Calvin's interpretation of the second petition signal and reinforce his overarching judgment that it is "in the person of Jesus Christ the eternal King, [that] the spiritual Kingdom and the earthly Kingdom are ultimately joined together."[29]

Further, there is no question that Calvin conceives the reality of the supplicant as one already determined by the campaign of God's electing and regenerating grace in the world being waged by Word and Spirit, the telos of which is eschatological victory. The situation of the one who prays is fundamentally shaped by the adventitious and agonistic realities of sin and divine grace.[30] As Calvin's account makes patent, the person who petitions for the coming of the Kingdom is decisively implicated in an eschatological contest in which individual, church, and world are all ultimately at stake. The time of the praying church is enfolded within the unfolding of the parousia. As Quistorp observes, for Calvin, "the whole span of time subsequent to the

27. See Quistorp, *Calvin's Doctrine of the Last Things*, 165.
28. Quistorp (ibid., 192–93) observes that Calvin's theology displays "a certain tension between his loyalty to the Biblical message of the return of Christ and of the Kingdom of God as a visible all-embracing reality, and on the other hand his humanistic tendency to confine and spiritualize the hope in the direction of the salvation of the individual."
29. Niesel, *Reformed Symbolics*, 299.
30. For a fuller account of this, see chap. 10 below.

epiphany of Christ, however protracted it may be, is the last hour."[31] That the Kingdom comes by way of the undoing of the false and disordered anti-God powers—of darkness, sin, death, Satan, the devil, the antichrist, *and* our conscripted sinful desires—bespeaks Calvin's understanding of God's reign as the good news of human redemption. This prayer goes up, then, in a time and place wherein Christ as Lord is already extending his dominion of grace, from people who even as they "bear the cross" are freed to hope in the assurance that finally "there is no power which can resist His."[32]

Barth

Karl Barth offers two focused discussions of the second petition of the Lord's Prayer: the first, as part of a set of seminars offered between 1947 and 1949 on prayer as a theme in the theology of the Reformers; the second, in texts written between 1959 and 1961 as the basis for the last paragraph of the *Church Dogmatics* (§78, "The Struggle for Human Righteousness") within his unfinished ethics of reconciliation.[33] We will briefly consider each in turn, looking to bring out the distinctive theological contours of Barth's interpretation and commentary in relation to our theme. It is highly signifi-cant that Barth explicitly sets out from the judgment that the Reformers

31. Quistorp, *Calvin's Doctrine of the Last Things*, 117, citing Calvin's glosses on 1 John 2:18–19.

32. Calvin, *Institutes* (1541), 483. Several features of Calvin's account are paralleled in contemporary Lutheran and Roman Catholic catechetical expositions of the second petition, yet also find echoes in subsequent Reformed catechisms, including the Heidelberg Catechism and the shorter and longer versions of the Westminster Catechism. The Heidelberg Catechism, q. 123, in Torrance, *School of Faith*, 94, teaches that prayer for the coming of the Kingdom seeks God's present preservation and governance of the church by Spirit and Word, and as its corollary, the destruction of the "works of the devil" and all powers set against God, "until the fullness of [God's] Kingdom arrives, in which [God] shall be all in all." These sentiments are echoed in Craig's Catechism, which identifies the coming of the Kingdom with the time "when the Spirit reforms and rules our hearts" even as the "tyranny of Satan may be beaten down" (Torrance, *School of Faith*, 140). See also the Larger Catechism and the Shorter Catechism, in Torrance, *School of Faith*, 231–32, 277. For the Catholic exposition, see "Thy Kingdom Come," in *Catechism of the Council of Trent*, 458–67. Common is discussion of the differentiated modalities of the Kingdom of grace and of glory, the identification of the former with the church and its mission, and a vision of the progressive overthrow of the re-bellion of Satan, sinners, and heretics by God's untrammeled power. The repeated emphasis on the instrumentality of "Word and Spirit" in the Reformed texts supplants, however, an explicit Catholic appeal to the "interior virtues of faith, hope, and charity" as the particu-lar instruments of Christ's present reign "in us." For Luther's gloss, see Large Catechism, §§53–54, in *Triglot Concordia*.

33. K. Barth, "Prayer in the Reformation," "Christian Prayer according to the Reformers," and "Interpretation of the Lord's Prayer," in *Prayer and Preaching*, 9–63; K. Barth, CD IV/4. On the latter, see also my essay "'To Pray, to Testify, to Revolt.'"

themselves did not adequately grasp the properly eschatological character of the Kingdom.[34]

Barth's first exposition leads with a fully eschatological definition of the Kingdom as God's "effective and appointed defence" of humanity and victory over sin; as such it is equivalent to the reconciliation of the world with God; it is the enactment of God's own righteousness, his sovereign realization of the world's "destiny and purpose," which sees all creaturely reality ultimately "enfolded by the peace of God."[35] From this definition, two crucial things follow. First, the coming of the Kingdom can only be something for which we pray since it infinitely exceeds both our imagination to conceive and our power to achieve. The Kingdom comes by way of the action of God as Creator and Lord, or it does not come at all. This, rather than its temporal finality, is what constitutes its eschatological character. Second, and no less crucially for Barth, God has already established his Kingdom in and through Jesus Christ. As he explains, in Christ "the world has reached its end and its goal" such that in him the final judgment is an event that is "already behind us": "We proclaim the Word made flesh and the Kingdom of God which has come." The "last word" on which our very life depends has been uttered by God in Christ, whose coming, dying, and rising have opened the final age.[36] Not only must God alone do it: God alone has done it.

This realized eschatology appears to make the petition "Thy Kingdom come" a very strange thing to pray indeed. It may suggest that the petition must in fact be understood as a form of indirect proclamation, since the meaning of the prayer, as Barth states, amounts to "*Thy Kingdom has already come. . . . Thou, God the Father, hast accomplished all things in Jesus Christ!*" And yet, Barth contends paradoxically, precisely when it is understood in this way, it becomes all the more necessary to offer up the prayer *as petition*. Why? Because to pray for the coming of the Kingdom means to ask God to make the hidden truth of this *already* manifest even now, to "remove the covering," to lift "the veil behind which reality lies," to make visible to sight what is currently invisible and grasped only by faith.[37] In short, Barth explains, the petition must be understood as a plea to disclose to plain sight the Kingdom that has already come.

But perhaps not only that. For he also writes of how this petition asks that the Lord resume his "great [saving] initiative for humankind" in our own time

34. K. Barth, "Interpretation of the Lord's Prayer," 35.
35. Ibid., 36.
36. Ibid., 37–38.
37. Ibid., 38, italics original.

and place, and act to make the reality of Easter "actual for all the world."[38]
There is a critical connection between knowledge and actualization here,
a conception of the *revelation* of the Kingdom as itself an effective event.
Revelation, for Barth, is a matter not only of epistemology but always also of
divine pragmatics. At this juncture Barth's citation of 1 Peter 1:13 is notable:
"Set all your hope on the grace that Jesus Christ will bring you when he is
revealed." This verse suggests that the advent of saving grace is coincident
with Christ's self-revelation (his own "apocalypse"). In this connection notable
too is Barth's remark that the marginal Lukan variant of the petition—"May
your Holy Spirit come upon us and purify us" (Luke 11:2)—provides a "fitting commentary" on the meaning of the petition, but only if the advent of
the Spirit is understood eschatologically to mean that power by means of
which "the end of the whole present order and the advent of the new order
of existence" is realized. "*Thy Kingdom come—this Kingdom that has come
already!*" is thus the meaning of the petition in Barth's account.[39]

Two things are clear: first, that Barth explicitly identifies *without remainder*
the Kingdom with the person and accomplished work of Jesus Christ; and
second, that he insists—not in spite but precisely therefore—on a fully eschatological understanding of the content of the petition. Those who pray for
the coming of the Kingdom have the Kingdom's hidden reality already behind
and around them as the object of their faith, and they have the Kingdom's
open manifestation and actualization ahead of them as the object of their
hope. Thus the prayer itself arises from faith in the reality of the Kingdom's
presence. It does not intimate its absence.

These motifs are reiterated and enlarged in the dramatic exposition of the
second petition that Barth offers in the fragment of the ethics of reconciliation
published posthumously as *The Christian Life*. Here the overarching context
is provided by the task of setting out the fundaments of a moral theology ori-
ented to the reality of divine reconciliation, in which prayer—specified as the
invocation of God—is the archetypal human action. For Barth, to prosecute
this task demands that we "orient ourselves further to [the] being of God in
Jesus Christ, the concept of the kingdom of God, [and] of the divine seizure
and exercise of power."[40] He explains:

God's kingdom is God himself . . . as he *comes*. The concern of the second
petition is precisely with this coming. As God's kingdom is God himself, so
God is his kingdom in his own coming: his coming to meet man, to meet the

38. Ibid., 30.
39. Ibid., 40.
40. K. Barth, *CD* IV/4:15.

whole of the reality distinct from himself. The second petition looks forward to this special dynamic reality, to the coming of God's kingdom as the coming of God himself. . . . He comes in the deed in which he acts and deals on and for and with them as their Lord and King, in which he acts directly as such and proves himself to be such. . . . He comes and creates righteousness.[41]

More tersely, Barth suggests that the Kingdom is "God himself in the act of normalizing human existence, . . . God himself in the victorious act of overturning the disorder which still rules humanity."[42] As before, this act of God is identified fully with Jesus Christ: it is *he* who is God's coming, such that "speaking about God's kingdom could only mean telling his story."[43]

Barth thus identifies the Kingdom with the enactment of divine salvation as such, stressing the complete identity of the action of God with God "in act." Here he fully exploits the New Testament's agonistic grammar of competing "lordships," setting the gracious and salvific lordship of God against the oppressive captivity of the false, yet actual, dominion of what he memorably styles here as "the lordless powers." Taking cognizance of the reality of these "lordless forces" is crucial, Barth argues, because otherwise Christians would "not know what we are doing when we pray 'Thy kingdom come,'" namely, that negatively at least, we are asking for the gracious unmasking, overcoming, and ultimate abolition of these absolutisms that rule us *per nefas* [improperly]."[44] In all this, Barth consistently draws out from the trope of the Kingdom the governing motifs of salutary divine *power* and *order* and applies them to humanity as such and to the world as a whole; the matter of the Kingdom's significance for the lives of individual believers and the church community is dealt with implicitly and derivatively from within this total eschatological perspective. Christians pray for the Kingdom not "from an alien or neutral place" but "from the enacted and present coming" of divine power and order in Christ.[45]

It is fascinating to consider whether Barth's talk of "the lordless powers" owes anything to Calvin's remarks in his *Harmony of the Gospels*, where he says in connection with the second petition that the Kingdom of God is completely opposed to the world's disorder and confusion (ἀταξία, *ataxia*) because there is nothing "in the world well-ordered unless He arranges [it]."[46]

41. Ibid., 236.
42. Ibid., 212.
43. Ibid., 252–53. Karl Barth anchors this point by a serial repetition of "He is . . ." claims.
44. Ibid., 219.
45. Ibid., 247.
46. Calvin, *Harmony of the Gospels*, 208. The text of this passage mistakenly reads ἀταραξία for ἀταξία.

However that may be, materially both Reformed theologians discern that to pray "Thy Kingdom come" is to be drawn into God's own struggle to extend the good and salutary order of his gracious reign across the contours of a damnably inhumane and unruly world.

Unique to Barth's late exposition of the second petition is his appeal to the theme of *revolt* to explain the significance of the prayer in disposing Christian lives. Precisely because of the eschatological content of the petition, uttering it amounts to the first and "decisive action of their revolt against disorder."[47] Barth goes on to suggest that Christians take responsibility for their prayer for the Kingdom precisely by enacting "kingdom-like" parables that exploit the "relative possibilities" for realizing a provisional human righteousness, which even now celebrates and hopes for its consummation in that final divine righteousness that only God can make manifest.[48] Barth lays down the rudiments of a fascinating, even if frustratingly incomplete, Christian social and political ethic in these final few fragmentary passages of his *Church Dogmatics*.

Christians are active in correspondence to divine righteousness during this present time of the Spirit, "endowed and equipped with freedom for this," Barth concludes, and "grasp this promise, look and move forward, and pray, 'Thy kingdom come,' 'Come, Lord Jesus.'"[49] We do well to notice Barth's confident apposition of these two New Testament prayers, a possibility afforded him by that "highly distinctive sense of time" determined by the "whole content" of the Easter gospel, in which the Christ who is "perfectly past" is also "still perfectly future."[50]

Concluding Remarks

In this chapter, I have searched for the particular eschatological content and form of the second petition of the Lord's Prayer in conversation with its interpretation by Calvin and Barth. Allow me to summarize some key insights that have come to light.

First, the very possibility of taking the second petition of the Lord's Prayer as our own resides fully in the gift of the Lord and nowhere besides: it is only as those saved, summoned, and commanded by Christ the *Eschatos* that we

47. K. Barth, CD IV/4:212.
48. Ibid., 265. For concise discussions of the ethics that Barth develops in this way, see Gorringe, *Karl Barth*, 264–66; Webster, *Barth's Ethics of Reconciliation*, 207–13; McKim, "Karl Barth on the Lord's Prayer."
49. K. Barth, CD IV/4:256.
50. Ibid., 254–55.

may genuinely pray for the *eschaton*. Those who pray "Thy Kingdom come" do so under a double eschatological determination: they have behind them the accomplished saving work of Christ, of the One who is *autobasileia* and from whom this petition is received as gift and command; and they have before them the promise of the full and final reign in which Christ will have "put all his enemies under his feet" (1 Cor. 15:25). Christians may only be "bold to say"—*audemus dicere!*—this petition for the Kingdom's coming because they have been graciously enfolded within the eschatological economy of salvation. In Calvin's terms, the prayer goes up from within the present kingdom of grace; in Barth's idiom, the possibility of the prayer resides in that fact that it asks for "this kingdom which has come already." The prayer becomes Christianly intelligible within this eschatological environment, or else it remains misunderstood.

Second, coming as it does from the hand of Christ, the mainspring of the prayer for the Kingdom is the plenitude of the gospel. The prayer, we might say, is propelled by the grace that has been received, rather than pulled from the supplicant by despair in face of the world as it is. While it certainly involves a forthright acknowledgment of the "gap," as it were—between faith and sight (Barth) or between the dispensation of grace and that of glory (Calvin)—it does not speculate about that for which it pleads, nor is it anxious about the uncertainty of the outcome. This is because the eschatological hope animating the petition is substantiated christologically. "It is not what *God* could do and what *we* could do that forms the basis of our prayer for the coming of the kingdom, but what God *does* for us and what God will do for us again and again."[51] In Christ, faith knows and trusts the God whose righteousness it calls down on the world; it knows and entrusts itself to the outworking of that same righteousness by which it has already been seized. And faith prays humbly and joyfully during this long "last hour" (Calvin) and from within the open parentheses of Christ's parousia (Barth) for the advent of the Kingdom as the concluding act in the divine campaign of saving grace.

Third, the prayer draws the supplicant into an agonistic situation of spiritual and moral struggle. The reign of God comes on and against creaturely opposition—futile, absurd, and anarchic opposition perhaps, but actual, inhumane, and evil opposition nonetheless. As Bonhoeffer once put it, "the kingdom of Christ is a kingdom that has been lowered into the cursed ground from above."[52] The expositions offered by both Calvin and Barth highlight this in their own way. Calvin concentrates more fully on the internal opposition of

51. Bonhoeffer, "Thy Kingdom Come!," 291.
52. Ibid., 289.

personal sin and unbelief that is being mortified under the present governance of Word and Spirit. But this is set firmly, as microcosm in macrocosm, within the full eschatological horizon of victorious struggle with the inimical and disorderly powers of Sin, Death, and Satan. Barth too especially lifts out the agonistic situation into which the Christian is actively drawn as a petitioner for the Kingdom. So much so, in fact, that the defining posture of the Christian life can be characterized in this context as *revolt* and *resistance* against the "lordless powers" of the present age. Prayer for the Kingdom of God enjoins faith's allegiance and creaturely obedience in just such struggle.[53]

In both cases, the understanding of this conflict is fundamentally disciplined by the christological concretion of the Kingdom and its coming: for Calvin, the means of the reign of grace—Word and Spirit—are the defining divine instruments of this eschatological struggle, and the transposition from grace to glory is effected by Christ, whose coming again is coincident with the final and full realization of divine righteousness. For Barth—even more explicitly and as a point of particular emphasis—the meaning and means of the Kingdom are identified with what God in Christ is and does for humanity: the eschatological horizon is identical with the horizon of the world already remade between Christmas and Easter, and final righteousness identical with the gracious rectification of all things, which is the accomplished work of Christ's cross. Christian hope in the struggle for the future is hope that it is and will be "the future of the One who has Come."[54] As Lochman has observed, in the end "to whom the final word belongs in our ambivalent world and among us ambivalent people is not in any sense unclear. Jesus Christ is Lord. . . . To him the future belongs."[55]

In a recent essay theologian and ethicist Hans Ulrich has argued that the very ethos of the Christian life is founded in the "apocalyptic-messianic reality" that is at once the environment in which we pray "Thy Kingdom come" and also the reality for which we hope and plead.[56] Our theological reflections on the second petition here suggest nothing less. To offer this petition is to commit oneself in discipleship to "constantly trying to confront situations with promises and promises with situations" so that all our problems are firmly placed and grasped "in the context of the Kingdom of God."[57] More

53. For trenchant reflections on the character of prayer as "combat" worked out in proximity to Karl Barth's sensibilities here, see Ellul, *Prayer and Modern Man*, 177–78.

54. From the title of Walter Kreck's valuable study of eschatology, *Die Zukunft des Gekommenen*.

55. Lochman, *Lord's Prayer*, 165.

56. Ulrich, "Messianic Contours of Evangelical Ethics."

57. Lochman, *Lord's Prayer*, 62.

than that, it is to be freed in obedience to think, speak, and act in ways that openly deny and repudiate as false and usurpatious the dehumanizing disorders of the present age. In sum, it is to inhabit a radical hope suspended and sustained by the promise of that time when "the kingdom of the world has become the kingdom of our Lord and of his Christ" (Rev. 11:15).

In view of all this, we can well appreciate the almost comical depth of Joachim Jeremias's understatement when he observes that "the Lord's prayer teaches us how to ask for the great things."[58]

---

58. Jeremias, "Lord's Prayer in Modern Research," 146.

7

The Final Triumph of Grace

The Enmity of Death and Judgment unto Life

Justice and Immortality: Toward an Evangelical Framing of the Question

There is, in Kant's moral philosophy, an important connection between the concept of immortality and the matter of final divine justice. As is well known, both the existence of God and human immortality are a priori postulates of practical reason: concepts to which reason is necessarily committed as the very conditions of possibility of there being a moral world at all. Human finitude and weakness seemingly frustrate ethical reason, confronting us with fragmentary and incomplete enactments of the moral law as well as manifest disjunctions between moral rectitude and human happiness. Yet, if it is to be rational for us to pursue the highest good as the proper object of our will, then right conduct and happiness *must* finally align, and a full and perfect enactment of the moral law *must* be possible. These demands are met by postulating as "subjective necessities" both the existence of God as the all-powerful moral lawgiver and judge, and human immortality as the provision of "a duration befitting the complete fulfilment of the moral law."[1] In short, a happy conspiracy of the supreme power of moral order and the infinite extension of the time of our autonomous moral agency renders intelligible the moral world and our lives within it.

1. Kant, *Critique of Practical Reason*, 140, 201, 246–47.

Notice that on Kant's account, immortality is instrumentally ordered to justice: eternity is simply that quantity of time a human life requires to guarantee
that it can attain to the ultimate ends of moral life. Further, as a postulate of
practical reason, the concept of immortality may signify nothing beyond that
which moral reason itself specifically necessitates. It thus comprises *nothing
but* infinite temporal duration as is "required for conformity with the moral
law," and "any further dissemination of its meaning" would be "a mere fig-
ment or fiction."[2] It is, on Kant's view, liable to no legitimate amplification
of meaning; it can undergo no broadening of reference; its characterization
cannot be further enriched. Kant's concept of immortality is as conceptually
astringent as it is fundamental to his project.[3] The solution to the problem
of perfecting the autonomous moral will in the rational world that the divine
Legislator oversees is simply that, as a matter of practical necessity, we believe
there will always be *more time*.[4]

Adjudged theologically, Kant's moral religious vision is soteriologically
anemic: the self-saving subject is afforded neither aid nor grace but only
authorized to "believe in" there being space to continue to struggle on ad
infinitum. Here we are not so much saved by the bell as saved by the fact that
the bell never rings to call time on our moral endeavors to realize the highest
good and marry justice with happiness. In short, where it is held—as Kant
does—that "the right way to advance is not from grace to virtue, but rather
from virtue to grace," rational belief in immortality serves only to hold open
law's laboring indefinitely.[5] Immortality is the moralist's optimistic wager
on there yet being more time to succeed.

A Christian theology riveted to the gospel of Jesus Christ will see the matter
otherwise. Constrained and yet also warranted and impelled by the reality of
God's self-revelation in Christ, evangelical dogmatics is given to approach and
understand the reality of eternal life—together with the narrower question
of human immortality that it encompasses—within a markedly different and
much more robust soteriological framework. For Kant, the fragile finitude of

2. Ibid., 241; Firestone and Jacobs, *In Defense of Kant's Religion*, 31.
3. As Pamela Sue Anderson observes, by this mode of argument neither immortality nor
God is made "cognizable" anyway—and they are certainly not hereby vindicated as objects of
theoretical reason indirectly (*Kant and Theology*, 61–63).
4. On the critical importance of the doctrine of the postulates for Kant's moral philosophy,
see Sprute, "Religionsphilosophische Aspekte," 295. A similar astringency and importance also
marks Kant's doctrine of God, which, in the hostile characterization of John Milbank, "only
lures the will to know more of its own empty assertion" ("Invocations of Clio," 16). Cf. Gray,
Immortality Commission, 22–31, who discusses how this view profoundly shaped the life and
work of the leading Victorian moralist, Henry Sidgwick.
5. Kant, *Religion within the Boundaries of Mere Reason*, 191.

the moral will is the problem to which immortality (as indefinite extension) provides a rational solution. Theology acknowledges that both the problem and its solution are far more radical. As with Kant, there is again a crucial connection between eternal life and the matter of ultimate justice. But theology must conceive the nature, ordering, and significance of that connection distinctively. Approached evangelically, eternal life stands as the crowning gift of the unimaginably gracious advent and realization of ultimate divine justice upon and for us, rather than being merely structurally instrumental to its human pursuit. *Pace* Kant, the determinative movement really is and can only be "*from* grace to virtue." If this is so, then the primary theological task is to understand the nature and role of saving divine judgment as the necessary and creative ground and source of eternal life. As we will see, pursuit of *this* task quickly makes clear that the theological question of eternal life concerns not merely the *quantity* of human existence but much more fundamentally its comprehensive eschatological *quality*.[6]

Question 52 of the Heidelberg Catechism asks, "What comfort does the return of Christ 'to judge the living and the dead' give you?" and answers: "That in all affliction and persecution I may await with head held high the Judge from heaven who has already submitted himself to the judgment of God for me and has removed all the curse from me; that he will cast all his enemies and mine into everlasting condemnation, but he shall take me, together with all his elect, to himself into heavenly joy and glory."[7]

In this chapter I consider the efforts of two contemporary Protestant theologians, Eberhard Jüngel and Jürgen Moltmann, to expose and exposit the connection between the advent of saving divine justice and the reality and promise of eternal life as set out here in the catechism. Whereas Kant could only conceive of divine justice as the ultimate vanishing point of autonomous human moral striving, these theologians can and must conceive of divine justice in strict and materially decisive reference to the "last judgment" and the event of Christ's crucifixion and resurrection as God's saving acts. By thinking through the links between cross, resurrection, justification, and final judgment, these writers try to attain to an understanding of eternal life adequate to the gospel. Their common aim is to offer responsible dogmatic commentary on the testimony to Christ's death and resurrection as that salutary act of God ensuring that "grace might exercise dominion through justification leading

6. It is interesting to notice how lines of eschatological thinking, when invested in the question of human agency and active moral reconciliation between persons, tend to be led in this Kantian direction toward affirming the instrumental necessity of something like the afterlife. See, e.g., Volf, "Enter into Joy!," 264.

7. Heidelberg Catechism, in Presbyterian Church, *Book of Confessions*, 66.

to eternal life through Jesus Christ our Lord" (Rom. 5:21). The question of
eternal life is thus rightly bound up with that of God's righteousness and so
with the final justification of God and the rectification of all things. In doing
so, they particularly emphasize the *philanthropic* dimension of divine judgment announced in the first half of the catechism's answer.

I will then go on to argue that for this philanthropic emphasis to be fully
worked out, we must also attend directly to the other motif invoked by the
catechism: the divine victory over inimical powers, "God's enemies and mine,"
of which Death itself is the final and ultimate enemy (1 Cor. 15:26). A forensic
emphasis on saving divine judgment admits and demands this crucial cosmological supplement. For eternal life, if it is to emerge at all, can and must
be understood to emerge miraculously from out of the inhumane cauldron
of death's enmity and sin's bondage.[8] We appreciate most fully both the
radically gracious and mercifully humane character of eternal life, I suggest,
when we acknowledge that life to be the fruit of God's redemptive overthrow
of humanity's utter usurpation by Sin and Death. The last judgment is a
judgment unto life—*eternal life*—not least because it is the terminal defeat
of death's annihilating enmity.

Divine Judgment for Life's Sake: Jüngel and Moltmann

Moltmann and Jüngel approach the question of the last judgment with special
interest in the features that mark it out as a specifically *Christian* dogma. What
commonly concerns them is the soteriological integrity of the doctrine, the
way it can be understood to cohere with fundamental evangelical teaching
concerning salvation by grace through faith in Christ alone. In this endeavor,
unsurprisingly, the christological determination of God's righteousness proves
decisive, forging material links between justification and judgment that anchor
and recast the meaning of the latter. The result is to call out the fundamentally
salutary character of the last judgment as a servant of the new creation and
the establishment of eternal life.

Aspects of Moltmann's thinking on this matter are already adumbrated
as early as his work *The Theology of Hope*. There he identifies divine righteousness with the creative fidelity of God that establishes and sustains the
historic, harmonious ordering of relationships "founded on promise and faithfulness" that justify life and make possible "existence as such."[9] Faith in the

8. For a developed Thomistic vision of the nature of eternal life's emergence that sees the
matter rather differently again, see Hoye, *Emergence of Eternal Life*.
9. Moltmann, *Theology of Hope*, 203–4.

gospel of Christ's dying and rising entrusts our lives to this divine righteousness as the sole power able to set all things to rights with God and creatures and thus makes justifying righteousness "the summary expression for a universal, all-inclusive eschatology which expects from the future of righteousness a new being for all things."[10] God's righteousness takes concrete form as the outworking of reconciliation toward a final redemption overreaching death and "quickening" to new life; even now, the gift of righteousness brings with it an experience of the re-creative "power of the Giver" in and over our lives.[11]

Particularly important for our purposes is Moltmann's developed insistence that an evangelical account of God's righteousness must be fundamentally eschatological. It is so because it grasps Christ's enactment of divine saving righteousness for us in his passion and resurrection as an anticipation, a prolepsis, of the final enactment of righteousness, as the "sending forward of God's future," his "historical descent from the future to the present," as it were; in and by these events begins God's "eschatological subjugation" of all things.[12] As Moltmann explains, the forward movement of the Christian life from "the presence of salvation to the consummating future . . . is comprehended and enclosed by the converse theological 'descent' from the eschatological sole lordship of God to the provisional lordship of Christ."[13] In short, the justifying work of Christ is a real and effective prolepsis of God's exercise of final judgment, "already realising today what is to be tomorrow."[14] For this reason, we are warranted in identifying the *content* of the last judgment with Christ's rectifying work by cross and resurrection: that *is* this, differing only in mode and manner of our participation, but not at all in fundamental reality and meaning.

It is this commitment that animates and informs two recent and overlapping essays in which Moltmann addresses himself directly to the question of the last judgment and eternal life.[15] Rather provocatively, he suggests that "it is high time to Christianise our traditional images and perceptions of God's final judgment" and to "evangelise their meaning for the present day."[16] Negatively, this demands that we reject the idea that divine judgment is retributive as a view properly alien to biblical faith, despite being widely

10. Ibid., 205, 204.

11. Ibid., 206.

12. Moltmann, "Trends in Eschatology," 30–31.

13. Ibid., 31.

14. Ibid., 47.

15. Moltmann, "Final Judgment"; Moltmann, "Sun of Righteousness." There is also related discussion of these themes in Moltmann, *Coming of God*, esp. 47–95 and 235–37. For some discussion of our themes, see Harvie, "Living the Future," 156–59.

16. Moltmann, "Final Judgment," 569–70; Moltmann, "Sun of Righteousness," 135.

held and deeply integrated into Christian traditions. No such reduction of righteousness to punitive retribution is warranted or indeed theologically cogent since it forfeits the biblically specific semantics of divine justice and instead conjures up a damaging image of a capricious, hostile, and wrathful God. Modern revisionist accounts of the judgment that do away with this picture of God but retain the logic of retribution turn God into a mere "symbol for the ultimate endorsement of our free will," whether as its "executor or accomplice."[17] Notably, in all cases retributive justice *is its own end*: that idealized moment in which we all get what is coming to us (*suum cuique!*).

Positively, Moltmann suggests that a properly Christian account of the last judgment must begin by recollecting both the concrete identity of the Judge and the scriptural concept of creative divine righteousness. It is Christ, who bears the sins of the world so that "grace also might reign through righteousness to eternal life" (Rom. 5:21 RSV), to whom humanity goes for final judgment; it is his "judgment seat" and his "day" (2 Cor. 5:10, Phil. 1:6). And he will be manifest then as the One he is: not a "divine avenger" or "final retaliator" but rather the "crucified and risen victor over sin, death and hell."[18] As such, Christ will render the selfsame divine righteousness that has already erupted proleptically in his death and resurrection: a righteousness that creates justice, reconciles all things to God, and rectifies the distorted field of sinful relations.[19] This is a creative, salutary, and healing righteousness—the work of the cross—that brings about liberation on all sides: justice and restoration for victims, transformation and rectification for perpetrators, genuine creaturely freedom for all.[20] It is an act of love that "burns away everything which is contrary to God so that the person whom God has created will be saved."[21] *This* is judgment that one might actually implore and await with "head held high."

Whereas a final retributive justice would be an end in itself, Moltmann suggests that an evangelical account rightly construes the execution of divine

---

17. Moltmann, "Final Judgment," 569. As an instance of this, Moltmann cites both art. 1037 of the *Catechism of the Roman Catholic Church* and a 1995 report by the Doctrine Commission of the Church of England, which asserts, "It is our conviction that the reality of hell (and indeed of heaven) is the ultimate affirmation of the reality of human freedom" (Moltmann, "Sun of Righteousness," 134).

18. Moltmann, "Sun of Righteousness," 136.

19. See Moltmann, *Coming of God*, 236. These remarks are also anticipated in Moltmann, *Way of Jesus Christ*, 335.

20. For brief discussion of this in the work of other modern theologians, see Thiselton, *Last Things*, 166–71.

21. Moltmann, "Sun of Righteousness," 137; Moltmann, "Final Judgment," 571. Cf. 1 Cor. 3:15.

judgment as a forward step in bringing about another end, namely, the establishment of eternal life. He explains:

> So the last judgment is not the end of God's works, nor is it the last thing of all; it is not last, but penultimate, it is only a first step in a transition from transience to non-transience. What is final is only the new, eternal creation, which will be brought into being on the foundation of righteousness. Because the judgment serves this new creation of all things, its righteousness is not a righteousness related to the past, which merely establishes what is done and requites it. It is a creative righteousness related to this future, a righteousness which creates justice, heals and rectifies. The judgment is not at the service of sin and death, as if it were the great settling of an account. It serves the new creation; . . . through and beyond that judgment [is] God's new world.[22]

Final divine judgment puts things to rights *for the sake of an unhindered future for creaturely life*. Identical in substance with the saving work of Christ, its essence is positive and generative: God judges to save and fulfill. And the eternal life to which it gives rise is shorn of all that would threaten, truncate, and undermine true life with and for God, a life founded ultimately beyond the entire "dissolution of the world of evil."[23] It is, in short, the gift of life made true by God's righteousness, life that God has graciously honored and dignified, a manifestly and irrevocably *justified* life.

Eberhard Jüngel operates with a markedly different eschatology from Moltmann, yet it is also one that secures the identity of the content of the last judgment with the saving work of Christ's cross and resurrection. This effort pivots around the theological category of "the new."[24] This idea—the advent of that which in no way emerges from the old and for that very reason calls the old into question, of that which ever remains "unique, never to be surpassed, and never to become antiquated"[25]—is core to the logic of Jüngel's account of revelation. As the saving act of God, Jesus Christ is *the* new thing—*definitive*, *final*, and graciously *generative*. The saving work of this "new Adam" gives rise to a renewed humanity, a "new creature in Christ [that] no longer grows old."[26] New in this sense, Christ is the *Eschatos*, who disposes over time. As the crisis, judgment, and savior of time, Christ's reality determines what will pass away and what "even if it is past, ought to have a future, an *eternal*

---

22. Moltmann, "Sun of Righteousness," 138. A closely parallel passage appears in Moltmann, "Final Judgment," 572.
23. Moltmann, "Final Judgment," 573.
24. Jüngel, "Emergence of the New," 35–58.
25. Ibid., 49.
26. Ibid., 51.

future." The salutary novelty of Christ and his justifying work show themselves precisely in the divine "*creative power of renewal*," which he exercises and by which all things shall be made new.[27] As Jüngel explains,

> The justifying judgment distinguishes and sets up two opposites: the being of the person as it is determined by that person's past and as it is determined by that person's future. . . . On the one hand there is power that determines the being of the person, the power of his or her guilt-laden past which is self-made, and which, by the death of Jesus Christ, had been forever condemned to perish and is therefore perishing. On the other hand there is the future, with all its eschatological possibilities, which has been granted to us by God and can thus never date. It has already been opened to the believer by the resurrection of Jesus from the dead.[28]

This account of saving revelation makes the event of Christ's historic cross and resurrection the decisive and unsurpassable determinant of the quality of creaturely life ultimately promised to faith. Creaturely life is secured for an *eternal future*, Jüngel says, in virtue of its gracious involvement in the eschatological character of Christ's own ever-new life. Jüngel contends that our hopes for this future life are "guided entirely by that participation in God's eternal life which has *already been achieved* in Christ and which is *even now possible* through the bounty of the Spirit."[29]

And this same mode of eschatological argument bears directly on the question of the last judgment. Once again, as with Moltmann's invocation of prolepsis, we have here an argument of the form "this *is* that" which effectively disciplines Christian understanding of the last judgment by tethering it tightly to the saving work of Christ's dying and rising. For Jüngel, it is the logic of the revelation of "the new" that secures this identity: we may admit that the last judgment is "an unexpected act of surpassing excellence," and yet it cannot be thought of as an act that either "relativises or thwarts" the work of reconciliation already accomplished in Christ.[30] In fact, Jüngel argues that the analogy between the present and future in this case should be conceived not as "already / not yet" but rather more strongly as "*even now—only then completely.*" On this basis he concludes that evangelical theology must construe the last judgment without hesitation or caveat "as an act of grace."[31]

27. Ibid., 54–55.
28. Jüngel, *Justification*, 224–25.
29. Jüngel, "Last Judgment," 390.
30. Ibid.
31. Ibid., 391.

What does this characterization mean, and what does it entail for understanding the relation between the final judgment and eternal life? In the first instance, it announces the fundamental importance of the identity of Jesus Christ as the Judge who "has been judged in our place." Judgment day will be *his* day (1 Cor. 1:8; 2 Cor. 5:10; Phil. 1:6). This being so, the last judgment is not only compatible with Christ's work of justifying "the sinner *sola fide*"; it is in fact decisively linked with and "founded" on it.[32] Our understanding must be led by the fact that the last judgment may only be conceived "within the horizon of the Good News." Salvation involves suffering the work of Christ's loving death and resurrection, so Christian hope in the final judgment is "something quite different from hope in endless continuity."[33] As a work of the "One who brings salvation," final judgment will itself be a grace, for "to be judged *by* Christ is a *blessing* which befalls humanity."[34] The philanthropy of judgment follows from the identity of the Judge who is love, a love made manifest "in the unity of life and death in favour of life"[35] for the sake of the wayward creation.

Jüngel explicates the philanthropic reality of divine judgment as an event of *dignifying truth* and *vivifying peace*. It is, first, an event of dignifying truth because its "severe illumination" of all things in the light of the gospel takes human life and history with the utmost seriousness, ascribing to it real value and so honoring humanity as the creature that divine love is concerned to bring into the truth.[36] The final judgment's elucidation of the lives we have actually led cannot be thought to be "indifferent" and "merciless" because its light is that of the One who came into the world not to condemn *but to save*; it is therefore a *glorifying* light. "Humanity," Jüngel says, "is *glorified* unto judgment."[37] Appeal to Christ's identity once again proves to be key: faith cannot conceive of Christ like the blindfolded—and thus indifferent and inhuman—judges that commonly figure justice in both the ancient and modern imagination.[38] His office is not coldly retributive, for Christ himself

32. Ibid., 394–95. For critical discussion of the adequacy of thinking along such lines, see Volf, "Enter into Joy!," 259–65.

33. Jüngel, *Death*, 120.

34. Jüngel, "Last Judgment," 395–96, emphasis added. Cf. K. Barth, *CD* IV/1:217.

35. Jüngel, "Last Judgment," 404.

36. Ibid., 396–97, 399.

37. Ibid., 397. As he explains elsewhere, "It is as finite that man's finite life is *made eternal*. Not by endless extension—there is no immortality of the soul—but through participation in the very life of God," for resurrection and final judgment concern "the life man has actually lived. It is this life which will be delivered and honoured" (Jüngel, *Death*, 120–21). Cf. Jüngel, *God as the Mystery*, 215n58.

38. Jüngel discusses these menacing images at the outset of the essay "Last Judgment," 391–93; interestingly, Moltmann offers some similar discussion of ancient Egyptian conceptions ("Sun of Righteousness," 129–31).

is the intimate advocate of those he judges. The truth delivered by the *lumen gloriae* (light of glory), the truth of the verdict of the last judgment, is the effectual truth that sets sinners free.

This leads directly to the second characterization of the judgment as an event of *vivifying peace*.[39] God in Christ reveals himself to be the One "who establishes justice, who by suffering injustice banishes it from the world and brings peace"; the rectifying work of cross and resurrection realizes an "eschatological juridical order of peace," which the last judgment will complete and establish.[40] In this it becomes plain that "God's righteousness is a power that penetrates into the fallen world in order to make over anew the world's unrighteous relationships."[41] In Christ, as at the last, this righteous work of judgment sees that God's "holiness is burdened with our unholiness" in order to save both victims and perpetrators from what has become of them in a traumatized world of sin.[42] The last judgment consummates justification in a redemption that delivers sinners from the agonistic captivity to self-righteousness *and* self-condemnation that still besets us in the present. The ultimate horizon of Christ's justifying judgment is the restoration—better, re-creation—of "those relationships in which alone human life can find its fulfilment," what Jüngel calls the ultimate achievement of an "unimpeachably" human condition, a vital and unshakeable peace won out of the maelstrom of sin and death by virtue of the creative power of God's love.[43] For Jüngel, this vision of righteous peace is at the heart of the very meaning of eternal life: the *intensity*, *fullness*, and *durability* of eschatological life are all functions of it being "*peaceful* existence"; for if "whatever exists in peace, does not suffer loss," as he explains, then we must think that "eternity is the *peace* of being."[44]

"God's Enemies and Mine": Making an End of Death's Enmity

To this point, I have endeavored to highlight the essential arguments in the work of Jüngel and Moltmann that account for the joyful confidence that the student of the Heidelberg Catechism has before the prospect of the final judgment. Both theologians follow the catechism's line by anchoring this joy primarily in

39. On this generally, see Jüngel, "Die Ewigkeit des ewigen Lebens," 352–53.

40. Jüngel, "Last Judgment," 397–98. "It is the work of the judge to establish the order of peace by means of that justice which makes God's grace into justice and thereby acquits the sinner" (403).

41. Jüngel, *Justification*, 64–65.

42. Jüngel, "Last Judgment," 398, 400–401.

43. Jüngel, *Death*, 89–90.

44. Jüngel, "Die Ewigkeit des ewigen Lebens," 352–53, emphasis original.

the identity of Christ as the Judge, who "has already submitted himself to the judgment of God for me and has removed all the curse from me." On this basis, both then draw out the creative, restorative, and liberating character of divine righteousness in a way that conceives of the last judgment as the consummation of the saving work of Christ's cross and resurrection; rather than being merely a retrospective cementing of the fates that human beings have worked out for themselves, the last judgment is actually another decisive step in the outworking of God's gracious salvation. The upshot for both is a substantive understanding of the gift of eternal life as a consummate fruit of final divine judgment.

Now, to conclude, I here remark briefly on the importance of the "second plank" of the catechism's hope: its vision of the final judgment as the divine victory over the inimical powers of Sin and Death, which it styles memorably as "God's enemies and mine." It is precisely the tight material connection between Christ's death and resurrection and the last judgment that makes this second theme an inalienable part of any fully evangelical account of the latter.

As argued above, among the soteriological idioms of the New Testament, perhaps the most radical is that of Pauline apocalyptic, for it conceives of human beings as captive to anti-God powers that have "rendered humanity incapable of repenting, seeing God's forgiveness, and resolving in future to do what is right."[45] Chief among our slave masters of "this present age" are Sin, Death, and the Devil, rogue cosmic agents inimical to God and God's purposes and to whom humanity has been, as Paul says, "handed over."[46] Sin and Death "reign" (Rom. 5:14, 17, 21). The situation is one of fundamental captivity and within that captivity also of baleful complicity as humans have become the "settled inhabitants" of the world of Sin, "actively habituated," as previously argued, to its ways as subjects devoted to the service of its false gods.[47] One might well call this state of affairs "total depravity."

Envisaged in this way, salvation can come only through a divine incursion from without, the invasion of divine grace, because what humanity needs is ontic and ontological rescue, "not merely repentance and forgiveness, but liberation from its captivity and, indeed, new creation."[48] God's saving work in Christ is here the ransom, redemption, and liberation of human beings out from under the terminal enmity of death and sin in an exchange of lordships that constitutes the very "turning of the ages." The saving work of the

45. Gaventa, "'Neither Height nor Depth'—Cosmos," 198. Galatians, the Corinthian Epistles, and Romans—esp. the central chaps. 5–8—are prime sites of this material.
46. Romans 1:24–28. For a compelling reading of this passage, see Gaventa, "God Handed Them Over," in *Our Mother Saint Paul*, 113–23.
47. See chap. 4 above.
48. Gaventa, "'Neither Height nor Depth'—Cosmos," 199.

cross and resurrection is the world's rectification by the Christ of God, whom death could not hold (Acts 2:24). It comes to expression as rescue from "the present evil age" (Gal. 1:4), the triumphant disarming of the powers of the age (Col. 2:15), a remaking of godless creatures (Rom. 5:6), the bringing into being anew of human partners who were as good as naught (Rom. 4:17), the making alive of those dead in Sin's service (Eph. 2:5)—in short, it is the advent of "a new creation" (2 Cor. 5:17) by incorporation into the living lordship of the Crucified One.

It is really only in this context that we can approach Paul's eschatological vision of Christ's triumphant subjugation of "all his enemies under his feet," culminating in the destruction of death itself, the final and ultimate enemy (1 Cor. 15:25–26). That Paul sees the upshot of Christ's sovereign eschatological judgment to be the *final victory* over death—"Death has been swallowed up in victory" (1 Cor. 15:54)—is of a piece with this apocalyptic vision of Christ's saving work as the prosecution of a "cosmic war between the powers of sin and death on the one side, and God's powerful rectifying, life-giving grace on the other."[49] Eternal life is life won from death's tyranny; thus the final work of divine judgment must bring to an end once and for all the usurpatious reign of death for the sake of God's beloved creatures. Moltmann summarizes the logic, clearly if rather abstractly: "The negation of the negative constitutes a position of the positive, which cannot be destroyed."[50]

Though it is not their controlling concern, Jüngel and Moltmann both attend to this important motif in their expositions of the final judgment, and Paul's apocalyptic grammar inevitably (and properly) shapes aspects of their understanding of God's rectifying grace. So, for example, Moltmann points up Christ's resurrection, in a somewhat Hegelian idiom, as the "negation of the negation of God" by way of God's own creative judgment, further characterizing it as an eschatological act that conquers the "deadliness of death" and over-reaches "all that is dead in death." In Christ's rising we meet the "beginning and source of the abolition of the universal Good Friday, of that god-forsakenness of the world that comes to light in the deadliness of the death on the cross."[51] Elsewhere Moltmann can declare that in the end, "what will be annihilated is nothingness; what will be slain is death; what will be dissolved is the power of evil; what will be separated from all created beings is separation from God,

---

49. De Boer, *Defeat of Death*, 179.
50. Moltmann, "Final Judgment," 574.
51. Moltmann, *Theology of Hope*, 211. For instance, references to Käsemann's scholarship on divine rectification, Pauline apocalyptic, and the central place of Christ's contest with and lordship over death are found at key junctures in the argument of that book, e.g., 206–7, as well as the later programmatic essay "Trends in Eschatology," 23–31.

sin."[52] Our ultimate salvation can in this vein be aptly summarized simply as "the annihilation of the destiny of death."[53] Remarks of this sort signal Moltmann's sensitivity to the role played by the overthrow of the atheistic enmity of death in the saving work of divine judgment unto eternal life.

The theme is even more sharply present in Jüngel's theology. Evangelical faith obediently trusts that "the God who in participating in man's death *gains victory over death*" has done so *for me*.[54] As Jüngel sees it, the antithesis between God and death structures the gospel itself. "God and death are opponents," he writes, "they are enemies. The style in which God deals with death, and in which death also has to deal with God, is the history which faith tells about Jesus Christ."[55] As the annihilating power and consequence of sin, death is aggressively active, "repudiat[ing] life by hopelessly alienating men and God from one another."[56] Salvation is the business of dealing with death, as it were. For Jüngel, the death of Christ accomplishes the *death of death*: in the identity of the living God with the dead man Jesus, God meets death, taking its enmity and contradiction into himself in virtue of his own divine life.[57] Death is thus overcome in and by the outworking of the eternal vitality of God's love. When this victory is consummated, "*even then*" in the final judgment, human beings will be given to know that it is by grace that they are "undying, or better . . . plucked from out of death."[58]

The final judgment is judgment *unto eternal life* because it means final deliverance from that annihilating power of death, which is "God's enemy and mine." And we should recognize that it is exactly the apocalyptic form of the saving work of cross and resurrection and its close identification with final judgment that makes it possible and then necessary to link the philanthropy of saving divine justice with the vision of God's ultimate triumph over death's inimical misanthropy.

At an End

God's final veridical judgment—"public, definitive and irrevocable"[59]—will establish the ultimate conditions under which humanity and God may enjoy

52. Moltmann, "Final Judgment," 574.
53. Moltmann, *Theology of Hope*, 206.
54. Jüngel, *Death*, 115, emphasis original.
55. Ibid., 81.
56. Ibid., 79.
57. Ibid., 116, 108, 112.
58. Krötke, "Hope in the Last Judgment and Human Dignity," 279.
59. Thiselton, *Last Things*, 176.

unhindered, undisrupted, and undissipated community, a state tradition-
ally characterized as one of plenary sanctification and glorification.[60] The
justifying work of cross and resurrection is indissolubly and determinatively
linked to the substance and form of the last judgment, as two moments of
this single eschatological work of the one Savior, Jesus Christ. God's way of
judgment is a path on which the truth of our lives is illumined and decided
by the only One competent to do so; it is a path on which everything we are
that is born of death is repudiated in love and set aside forever; it is a path on
which Christians may walk with "heads held high," confident that "our true
humanity will be realised in our being together with God" forever because of
Christ's once and future triumph over death, a triumph won by the power of
divine love in which he, the judge, is given into judgment *for us*.[61] Faith thus
rightly yearns for the final judgment as the "public, glorious, incontestable,
and irrevocable justification of man through God's grace."[62]

Pace Kant, the only movement that finally matters is and can only be the
one "from grace to virtue," or best and evangelically most apt, from grace to
eternal life. For even "the end is also an act of grace."[63]

60. Heppe, *Reformed Dogmatics*, 695–712.
61. Krötke, "Hope in the Last Judgment and Human Dignity," 281.
62. M. Barth, *Justification*, 82.
63. Jüngel, *Death*, 90.

PART 3

Living Faithfully at the Turn of the Ages

8

Creation, Redemption, and Moral Law

The concept of the natural must be recovered from the gospel itself.

—Dietrich Bonhoeffer, *Ethics*

In this chapter I explore two distinct efforts within modern Protestant theology to ask and to answer the question of the "consequences of the Christian faith for establishing and observing law."[1] The aim is to scrutinize the dogmatic framework within which the question of human law is set and within which answers to this question are ultimately formulated and proposed. The works of American theological ethicist Paul L. Lehmann and Scottish theologian T. F. Torrance serve as my exemplars. Both are Reformed Christian thinkers of substance and influence; both approach the question of human law on the basis of themes close to the material heart of their respective projects: Torrance with reference to the contingency of both physical and moral creaturely reality upon divine reality, Lehmann by way of a christologically concentrated and eschatologically inflected theological ethic. Each in his own way is centrally concerned to connect the actuality of human law to the decisive and salutary reality of divine sovereignty, though they differ significantly regarding how this connection is best acknowledged and described. The difference concerns the proper dogmatic location of the question of human law. This difference trades on a wider disagreement over the dogmatic location of the "world" within Christian theology, and it tells importantly in the

1. The phrasing is that of Pannenberg, "On the Theology of Law," 23.

fundamental conceptions of the Christian life. Both Torrance and Lehmann are rightly convinced that much is at stake, Christianly and humanly, in doing theological justice to the question of the basis and nature of human law.

T. F. Torrance: The Reality of Law within Creation

We do not commonly think of T. F. Torrance in connection with the theme of theology and law. Yet the famous historical and dogmatic theologian turned his hand to the question of the nature of law in two significant essays: the first is a short monograph titled *Juridical Law and Physical Law* (1982), characterized by one reviewer as "a pungent tract for the times";[2] the second is his 1995 Warburton Lecture, delivered at Lincoln's Inn and published the following year as "Revelation, Creation and Law."[3] Both texts share a common aim: namely, to diagnose the positivism of contemporary British legal thinking and to venture a theological alternative. Torrance adjudges legal positivism—and constructivism and utilitarian rationality, which are its close corollaries—to be the cause of the "highly volatile state" of contemporary legal institutions because this regnant philosophy of law sees to it that the "laws we formulate and put into effect are ultimately no more than patterns of self-centred human subjectivity within which we imprison ourselves."[4] For the idea of "truth in law" has long since been displaced by pursuit of "impeccable logical correctness," as the object of legal science has been positively reduced to "law as it is" and thus jurisprudence reduced to adjudication of "what is formally right."[5]

All this, says Torrance, is a "recipe for frustration and lawlessness" a long time in the making.[6] Arising on the ground of early modern nominalism and dualism, the theoretical contributions of first John Locke and then Jeremy Bentham bequeathed to British legal philosophy a thoroughly conventional and external view of laws as the utilitarian outworking of that "first and fundamental positive law" of the nation, namely, the sovereignty of legislative power.[7] The common law tradition, despite its salutary inertia, was progressively overtaken by this trend. Over time it became a commonplace that law is simply *made*, rather than being discovered or articulated, and "in so far as

2. W. A. Whitehouse, review of *Juridical Law and Physical Law*, by T. F. Torrance.
3. Torrance, *JLPL*; Torrance, "Revelation, Creation and Law."
4. Torrance, *JLPL* xi.
5. Torrance, "Revelation, Creation and Law," 277.
6. Torrance, *JLPL* xi.
7. See John Locke, *Second Treatise of Government*, chap. 11, 69–76. For all this, see Torrance, *JLPL* 6–21.

legislation is the sole source of law, it is a self-contained and self-grounded system."[8] Of a piece with this is the loss of any distinction between law and rules of social organization. This has and continues to fuel a vast multiplication of laws whose sheer volume tends to diminish the authority of law.[9] Finally, Torrance understands all this to be compounded by the fact that in the United Kingdom such legal positivism is as good as "built into the constitution itself." For the reduction of law to legislated contrivance is the essential corollary of the absolute sovereignty of Parliament and the practice of what Lord Hailsham memorably characterized as "elective dictatorship, absolute in theory, if hitherto tolerable in practice."[10] Such is the diagnosis.

The alternative Torrance advances to all such positivism is, not surprisingly, thoroughly realist in character. Indeed, his aim is nothing less than a "realist reconstruction of the ontological and epistemological structure of our law" and thereby the establishment of a "deeper and more dynamic concept of *natural law*."[11] His proposal trades on a close analogy, or even univocity, between physical laws and juridical laws and so also between the operations of natural science and those of jurisprudence. Fundamentally, legal science must regain its "objective ground" in the same reality that establishes and sustains all creaturely reality: the "ultimate Truth and Rightness of God Himself."[12]

It is not necessary here to provide a full explication of Torrance's views on the pivotal contributions of Einstein, Michael Polyani, and Clerk Maxwell to developments within the philosophy of natural science in particular and epistemology more generally.[13] For our purposes, we can make do with Torrance's summary of their "far-reaching implications" for all human knowledge. As he explains, they involve

> the integration of ontology and epistemology in rigorous fidelity to the fact that empirical and theoretical factors are found already inhering in one another in objective reality. Thus the only acceptable structures of thought are those which arise in our minds under the compulsion of the objective structures of the field into which we are inquiring, unencumbered by a priori assumptions or antecedently reached or formalised conceptions. We work only with appropriate

---

8. Torrance, *JLPL* 17.

9. Ibid., 20. He has arguments from Hayek's *Law, Legislation and Liberty* in view here.

10. Lord Hailsham, *Elective Dictatorship*, 5. Cited by Torrance, *JLPL* 19.

11. Torrance, *JLPL* 22, xi; Torrance, "Revelation, Creation and Law," 277: "This surely calls for a basic change in jurisprudence, and in the relation of statute law to common law, in which we recover a realist instead of positivist understanding of law, and its practice in the courts."

12. Torrance, *JLPL* x.

13. On this see Torrance, "Theological Rationality"; Torrance, "Concept of Order"; Torrance, *Divine and Contingent Order*.

concepts that are formed on the ground of actual knowledge and in accordance with what is prescribed by the nature of the given realities. . . . In this way we replace a dualist frame of thought with a unitary basis on which there arises a polarity of ontic and noetic structures in which empirical and theoretical factors while distinguished remain integrated.[14]

In short, the intelligibility and order of things comes into our purview together with the things themselves, and we are thereby made subject to the "compelling claims of the reality being investigated."[15] The struggle for knowledge, as Polyani styles it, is a struggle "to submit to reality."[16] Accordingly, whatever concepts or "laws" we formulate about the orders of things are fully contingent upon the realities they indicate: knowledge is provisional, always laid open to revision by the field of reality that governs it. This limits the degree to which truth claims can be formalized into systems of logical certainty since their truth lies in the "real structures" of the world.[17] But more than this, Torrance is deeply convinced that reality as a whole is itself *contingent* and hence "not self-sufficient or ultimately self-explaining but . . . given a rationality and reliability in its orderliness dependent on and reflecting God's own eternal rationality and reliability."[18] Whatever orderliness we may discover in the nature of things has its sufficient reason and final basis only in God.[19]

Now in light of all this, what about law? Torrance avers that "in legal as in natural science our task is to detect and elicit the hidden patterns of order which we acknowledge to have normative force over our behaviour and to give them coherent and consistent formulation in a way that is invariant with respect to our many individual differences."[20] Understood aright, laws "are discovered, not contrived": positive lawmaking arises from recognition of the "basic patterns intrinsic to the given realities in the fields of moral and legal

14. Torrance, *JLPL* 24–25.
15. Torrance, "Revelation, Creation and Law," 278.
16. Polyani, *Personal Knowledge*, 63. Cf. Torrance, *JLPL* 4.
17. Torrance, "Revelation, Creation and Law," 276. In relation to this point, Torrance consistently invokes Einstein's paper "Geometry and Experience": "As far as the propositions of mathematics refer to reality, they are not certain; and as far as they are certain, they do not refer to reality."
18. Torrance, "Revelation, Creation and Law," 274; cf. 276. See also Torrance, *JLPL* 36–37.
19. "In the last resort meaning and truth in natural and moral and legal science depend on an epistemic correlation between [wisdom and knowledge]. Behind that correlation is the intersection of symmetries between an ultimate ground of order and an immanent ground of order, or between divine order and contingent order" (Torrance, "Revelation, Creation and Law," 281). Cf. Torrance, *JLPL* 36–37, 52–53.
20. Torrance, *JLPL* 29; cf. 38–39.

experience" in order to be able to "articulate and make public the hidden regulative principles" that give shape to the human obligation to "*behave strictly in accordance with the nature of things.*"[21] All aspects of the practice of law, just as in other fields of human endeavor, are subject to "the compelling claims and regulating standards of a transcendent rational order," exposed to the "commanding intelligibility of the universe," and called on to respond "to the imperious constraint of a single transcendent reality which we cannot rationally or morally resist."[22] This requires us to accede that laws have an "open structure" and so do not have their truth and justification "in themselves or in their systematic coherence and formalization," but only finally in their "informal non-logical reference to objective reality beyond themselves."[23] And just as the physical cosmos finds its sufficient cause only in God, so too does moral-legal reality. Of this Torrance writes,

> The contingent nature of the order embedded in the ontological structure of interpersonal human relations, within the wider realm of contingent order or empirical reality, points all human law-making beyond itself to a normative source and self-sufficient ground in Almighty God. It is through controlling reference to divine justice as the universal Constant that the contingent intelligibility presupposed by juridical law invites confidence and trust in its integrity, consistency and reliability. Without that final Constant there would be no universal standard of justice in the world and everything would be engulfed in relativism, so that there would be no real ground for objectivity in the making of law or for impartiality in the practice and interpretation of law.[24]

In short, Torrance argues that only acknowledgment of the *uncontingent* reality of divine justice can finally underwrite and sustain a humane "system of law which is itself subject to the justice it intends to promote and which thereby acknowledges its own limitations in defining justice."[25]

As these remarks make plain, Torrance sets his account of law firmly within the scope of a doctrine of creation, and elements of this doctrine provide the relevant dogmatic basis for his realist proposal. Indeed in the Warburton Lecture, Torrance develops the motif of contingent rational order explicitly from patristic accounts of creation and the relation between uncreated and created light.[26] Both the intrinsic incompleteness and ordering of the created

21. Ibid., 26, 28.
22. Torrance, "Revelation, Creation and Law," 280–81.
23. Ibid., 282.
24. Torrance, *JLPL* 53.
25. Ibid., 66.
26. Torrance, "Revelation, Creation and Law," 273–75, 282.

world belong to "our ultimate beliefs, apart from which there can be no rational inquiry."[27] In fact, Torrance ascribes the very possibility of modern science to the capacity of a Christian doctrine of creation to secure and sustain "confidence in the rational integrity and authentic reliability of the empirical world."[28] As has been noted, the same holds good in the sphere of law, where the dual affirmation of divinely contingent order *and* intrinsic intelligibility of the realities of human right and obligation gives rise to a proper "confidence and trust" in law's "integrity, consistency and reliability."

Torrance's depiction of the nature of creation, as contingent and ordered, remains highly schematic. Yet the proposal implies both the possibility and necessity of producing a more doctrinally substantial detailing of something like the "orders of creation," that is, a detailed depiction of the "ontological structures of interpersonal human relations" that positive law seeks to articulate and to which it is responsible for its truth and right. The obvious rubric under which to pursue such an undertaking is, of course, natural law. However it might be styled, the burden of such a project on Torrance's view is the "supreme meta-juridical task" of "testing the bearing of . . . laws, rules and interpretations upon sheer justice."[29] This task would never be accomplished fully or settled because of the relentless dynamism, "depth and range of intelligibility that characterize contingent order." Torrance imagines such top-tier jurisprudential reflection continuously driving critical and creative reform within positive law for the sake of a better and more humane iteration of human right and obligation. As he concludes, only if "juridical law is regarded as no more than a human attempt to express and serve the will of God, will it be promulgated, taught and practiced in a way appropriate to the human children of God."[30]

The force of Torrance's argument is largely borne by the strong analogy—pressed almost to the point of identity—between moral-legal reality and natural-physical reality and the corresponding similarities in the forms of their respective sciences. If this comparison holds, then the proposal to recover the ontological realism of jurisprudence emerges, perhaps surprisingly, as *progressive* rather than reactionary, and the continued presence of legal positivism is cast as an anachronism reflecting legal theory's continued allegiance to early

27. Accounts esp. of Basil and of John Philoponos; see Torrance, "Revelation, Creation and Law," 274.

28. Torrance, *JLPL* 28. Cf. Torrance, "Concept of Order," 23–24. It does so against its historic depreciation by "ancient science and the long tradition of Augustinian culture," even as it resists any metaphysical subjugation of nature to "arbitrary necessities and timeless patterns."

29. Torrance, *JLPL* 65.

30. Ibid., 67.

modern scientific paradigms long since surpassed within the physical sciences themselves. Moreover, the proposal embeds at the heart of legal science a self-critical principle whose mainspring is not ideological suspicion but scientific commitment to the principle of *nullius in verba* (take nothing on the word of another)—the relentless pursuit of an ever better grasp of the nature of human right and obligation solely on the basis of the "intrinsic intelligibility" of these realities themselves.[31] When Torrance speaks of the *dynamism* of this view of natural law, he has these key features of his account in mind.

While it is true that the doctrine of creation provides the explicit dogmatic location for this account of law, the argument is theologically minimalist. Torrance elects not to bring any of the fulsome dogmatic resources of his trinitarian theology to bear upon the question of law. Neither does he draw the question into the arena of the doctrines of grace and salvation. Rather, he relies on the barest affirmations of divine creation ex nihilo to establish his two realist claims of the open contingency and intelligibility of moral-legal order. Contingency needs only a countervailing transcendence to secure it, something for which the word "God" will do quite nicely. But the matter of intrinsic order requires more than this. Here Torrance must go on to specify that legal order is a function of the "commanding Word or Logos" of God.[32] In the texts we have been considering, he goes no further, content to hold the question of law within a discussion of the "social transcendental" supplied by the doctrine of the presence of the Logos within creation.[33]

Elsewhere, however, he offers further comment, expressing his full agreement with John Polkinghorne that "behind the intelligibility of the universe, its openness to the investigation of science, there lies the fact of the Word of God. The Word is God's agent in creation, impressing his rationality upon the world. That same Word is also the light of men, giving us thereby access to the rationality that is in the world."[34] Yet Torrance must also admit that the Word is also the architect of another kind of order about which Christians are greatly concerned: the "order of redeeming Love" disclosed in the incarnation. And this is no idle admission. For, in the end, the hope of the renewal of legal science would seem to turn on it, since it is only when the "order that impregnates nature and pervades the whole universe is correlated with the Word of God incarnate in Jesus Christ that it becomes articulate beyond what

31. *Nullius in Verba* is the motto of the Royal Society: "On the word of no one!" Cf. Torrance, "Revelation, Creation and Law," 278.

32. Torrance, "Revelation, Creation and Law," 275.

33. A similar approach is advocated by Dan Hardy in his essay "Created and Redeemed Sociality," 202–5.

34. Torrance, "Concept of Order," 26, citing Polkinghorne, *Way the World Is*.

it is capable of in itself, and as such becomes not only a sounding board, as it were, for the message of the Truth and Love of God in Jesus Christ, but the means whereby that message may be received, understood and actualised in human life and civilisation as perhaps never before."[35] These remarks point well past the unfolding of an account of the "orders of creation" and indicate how Torrance envisages that the question of law is finally and fundamentally, like all creaturely reality, decisively impinged on by the "order of redemption" because the "commanding Word or Logos" at issue is not simply the principle of creation's intelligibility but more fundamentally the gracious divine agent of its salvation.

Paul L. Lehmann: Putting Human Law in the Context of the Gospel

In a sense Paul Lehmann's approach to the question of law begins precisely where Torrance's account leaves off. Indeed, Torrance's solution to the problem of law—the theological invocation of an idea of natural law—is the particular problem from which Lehmann sets off. Lehmann stands firmly within a trajectory of those twentieth-century Protestant theologians for whom the crisis of confidence in the coherence of law amid the trials of their time could only be adequately met by establishing law upon the revelation of God in Christ.[36] In this they overleaped even the Reformers themselves, who on matters of state, social ethics, and the *res publica* left long-inherited patterns of argument from natural law largely undisturbed, something Lehmann considers a loss of theological nerve.[37] As he describes it, "Almost immediately after the Reformers had made their attempt at a theology adequate for a gospel of forgiveness," the focus of the problems of ethics and law was "returned to the point from which they had deflected it."[38] The effect was to keep questions in these fields, including the question of the basis of juridical law, firmly within the ambit of the doctrines of creation and providence, abstracted (or insulated) largely from the radical cardinal dogmas of emerging Protestant faith. In short, on

---

35. Torrance, "Concept of Order," 26–27.

36. The leading figures are the likes of Karl Barth, Bonhoeffer, Ernst Wolf, Visser 't Hooft, et al. On this, see Pannenberg, "On the Theology of Law," 24, 36–38.

37. Lehmann, *Ethics in a Christian Context*, 78n2. See McNeil, "Natural Law in the Teaching of the Reformers." More recently, this continuity has been emphasized by Grabill, *Rediscovering the Natural Law in Reformed Theological Ethics*; and in two related essays by David VanDrunen, "Context of Natural Law" and "Two Kingdoms Doctrine."

38. Lehmann, "Toward a Protestant Analysis of the Ethical Problem," 1–3, a judgment frequently echoed in later writings. In this he follows Troeltsch's historical account; see Troeltsch, *Social Teaching of the Christian Churches*, 494–95, 528–29, 602–3, 673–74, 999–1000. See also Lehmann, "Law," 205–7, and "Law as a Function of Forgiveness," 109–10.

such matters as these, Lehmann contends that "Protestant theology has never sufficiently regarded the world in the light of the victory of Christ."[39]

Lehmann's own theological ethics is ambitious to regard the world strictly in light of this divine victory won in Christ for the sake of wayward humanity. What Torrance was content to denote simply as the "Logos of God" must, in Lehmann's view, be much more precisely specified as the very "presence and formative power of Jesus Christ in this world."[40] Torrance's leading motifs, divine sovereignty and the intrinsic and intelligible ordering of things, must be inflected christologically. The crucial point of dogmatic orientation for Lehmann is not so much creation and the transcendence of the Creator as it is redemption and the lordship of the Savior. In ethics generally, and so too on the question of law, the approach must be thoroughly christological. Where it is not, Lehmann muses, Christian inquiry inevitably gets snagged in a dilemma between "a capricious doctrinal selectivity, on the one hand, and the abandonment of its theological character, on the other."[41]

In this, Lehmann shows his close fidelity to impulses from the fragmentary ethic authored by his friend Dietrich Bonhoeffer.[42] Lehmann sees himself as standing in the trajectory that carried Bonhoeffer's own thinking from "the response to the Lordship of Christ in the church to the response to the Lordship of Christ in and over the world." The upshot thereof was that in his late *Ethics* and *Letters and Papers from Prison*, Bonhoeffer considered the world with increasing clarity "as the sphere of the *regnum Christi* [reign of Christ]."[43] In his own *Ethics in a Christian Context*, Lehmann asserts that the significance of the *regnum Christi* for the question of law is best grasped by focusing on two christological motifs, both of which have concerned us already in previous chapters of this book: first, the threefold office of Christ and, second, the identification of Christ as the second Adam.[44]

Lehmann's interest in the threefold office of Christ is itself centered, as one might anticipate, on the royal office: Christ's kingship is the motif that

39. Lehmann, *Ethics*, 115.

40. Lehmann, *Christologie und Politik*, 8. Lehmann authored a new preface for this German translation and abridgment of *Transfiguration of Politics*, from which I cite here in my own translation.

41. Lehmann, *Ethics*, 105.

42. Lehmann, *Christologie und Politik*, 14, my translation.

43. Lehmann, "Faith and Worldliness in Bonhoeffer's Thought," 38, and then at that same place citing Bethge, *Dietrich Bonhoeffer*, 805–6. On this, see Bonhoeffer's manuscript "Christ, Reality and the Good" with its polemic against "thinking in two spheres" (Bonhoeffer, *Ethics*, 56–61).

44. Lehmann, *Ethics*, 105. Trinity and second advent are more tersely handled in the section that follows.

best expresses the effectiveness and scope of his saving work; it indicates that the order of salvation is the context and foundation of the ethical question of human right and obligation.[45] By drawing attention to the "the political character of what God is doing in the world," Christ's royal office clarifies for faith the "environment and direction" of all human activity, including lawmaking.[46] Unless one is willing to delimit the Pantocrator to being "governor of a clearly limited province" like the church, this doctrine requires theologians to acknowledge the decisive importance of Christ "not only for those who recognize him but for the whole world."[47] As Lehmann explains,

> the recovery of the doctrine of the threefold office of Christ safeguards against the peril of a double standard. The christological focus and foundation of behavior mean that believer and unbeliever are both alike in the same ethical situation. Both believer and unbeliever belong to Christ. Both believer and unbeliever are promised in him the secret and the power of maturity. Both believer and unbeliever are being confronted, in the environment being shaped by Christ's royal and redemptive activity, by the decision to accept or to reject the conditions of a new humanity on Christ's terms, not their own. The difference is that for believers, as members of the koinonia, the kingship of Christ is revealed; in the world (that is, among unbelievers) it is hidden.[48]

One significant effect of specifying the nature of present divine sovereignty as the lordship of the risen and ascended Christ is to make plain that from the perspective of Christian faith, "all [persons] are involved in the situation defined by the gospel."[49]

Lehmann's second leading christological motif is that of Jesus Christ as the second Adam.[50] The function of this theme is twofold. First, by focusing the question of humanity on the eschatological humanity of Jesus, it removes

45. Ibid., 115; cf. Calvin, *Institutes* 2.15. On the resurgent importance of the royal office of Christ in Protestant theology during the first half of the twentieth century, see Visser 't Hooft, *Kingship of Christ.* Lehmann himself may well have heard the Stone Lectures of 1947, on which this text is based.

46. Lehmann, *Ethics,* 116.

47. See Visser 't Hooft, *Kingship of Christ,* 18. Visser 't Hooft notes that Schleiermacher could delimit the exercise of Christ's royal office to the church: "Christ commands only the forces of the church" (*Christian Faith,* §105). For an account of Turretin and Rutherford as earlier examples of this countervailing tendency within Reformed theology to strongly distinguish the *regnum Christi* into a "twofold kingdom" of the "natural or essential" and the "mediatorial and economical," corresponding strictly to the distinction between the work of creation and that of reconciliation, see VanDrunen, "Two Kingdoms Doctrine," 749–54.

48. Lehmann, *Ethics,* 116–17.

49. Lehmann, "Law as a Function of Forgiveness," 105.

50. On this, influentially for Lehmann, see K. Barth, *Christ and Adam.*

the "last possibility of a surreptitious resort to [general] anthropology in Christian ethical reflection."[51] Second, and positively, theological ethics is hereby afforded a material focus, since the new humanity constitutes both "the subject and the aim or goal of ethical action." Human acts and institutions (including law) are, strictly speaking, not significant in themselves but as "pointers to or bearers of the new humanity which in Christ has become a fact in the world and in which, in consequence of what Christ is and is doing in the world, we participate."[52] Lehmann goes on to explain:

> The immediate and direct theological presuppositions of Christian ethics have to do with the context and actuality of the new humanity in Christ, not with humanity in general, humanity apart from Christ. . . . The Christian character of behaviour is defined not by the principal parts of an act, but by the functional significance of action in the context of the divine economy and of the actuality of the new humanity. Thus behavior, as Christianity understands it, is not qualitatively but symbolically significant; . . . behavior is ethically defined not by perfections but by parabolic power.[53]

And since the Second Adam, and in him the new humanity, originates as the object of the eternal election of God, this electing action "gives foundational priority to freedom over order, purpose over policy, future over past, and destiny over devices," ensuring that the "new order of humanity, in which and by which the Christian lives," takes formative priority and gives rise to "its own way of looking at things and its own way of living out what it sees."[54] The dynamism of the reality to which law is indexed is eschatological.

So, what do Christians see when they look in their distinctive way on the phenomenon of human law? How does juridical law appear when considered within a human situation acknowledged to be "determined and understood only on the basis of the Word of God" thus understood?[55] Just what might we take to be law's "functional significance . . . in the context of the divine economy and of the actuality of the new humanity"? And what account of the basis of human law can be won on the explicitly christological grounds advanced here?[56]

---

51. Lehmann, *Ethics*, 120.

52. Ibid., 119.

53. Ibid., 121–22.

54. Lehmann, *Transfiguration of Politics*, 241; Lehmann, *Ethics*, 123.

55. Lehmann, *Christologie und Politik*, 7, my translation. This of course restates Barth's view that "the dogmatics of the Christian Church, and basically the Christian doctrine of God, is ethics. . . . It is the *answer*—this must be our starting point" (K. Barth, *CD* II/2:515).

56. Lehmann addresses these questions in several important essays in addition to the discussion in his *Ethics*. See also "Law," 203–7; "Law as a Function of Forgiveness," 102–12; "Christian Alternative to Natural Law," 517–49; and "Metaphorical Reciprocity between Theology and

Law, says Lehmann, is the "principle and operation of order in the world" and precisely as such raises a particular problem within Christian theology. The problem is this: how does such worldly order relate to the purposes and acts of God? The basic theological question about law runs thus: "In a world whose Creator and Redeemer is God, is law a self-evident expression of God's will and purpose or is law instrumental to another and different or higher expression of God's will and purpose?"[57] As we have already observed, the gospel of the reconciliation of all things to God in Christ provides just such a different and supervening divine purpose. The gospel does not merely affirm or supplement the world; rather it issues in a fundamental reordering of things: not the correction or completion of the existing orders but their fundamental "transvaluation" is at hand.[58] So we are not surprised to find him proposing to "finish what the Reformers started" by arguing that human law is strictly instrumental to eschatological reconciliation. Law, he says, is properly acknowledged to be "a function of forgiveness": it is the means by which "justice becomes the concrete occasion and context of reconciliation" between persons.[59] In other places Lehmann expresses this same basic idea of law as a serviceable means toward the gospel's humanizing ends by character-izing it as the "nexus of human reciprocity," as the discourse that "defines and directs the operation of human gratitude in society," when love eschews abstraction or mere sentimentality.[60]

For Lehmann, the truth about law's evangelical instrumentality becomes most clear when law's indicative function is brought to the fore. Of this he writes, "Human relations always veer toward the boundary on which the issue of the humanity or the inhumanity of man to man must be fought through, and the direction of God's activity must be sighted again. Law has the func-tion of exposing this boundary and in that sense is instrumental to the divine activity. This is the ethical significance of law, and in so far as a given law cannot be shown to perform this function, it violates Christian ethics and thus also the Christian understanding of law."[61] Or again, while no law "can be the norm or criterion of action in accordance with the will of God," for

Law," 179–92. The question is also addressed in *Transfiguration of Politics*, especially in the large central section of the work that begins at page 250. In *Transfiguration*, Lehmann in fact retrospectively characterizes the essay "Christian Alternative to Natural Law" as "a kind of first try at an indication of the correspondence between the biblical and the human meaning of politics" (342n27).

57. Lehmann, "Law," 204.
58. Lehmann, "Christian Alternative," 533.
59. Lehmann, "Law as a Function of Forgiveness," 110, 112.
60. Lehmann, *Transfiguration of Politics*, 250; "Law as a Function of Forgiveness," 111.
61. Lehmann, *Ethics*, 147.

their relation is precisely the reverse, law does lend order to human relations by "exposing crucial danger spots affecting human relations and also indicates the direction of humanization."[62] Remarks like these indicate that Lehmann conceives of human law in terms akin to those of the threefold "use of the law"—to condemn, to constrain, and to direct—within traditional Protestant doctrine. Lehmann's modification to this scheme, however, is to stress that when law is firmly set within the eschatological outworking of divine grace, its functions are more permissive than prescriptive, more indicative than imperative, and thus basically catalytic to the Christian venture of living faithfully before God. Within this formative context, in which Christ's reign and the pressing reality of the new humanity are constitutive, law's service is ever to "bend the things which have been towards the things which are to come"[63] by offering concrete, if provisional, indications of the forms of human right and obligations that bespeak it.

On the view Lehmann advances, neither legal positivism nor legal pluralism is inimical to the proper function of law. For all positive legal regimes are "functions of a sovereignty in action, fashioning by providential governance and experimentation, the conditions, sustaining and correcting . . . a community requisite for the humanization of human life."[64] If in a world made and actively governed by God with the aim of "giving human shape to human life, *law is the behavioral function of providence*,"[65] then Christians should expect the formation and revision of human law to have and to continue to unfold under what Lehmann elsewhere calls the "providential-eschatological pressure of reality upon human affairs."[66] Importantly, the substance of God's providential *gubernatio* (government) is conceived strictly in terms of the *regnum Christi*, and hence characterized as "providential-*eschatological*" pressure.

Lehmann stresses that while recognition of this is a "datum of the knowledge of faith," its "functional reality is independent of such recognition."[67] There is no need for the plurality of positive legal schemes to be either rejected or "subsumed under the inferences drawn by reason from a single confessional or rational faith" finally because, as Lehmann concludes,

in a world, in which Jesus of Nazareth has restored, by the full dimensions of his presence and activity, all created things to their proper subsistence

62. Ibid., 146–47.
63. Lehmann, "Christian Alternative," 535. On these themes, see "Law as a Function of Forgiveness," 106–7; and most fully, Lehmann, *Decalogue and a Human Future*, 15–29.
64. Lehmann, "Christian Alternative," 540–41.
65. Ibid., 541.
66. Lehmann, *Transfiguration of Politics*, 237.
67. Lehmann, "Christian Alternative," 541.

and centered all created things upon the priority and possibilities of human fulfilment, there is an order of things and times which sustains and effects a continuing reciprocity between responsible life and human life. This order bears the secret of a sovereignty which, as Augustine observed, is "hidden from us, but thoroughly known to Himself; which same order of times, however, He does not serve as subject to it, but Himself rules as lord and appoints as governor." In such a world, *law*, understood . . . as *primus usus legis* [first use of the law], means the primary order in which man's behavior is set, and by which his behavior is corrected and sustained. . . . Law is function, not a principle of order.[68]

The principle of order is the constancy of God's salutary reign in and through Christ; it is the function of human law in this time between the times to serve the humanizing purposes of this reign, whether by design or default, or despite itself.

For Lehmann, then, the issue around which everything turns regarding the matter of law is the nature and purpose of divine agency. Explicitly in connection with the matter of law, he puts it thus:

Is God upholding the world by changing it; or is God changing the world by upholding it? If God is doing the second, then the given patterns and structures are the fundamental supports indispensable to having any world at all; then order has taken priority over freedom and law over justice. . . . But if God is doing the first, then the concrete realities are those not yet given patterns and structures that are displacing patterns and structures that have been taken for granted; then freedom is the presupposition and condition of order, and justice is the foundation and criterion of law.[69]

As we have seen, led by the eschatological heart of the second christological article of the ancient creeds of the church, Lehmann himself takes the latter view. His approach to the question of human law within Christian theology is thus a strongly *teleological* one. Characterizing law's service, its *usus* or instrumentality, within and under the present reign of Christ becomes the decisive task. The hidden reality and ubiquity of this reign encompasses all actual human lawmaking, subjecting it ever to its formative "providential-eschatological pressure." Within the reality of this regime, the leading puzzle is less "Whence comes law?" than "What is law good for *here and now*?" The specific eschatological description given of the *here and now* in terms of the advent of Christ's reign turns out to make all the difference.

68. Ibid., citing Augustine, *City of God* 5.9.33 and 19.24.
69. Lehmann, *Transfiguration of Politics*, 263.

Some Conclusions and Questions

Both Torrance and Lehmann give accounts of the nature of human law that underwrite its immense human significance by anchoring law in that which is taken to be most real. They do this even as they relativize actual human legal achievements by stressing their contingency upon either the intrinsic created orders of human obligation (Torrance) or the impinging order of evangelical love and reconciliation (Lehmann). Both these Protestant theologians argue for a realist view of law capable of enjoining permanent and salutary criticism of extant legal regimes. The decisive thing this realism affords is a finally transcendent referent for law. For Torrance, this transcendence is a function of law's contingency upon the intrinsic order of created reality and finally the contingency of created reality itself on the will of its Creator. For Lehmann, law's transcendent referent is the effective eschatological reality of Christ's royal office. Correspondingly, the mainsprings of criticism and reform of law are markedly different: on Torrance's view, legal criticism is an iteration of the common scientific discipline of informal (nonlogical) falsification; on Lehmann's count, such criticism arises from present discernment of the incompatibility of the present order with the promise and patterns of the coming Kingdom.

Both authors also hope for an understanding of law that acknowledges and finally augments its humanizing power. Torrance intimates, as we have noted, that recovered appreciation for the objectivity and intelligible order of the field of legal reality ought to have humane consequences, because it holds the promise of moving human life more clearly with, rather than across, "the grain of the universe." Such a hope, of course, trades on affirmation of the anthropic benevolence of reality, on the affirmation of creation's abiding goodness. Among the strengths of Torrance's proposal is its apologetic power as a "middle discourse" that taps the cultural prestige and intellectual gravitas of the natural sciences for the sake of a juridical law, as he says, capable of being "promulgated, taught and practiced in a way appropriate to the human children of God." Yet I must admit to an evangelical hesitation before an account of human law that, in its strict recourse to the doctrine of creation, seems to concur with Thomas Aquinas's stated view that "the New Law had nothing to add as regards external action."[70]

In Lehmann's case the humanistic promise of law lies in the fact that under the present reign of Christ, law itself finds fitting service in the "hammering out" of the new humanity made possible by the forgiveness of sins.

---

70. Thomas Aquinas, *Summa Theologia* I-II, q. 108, art. 2.

The peculiar strength of what Lehmann proposes lies in its greater dogmatic density, its close proximity with themes at the heart of the Christian gospel, and perhaps—because of its focus on law's function rather than its essence or origin—its ability to cope with the challenge put to legal science by historicism.[71] His approach decisively shifts the question of human law out of the first patrological article of the ancient creeds, wagering instead that "the general power of the Spirit provides the kind of theological and ethical substance and sobriety which intrinsically links the divine economy with human maturity and puts believers and unbelievers upon a common level of integrity about what the struggle for human maturity involves."[72] While important questions also attend Lehmann's account—concerning, for instance, the sufficiency and development of this pneumatological reframing of relation of church and *saeculum* (the present age)—there is a peculiarly evangelical attraction to a view of law that, by virtue of being set firmly within the eschatological outworking of divine grace, ensures that the legal principle of *suum cuique* (to each their own) receives a revolutionary specification. For, seen Christianly, what we each deserve is not finally established by a natural but rather by a profoundly *unnatural right*, since by grace human beings are blessed to be those who bear a righteousness that is not their own (Phil. 3:9).[73]

71. On this see Pannenberg, "On the Theology of Law."

72. Lehmann, *Ethics*, 158–59.

73. On this theme, see Tanner, "Justification and Justice in a Theology of Grace," 510–23, esp. 522–23.

9

The Fate of Natural Law
at the Turning of the Ages

Retrieving Natural Law at the Present Time

There is at present a resurgent interest in natural law within Protestant theological ethics. Recent works by Stephen Grabill, J. Daryl Charles, David Van-Drunen, and many others argue for a rediscovery and retrieval of natural law as a tradition of moral theology marked by wide catholicity and unparalleled power to render Christian moral insight intelligible and persuasive within the public square. They contend against both revisionist and orthodox dismissals of natural law—the former reflecting the historicist and anti-metaphysical mindset of late modernity; the latter variously motivated by skittishness regarding natural knowledge of God, worries about soteriological synergism, or defense of the unparalleled virtues of the Christian community. The common aim of these authors is to revalidate an understanding of natural law that, as Charles puts it, "mirrors the moral order of creation, not salvation, and thus underscores the ethical *permanent things*—what applies to all people at all times and in all places," setting before us the sum total of those ethical truths open to unaided reason that "we all cannot *not* know."[1] Pursuit of this aim requires that certain "Protestant prejudices" that have displaced natural law in theological ethics be overcome and that the essential (and proper)

---

1. Charles, *Retrieving the Natural Law*, 113; VanDrunen, *Divine Covenants and Moral Order*.

continuity of the Reformers themselves with the Catholic tradition on this point be acknowledged.[2]

I do not wish to say more about this trend here. The dogmatic point at issue in this chapter is raised with perfect clarity in the words I have just cited from Charles, when he says that a Protestant natural law ethic must concern itself with permanent and universal rational truths because it is keyed to the abiding moral order of creation and "not salvation." Following on closely from the previous chapter and pressing further in the direction of its analysis, in what follows here I reflect on the theological cogency of insulating the moral order of creation from the impact of the outworking of divine salvation in this way. In particular I ask about the fate of the category "natural" within a hearing of Paul's apocalyptic gospel. As throughout this book, we are assisted in doing so by the insights of J. Louis Martyn, Martinus de Boer, Beverly Gaventa, and others.[3] As we have seen, this hearing of Paul lays particular stress on the essential cosmic dimensions of the apostle's witness to the gospel and so contends that the saving apocalypse of God in Christ unhinges the existing order of creation, an order that itself had already previously been unhinged by the Adamic incursion of sin. This particular history of the cosmos is ingredient in Paul's telling of the gospel and, if taken seriously, renders untenable claims that a rationally accessible moral order of creation simply "abides" undisturbed by all this. Renewed appreciation for Paul's apocalyptic theology thus raises critical challenges to the viability of natural law ethics within any Christian theology that hopes to keep faith with that twice-born apostle. It leads us to ask what the quest for moral order via natural law has to do with Paul's own ethical question "Who is Lord?" and its correlate, "Who owns the earth?"[4]

The Nature of the "Twice-Invaded World"

The disruption of the categories and strategies of natural law ethics is so thoroughgoing precisely because of the fundamentally cosmological register

2. See Charles, *Retrieving the Natural Law*, 111; Grabill, *Rediscovering the Natural Law*, 21. Whether this historical continuity redounds to the Reformers' credit may be queried, of course. As just discussed in chap. 8 above, Paul Lehmann considered it a "loss of theological nerve," since after making "their attempt at a theology adequate for a gospel of forgiveness" the focus of the problems of ethics and law was "returned to the point from which they had deflected it," namely, the natural law ("Toward a Protestant Analysis of the Ethical Problem," 1–3).

3. See the characterization of this group of scholars in James F. Kay's review of Douglas Harink, *Paul among the Postliberals*.

4. See Käsemann, "On Paul's Anthropology," 25.

of Paul's apocalyptic gospel. Paul's significance for ethics lies not in any distinctive answer he might give to the generic ethical question "What ought I to do?" but rather, writes Leander Keck, "in the way he transforms the situation of the doer."[5] An apocalyptic theology like his asks not only "What time is it?" but also "Where are we?" or, sharper yet, "What world is it?"[6] As Martyn succinctly puts it, the evangelical testimony leads us to answer that "we live in a twice-invaded world."[7] Both invasions—that of sin and that of God in his Christ—fundamentally shake the world. Overrun by sin, the world of creation first becomes "this world," whose very "form . . . is passing away" (1 Cor. 7:31), and in turn this fading world is again remade as "a new creation" (2 Cor. 5:17; Gal. 6:15) by the sovereign incursion of God's mercy in Christ.[8] While not of equal gravity, both disruptions are serially and massively determinative. They both bend creation around themselves in due proportion, and do so with real effect.

The cosmos itself thus has a history, in which decisive architectonic shifts occur, the first of which is caused by the eruption of sin into the creation. The account that Paul gives in his letters of Sin's career—what Gaventa has called "the résumé of sin"—insists that the human predicament is marked not merely by the existence of moral frailty and failures but also by bondage: men and women have come to exist under the power of "the present evil age" (Gal. 1:4), being captive "to beings that by nature are not gods" (Gal. 4:8), being "enslaved to sin" (Rom. 6:6), and having been "given over" into the power of sin (Rom. 1:24, 26, 28) by God for a time such that "sin exercised dominion in death" (Rom. 5:21).

To the question "What world is it?" the first partial answer comes forth: *this* world, the world whose form is passing away, the world that sin has unmade and within which all human beings ("in Adam") have become "without exception incompetent" to hear and obey God's claim and direction (Rom. 11:32). Handed over as they have been to anti-God powers, and being "under the power of sin, . . . both Jews and Greeks" (Rom. 3:9), human beings find that even the good and holy law of God has been, as Martyn writes, "hijacked" to their undoing, "employed by Sin to deceive and kill," having been corrupted and "indeed conscripted by Sin into a lethal alliance" with it.[9] For

5. Keck, "Justification of the Ungodly and Ethics," 200.
6. Martyn, "World without End," 119.
7. Ibid., 24.
8. Gaventa, "Cosmic Power of Sin," 128; see also Gathercole, "Sin in God's Economy," 158, which speaks of Paul's "history of Sin."
9. Martyn, "Epilogue," 179; Martyn, "*Nomos* plus Genitive Noun in Paul," 581. See also Martyn, *Galatians*, 370–77.

Paul, the true "discernment of sin's power is itself a result of God's invasion of the world in Christ" such that we cannot "take the measure of Sin apart from that redemptive event."[10] Yet positioned as it is precisely in the wake of that event, Christian theology has every reason to confess that all human moral schemes calibrated to this old world are vulnerably ignorant of their being "sold . . . under sin" and "conformed" to its distortions (Rom. 7:14; 12:2). As John Barclay observes, "Precisely what, in his contemporaries' eyes, made religion 'natural' and therefore right and true is interpreted by Paul as a regime of truth rendered false by the new creation of the Christ event."[11] Here then is the first serious complication for any positive idea of natural law.

But the gospel gives a second and asymmetrically more important reply to the apocalyptic question "What world is it?" It is that our world is one in which, by the power of the cross and resurrection of Jesus, the "new creation" has come upon us. In Paul's idiom, the gospel tells of how the Son and the Spirit of the Son come upon the scene—literally, are apocalypsed, that is, revealed and realized—from beyond. It traces the "invasive route God has elected" in order to rectify the world gone wrong by redeeming it out from under the thrall of sin.[12] In the words of a novelist much beloved by Martyn, salvation is won by "the action of grace in territory held largely by the devil."[13] It involves a death that takes sin down with it. Further, it entails the outpacing of death by divine life in Christ's resurrection. It sees Jew and gentile together "taken in hand" by the Spirit in Christ for the sake of the Kingdom of heaven. In short, God rectifies an oppressed world and then liberates its inhabitants through the exercise of the cruciform power of divine love, extending his effective rule over it once more. Indeed, for Paul, as we have noted above, any decisive change in human existence is a consequence of a change of lordship.[14] Such a martial and cosmological view of salvation further complicates appeals to the essential continuities of creation in the form of natural law.

An important and provocative piece of Martyn's work has been to make plain the connection that Paul forges between these cosmic incursions of sin and salvation and the problem of human knowing. This is directly relevant

10. Martyn, "World without End," 124.
11. Barclay, "Paul and the Philosophers," 177.
12. Martyn, "Apocalyptic Gospel in Galatians," 254–55.
13. Flannery O'Connor originally used these words to describe the subject of her fiction; see her *Mystery and Manners*, 118.
14. See Käsemann, *Commentary on Romans*, 43; see also Martyn, "*Nomos* plus Genitive Noun in Paul," 583.

to our present theme.[15] The emphasis on discontinuity that marks Paul's understanding of the world made, unmade, and remade redounds sharply in the sphere of epistemology.[16] If this world is no longer that world, and if the very form of this world is passing away (the things that are being "reduce[d] to nothing"; 1 Cor. 1:28), then the schemes of knowing that comport with it are made redundant and irrelevant. In landmark essays, Martyn has argued that the cosmic tumults of the gospel of God render intelligible Paul's strong repudiation of the putative continuities of both salvation history and wisdom. Neither finally comprises or "contextualizes" the gospel that Paul serves; rather, they themselves are undone when over-reached and outbid by the gospel as they are—counted as utterly lost (Phil. 3:7). They are both concluded within the cosmos that suffers crucifixion, as Paul puts it so graphically in Galatians 6:14–15. Martyn contends that the ontologically and noetically "lethal reach" of the cross is universal, extending over the "world of Sinaitic, orthodox, two-ways moral drama, the world of circumcision and uncircumcision" as well as the "whole pagan world."[17] Ingredient in the work of the cross, in other words, is its salutary power to rob us of our sin-governed world and to open up "fissures" beneath our knowing that drop it "into an abyss."[18] Martyn insists that "no one, and no one's way of understanding the world, is exempted from the geological fault created by God's foolish and scandalous act in the cross of Christ (cf. Rom. 3:9)."[19]

It is as the turning point of the ages that the cross destroys "the wisdom of the wise, and the discernment of the discerning" (1 Cor. 1:19). The cross is the event in which God, in his wisdom, discloses that "the world did not know God through wisdom" (1:21). It stands, writes Martyn, as "an epistemological watershed" and crisis, for "on a real cross in this world hangs God's own Messiah, the Lord of glory."[20] With the loss of this cosmos comes the dissolution of the structuring elements of the hitherto known world, the

15. The central essays are Martyn, "Epistemology at the Turn of the Ages" and "Apocalyptic Antinomies."

16. Paul's theological witness is apocalyptic primarily because it "shares with apocalyptic theology the *perspective of discontinuity*. Over against all theologies which see continuity between God and world (whether focussed on nature or the history of a people) Paul sees disjunction. God and the redemptive future stand over against the world and its history, including the history of Israel (Rom. 9–11) and the future of the church (1 Cor. 10:1–22). At the same time, God's freedom from the world makes possible a relation to it which is grounded solely in God's integrity" (Keck, "Paul and Apocalyptic Theology," 241).

17. Martyn, "Gospel Invades Philosophy," 30.

18. Martyn, "Apocalyptic Gospel in Galatians," 257.

19. Martyn, "Listening to John and Paul on Gospel and Scripture," 75.

20. Martyn, "Epistemology at the Turn of the Ages," 108–9.

ancient "antinomies." These are supplanted by the new unity in Christ and displaced by new and different apocalyptic antinomies that follow in the train of God's salutary invasion of the world.[21] Christians cannot continue to grasp the contours of reality "by the power of the flesh" (*kata sarka*) but must reconceive it now by the power of the cross, of Christ crucified (1 Cor. 1:23; 2 Cor. 5:16). It is striking that the scriptural and pagan category "wisdom" should receive so precise and so polemical a redefinition at Paul's hands when he baldly identifies Jesus Christ, the Crucified One, as the one "who became for us wisdom from God" (1 Cor. 1:30). Again, discontinuity is the predominant motif. The incursion of Christ as divine wisdom, Paul stresses, utterly disqualifies all other claimants to wisdom: "Has not God made foolish the wisdom of the world?" (1 Cor. 1:20). It is because wisdom, like the law, has been usurped and commandeered by sin in the fallen world that the gospel of salvation—the powerful announcement of the turning of the ages on the axis of the cross—cuts decisively across its grain. Human wisdom, writes Barclay, far from being confirmed as continuous with the "apocalypse of faith," is shown to be at cross-purposes (literally), because salvation involves "being reconstituted by . . . an event which bears its own criteria for truth-discernment."[22]

If God's rectification of the predicament of this world involves the inauguration of a new age by which, writes Martyn, "the foundation of the cosmos has been subjected to a volcanic explosion that has scattered the pieces into new and confusing patterns," then we may well ask whether anything like the given "moral order of the creation" is really available to be gleaned in the midst of a cosmos "subjected to futility" within the passing age (Rom. 8:20).[23] We may also ask to what extent any putatively natural law may in fact amount to a prudential articulation of the structuring rationality of that world, which has in fact been "crucified" to the believer in Jesus Christ.[24] Moreover, if this reading of Paul's apocalyptic gospel is correct, then the very notion of existing and enduring morally freighted contours of a steady-state world—a world, in effect, "without end"—has been displaced by the dynamic history of the twice-invaded cosmos.[25] We find ourselves twice removed from the world of creation per se. In light of Paul's witness, the endeavor of natural law ethics to treat only the moral order of creation and not of salvation seems ill-begotten,

21. Martyn, "Apocalyptic Antinomies," 118.
22. Barclay, "Paul and the Philosophers," 178.
23. Martyn, "Apocalyptic Gospel in Galatians," 256.
24. See K. Barth, CD IV/2:504. Barth argues that reliance on natural law entails that "either tacitly or openly we are subjected to other lords" alongside Christ.
25. Martyn, "World without End," 118.

as it corresponds to no actually existing world.[26] What world is it, then? Doug Harink has aptly summarized the issue:

> It is clear that Paul envisages the new creation neither as a gnostic nor as an enlightened liberal democratic cosmos. The old cosmos characterized by seemingly primordial antinomies is not replaced by one in which every distinction and difference is deemed illusory and evil (the gnostic cosmos), or irrelevant (the liberal cosmos). . . . Rather, the apocalyptic gospel absorbs, recontextualizes, and redefines these distinctions and differences according to a whole new order in which they are made to serve and bear witness to that gospel in the messianic community.[27]

Universality by Other Means

Taking its cue from Paul's eschatological gospel, theological ethics will, I suggest, quite properly despair of the presumption that a permanent and perspicacious moral order of creation lies before us, available for rational discernment. Rather, it will acknowledge that the history of the twice-invaded cosmos makes our world what it is: a world marked by what Martyn calls "startling and uncompromising discontinuity" between creation and "*this world*" and, all the more, between "this world" and the new creation that is the ripening fruit of the cross.[28] It will not do to claim adequate biblical warrant for natural law ethics on the grounds that, as Matthew Levering writes, "the creation of human beings includes [a] body-soul participation in God's wisdom."[29] Further, it is difficult to see how, on Pauline terms, one could admit the view of Thomas Aquinas that the coming of salvation altered nothing in this regard inasmuch as—in a passage already quoted in relation to our analysis of T. F. Torrance's view of human law—he concludes that "the New Law had nothing to add as regards external action."[30] Rather, the

---

26. K. Barth, *CD* IV/2:101: "There is, therefore, no natural religion, no natural theology, no natural law. In all these concepts 'natural' means apart from Jesus Christ, apart from the Son of God who became also the Son of Man, who is called and is also Jesus of Nazareth, who in His unity with Jesus of Nazareth has also human essence. The antithesis to this 'natural' is not in the first instance the concept of 'revealed,' but that of human nature once for all and definitively exalted in Jesus Christ, once for all and definitively placed at the side of the Father and in fellowship with Him."

27. Harink, "Paul and Israel," 377–78. See also Barclay, "Paul and the Philosophers," 178.

28. Martyn, "Paul and His Jewish Christian Interpreters," 6.

29. Levering, *Biblical Natural Law*, 42. Levering's case builds heavily on wisdom traditions, and yet nowhere in his carefully argued work is consideration given to the troubling Pauline claims set out in the Corinthian correspondence.

30. Thomas Aquinas, *Summa Theologia* I-II, q. 108, art. 2.

cosmos has become something else since its inception, and like Israel's Scriptures, it too, writes Martyn, "no longer reads as it did before the advent of
the gospel."[31] This is because God has not and is "not concerned to preserve
to eternity what was in the beginning, [a] *world* without end!" Instead, over
against sin's incursion God has shown himself to be "the invading God, the
God of action, the God of action now, the God whose invasion of the world
has unleashed the strange war of liberation that brings in the new creation
by taking its bearings from the cross as apocalyptic sign."[32]

Intriguingly, Paul's apocalyptic gospel might, however, be able to deliver part
of what contemporary advocates of natural law seek. As Martyn stresses, it is
the work of the Spirit to re-create a body of new creatures able freely to take
in and take up the imperatives that the gospel enjoins. These communities are
not generic but specific; they are churches rendered "significantly different from
humanity in general" because they are divinely fashioned into "*addressable
communities* able to hear God's imperative and to act on it because, as the
Spirit's soldiers, they have been called to the front trenches of God's life-and-
death war against the enslaving power of the Impulsive Flesh."[33] As Martyn
puts it, in the "earthshaking, invasive event which is the sending of the Spirit
into human hearts (Gal. 4:6), God has commenced *his own participation in
human morality*, and that participation has clearly brought radical changes
to the whole of the human moral drama."[34]

Martyn now is speaking of the "whole of the human moral drama." God's
salutary and sovereign invasion of his cosmos drives Paul and his readers
toward such universal claims. Although Paul himself clearly stresses the speci-
ficity of the bridgehead of the remade world—victory in life comes to "those
who receive the abundance of grace and the free gift of righteousness . . .
through the one man, Jesus Christ" (Rom. 5:17)—it is also true that God's
rectification of the world in Christ "leads to justification and life for all"
human beings (5:18). The totality of disobedience is met by a comprehensive
divine mercy that befalls all (11:32); the totality of death is met by the superior
totality of life (1 Cor. 15:22). The cosmological register of Paul's apocalyptic
theology makes itself felt once again precisely here.

Are we perhaps led to confess that the new creation is brought about as and
when "this world" is drawn into Christ and as his reign makes its way both
within and without the church? And where does Christ not so reign? Thinking
along such lines, the universality that our contemporary Christian ethicists

31. Martyn, "Listening to John and Paul," 77.
32. Martyn, "World without End," 129.
33. Martyn, "De-apocalypticizing Paul," 91.
34. Martyn, "Gospel Invades Philosophy," 28.

seek by a retrieval of natural law could be secured not by appeal to creation per se but rather by appeal to the one reality of the one world that has been remade at the turning of the ages, the reality of the twice-invaded world, and so by appeal to the "universality of the revealed God," to use Wolf Krötke's phrase.[35] Something like this is surely the force of Bonhoeffer's compressed observation that the church only "views the creation from Christ" because it acknowledges that "the world belongs to Christ, and only in Christ is the world what it is."[36] Thus, discerning "the natural" is a strictly evangelical possibility for theology, or it is no possibility at all. For it is the elemental interruption brought about by the Kingdom that is "at hand" that makes all the difference, deciding what the earth is and what really matters therein.[37] Recall from a previous chapter how Ernst Käsemann put the matter, when he wrote that according to Paul's witness a human person

> is never just on his own. He is always a specific piece of world and therefore becomes what in the last resort he is by determination from outside, i.e., by the power which takes possession of him and the lordship to which he surrenders himself. His life is from the beginning a stake in the confrontation between God and the principalities of this world. In other words, it mirrors the cosmic contention for the lordship of this world and is its concretion. As such, [human] life can only be understood apocalyptically.[38]

Some of the most important aims of the natural law tradition might then be pursued on the basis of recounting the reality of human life effectively

35. The title of Krötke's 1985 essay collection, *Die Universalität des offenbaren Gottes*, expresses the drift of much of the material collected therein. Like Krötke, I see this as the basic movement of both Karl Barth's and Bonhoeffer's ethics. So Barth: "What other [word] pronounces that unconditional *dominus pro et cum nobis* [the Lord for and with us], thus indicating that a new situation has already been created for all humanity, setting each man at this new beginning and pushing him on from this point?" (*CD* IV/3:108).

36. Bonhoeffer, *Creation and Fall*, 22; and Bonhoeffer, *Ethics*, 67. In a prefatory summary of the argument of his commentary on Genesis, Calvin voices a similar conviction, contending that knowledge of creation and the Creator is only to be had on the other side, as it were, of the "foolishness of God" (cf. 1 Cor. 1:21): "Nothing shall we find, I say, above or below, which can raise us up to God, until Christ shall have instructed us in his own school. Yet this cannot be done, unless we, having emerged out of the lowest depths, are borne up above all heavens, in the chariot of his cross" (Calvin, *Commentaries*, vol. 1, *Genesis*, 63–64). I am grateful to David Demson for drawing my attention to this passage.

37. See Jüngel, "On the Dogmatic Significance of the Historical Jesus," 89; see also Morse, *Difference Heaven Makes*. For a supple account of this point that nevertheless makes a case for the continued utility of the appeal of natural law, see Braaten, "Protestants and Natural Law," 26. Importantly, Braaten's account allows that "the eschatological perspective has so relativized natural law that it hardly deserves to be called natural law anymore."

38. Käsemann, "On the Subject of Primitive Christian Apocalyptic," 136.

superintended by Christ's exercise of his royal office and subjected to the mission of the Spirit who is the Lord (2 Cor. 3:17–18). Brought forward concretely into the second and third articles of the ancient creeds, out from abstract isolation in the first article, some leading ambitions of the natural law tradition could perhaps receive a properly evangelical—because thoroughly eschatological—treatment.[39]

Guided to hear Paul's witness in this way, contemporary Protestant ethics may leave off the temptation to chase an abstract vision of a world merely framed by an unchanging order; instead, it needs to pursue the task of discerning the reality of a world graciously governed by the present, world-making, and salutary divine action and ordering of Word and Spirit.[40] Much is at stake in this endeavor, for as Martyn observes in echoing the apostle, "to speak of a course of ethical action on the basis of a flawed perception of the cosmos, and of the human being's place in it, is to court disaster."[41]

39. In this regard, one may agree with John Howard Yoder's assessment that "it would not be too much to claim that the Pauline cosmology of the powers represents an alternative to the dominant ('Thomist') vision of 'natural law' as a more biblical way systematically to relate Christ and creation" (Yoder, Politics of Jesus, 159).

40. See Torrance, "Modern Eschatological Debate," 48.

41. Martyn, "De-apocalypticizing Paul," 102. See also Martyn, "World without End," 122: "To analyze this cosmic drama as though we did not live in a fundamentally flawed world is to walk about in the dark, with all the dangers attendant to doing that."

10

The Adventitious Origins
of the Christian Moral Subject

John Calvin

In this chapter we continue to reflect on the matter of the Christian moral life in relation to the apocalyptic gospel of God's grace. Moving on from consideration of questions of law, I now pose another fundamental question: Whence arises the moral subject of a Protestant theological ethic? What are the primary doctrinal coordinates of our perception and conception of this moral subject? Is there perhaps anything distinctively *Reformed* about the way theologians working in that Protestant tradition approach the question of the human being as subject and agent of the moral life? In this essay I reflect on these questions by exploring the themes of human nature, depravity, and regeneration in Calvin's theology in their close relation to uses of the law. I will argue that, while affirming the essentially formal architecture of the human subject as a creature possessed of reason and will by nature, more important by far is what becomes of this nature through the adventitious history of fall and redemption. For this history is the history of the unmaking and remaking of the moral subject, the transit of the human creature from the *status corruptionis* (state of corruption), in which genuine moral subjectivity is an impossibility, to the *status gratiae* (state of grace), in which it becomes newly possible solely by virtue of the effective working of Christ and Spirit on and in us. That sin's depravity fully undoes human moral competence is reflected directly in Calvin's account of the *primus usus legis* (first use of the law), in which the law neither finds nor can create its proper addressee. It is only the advent of salvation that constitutes the human as a *moral* subject, creating—if not exactly ex nihilo, then certainly *ex contrario* (out of what is contrary)—those to whom the law may be addressed again: women and men newly and miraculously competent to hear and to obey. What this suggests is that Calvin's work on these themes challenges Reformed moral theology to embrace a radical soteriology as "first moral philosophy," as it were.

Much debate about the moral subject in Reformed theology generally, and in Calvin's theology in particular, concerns the neuralgic question of human freedom. This question is most often engaged with predominant reference to the doctrines of divine predestination and providence; it readily modulates into arguments for or against the intelligibility of various compatibilist strategies.[1] While our grasp of human moral subjectivity might well be aided by recasting the doctrinal materials into the formal idioms of philosophical logic and analytical theology in these ways, here I look to win a different purchase on the problem of the moral subject by drawing Calvin's thinking back into proximity with the predominantly Pauline discourse from which it emerges and to which it ultimately seeks to do justice. In this way we come to see acutely how the adventitious and efficacious qualification of the human will by sin and grace respectively in the economy of salvation plays the decisive role in making human will *moral*. To this end, we begin with concise consideration of J. Louis Martyn's discussion of the constitution of the human moral subject within Paul's apocalyptic gospel.

Apocalyptic, Paraenesis, and Matter of the Moral Subject

In a series of late essays, Martyn advances a perceptive and persuasive account of the status of the human being as moral agent within Paul's evangelical testimony.[2] In the Hellenistic world of Paul's mission, he argues, the standard description of *tōn ethikōn* (the moral life) concentrates on moments of decision in which human agents are presented with a choice between two ways, exhorted to choose the better of the two, and then, in an exercise of freedom, do in fact so choose. Animating this account is a view of human agency like

---

1. For very recent examples of such efforts, see Crisp, "Reformed Accounts of Free Will."

2. Martyn, "Epilogue," "Gospel Invades Philosophy," and "Afterword: The Human Moral Drama." See also the relevant thematic excursuses in his *Galatians* and the essays collected in part 4 of his *Theological Issues in the Letters of Paul*, 231–97.

that exemplified in the teaching of Sirach: "[God] created humankind in the beginning, and he left them in the power of their own free choice. If you choose, you can keep the commandments, and to act faithfully is a matter of your own choice" (Sir. 15:14–15). Moral competence comprises precisely this ability to will and to choose freely, to know and then to will the good. Its exercise is a distinct, autonomous second step in the ethical event, one that follows on and responds to the presentation—divine or otherwise—of the possibilities of the two ways. The patterns and practices of late antique moral instruction and exhortation regularly presume just such moral competence of their addressees.[3]

Martyn observes that Paul paints a radically different portrait of the human moral drama. In his apocalyptic vision, human moral subjectivity is decisively superintended in the first instance by the suprahuman powers of Sin, Death, and "the Flesh." "In the Adamic moral drama as it actually exists," Martyn writes, "human beings are *not alone*; they have in fact company, not least the lethal company of Sin as a *cosmic power*."[4] Here the moral commandment meets the human being as one enslaved "under the power of sin" (Rom. 3:9), a complicit accomplice in enmity and revolt against God. On such a vision, the moral field is a battlefield, in which the decisive thing is not so much what human moral agents do as "what has been done, is being done and will be done *to* them"; conscripted by Sin, and delivered over to the Flesh by God, disobedience becomes and bespeaks moral incompetence "without exception."[5] Paul's vision and his apocalyptic moral grammar are remote from any scenario in which rational human agents know and freely choose between ethical possibilities undisturbed from without. As he makes clear in his discourse concerning the law in Romans and Galatians especially, moral exhortation, even in the form of the holy address of the divine law, is impotent within the sphere of creation usurped by sin, only serving—paradoxically, horribly—to aggravate human alienation all the more. Under such circumstances, the law sets forth moral prospects and directives that cannot and will never be chosen by those who have been turned—and remain firmly set—against their God, integral members of a "body of death" (Rom. 7:24). For persons thus "worked by the flesh" (cf. Gal. 5:19–21), to know the good is neither to will nor to do the good; for bound by sin human beings are *non posse non peccare* (not able not

3. Martyn provides a very concise account of this nearly ubiquitous "two-ways portrait" of the human moral subject in "Gospel Invades Philosophy," 16–20. He finds it widely attested in both pagan and Jewish sources contemporary with Christian origins.

4. Martyn, "Afterword: The Human Moral Drama," 161, emphasis original. For concise discussion of this critical motif, see Gaventa, "Cosmic Power of Sin."

5. Martyn, "Epilogue," 179–80; cf. Rom. 1:21–28; 3:9; 6:6, 12–22; 7:11.

to sin).[6] They are naturalized citizens of "this world" and fully domesticated in the service of the gods of "this passing age."

As Paul's evangelical proclamation makes plain, the plight of cosmic captivity is only disrupted and overcome by God's own coming in the salutary power of his creative grace. As Martyn emphasizes, the next act of the moral drama is opened up only when God acts:

> Far from allowing the human agent to stand alone at the road fork, this invasive God powerfully meets both the incompetent, enslaved agent and the powers that enslave him in their own orb, . . . not in a renewed word of exhortation, but rather in the *logos tou staurou* [word of the cross], the totally strange word-event that shatters "the wisdom of the wise and the discernment of the discerning," thus destroying prior images of the human agent as well as old-age images of God (1 Cor 1:18–19). And in that meeting the divine agent does something unheard of. Destroying old-age images of the human agent, God changes human agency itself![7]

Once again we register how the event of redemption and liberation has the force of nothing less than "new creation," in which the enslaved and incompetent human agent is remade in the image of the crucified Son by the gift of the Spirit. There appears, in short, a new human agent "in Christ," one wrenched free from the "body of death" and knit together into the "body of Christ," the church. Paul conceives of this *"corporate, newly competent"* agent as the proper addressee of his paraenetic discourse. Paul's exhortations and moral imperatives are all directed to a "community that is newly addressable because it bears Christ's form and is led by Christ's Spirit. . . . Every one of Paul's hortatory sentences presupposes the presence of Christ and the constant activity of Christ's Spirit, as it causes the church to be able to hear."[8]

In all this, creaturely reason and will are not the presupposed instruments of transformation; rather, they are themselves the objects of gracious redemption and re-creation. The emergence of faith signals "that we ourselves have been invaded by God's presuppositionless grace," such that "the locus of God's invasion is *especially* our will! Far from presupposing freedom of the will (cf. Hos 5:4), Paul speaks of the freeing of the will for the glad service of God and neighbor."[9] The victory of divine grace, Martyn concludes, involves the

---

6. Augustine, *De natura et gratia* 57 (PL 44).
7. Martyn, "Epilogue," 180, emphasis original.
8. Martyn, "Church's Everyday Life," 231–34, at 234. Cf. Martyn, "Epilogue," 181.
9. Martyn, *Galatians*, 272n173, emphasis original.

"*genesis of the newly moral community*," one that owes "both its birth and its sustained life to God's powerful act in the gospel and to nothing else."[10]

In what follows in this chapter, I want to suggest that in Calvin's theology we may discern a closely analogous account of human moral impotence under sin as well as of the radical remaking of the human ethical agent in the event of salvation that generates the "newly moral community." Particularly important is the priority placed on the efficacious agencies of sin and grace in the constitution of the moral field, and the resultant historicized account of human moral nature concomitant with it. We may begin to demonstrate this by attending in the first instance to what Calvin says about the nature and function of divine law in close connection with his account of human depravity.

The Unmaking and Remaking of Moral Agency in Calvin's Theology

> It is true that our Lord created us after His own image and likeness, but that was wholly defaced and wiped out in us by the sin of Adam; we are accursed, we are by nature shut out from all hope of life.
>
> —John Calvin, sermon on Deuteronomy 24:19–20

Calvin is a theologian of sovereign divine grace and for just this reason also advances a doctrine of far-reaching human sinfulness and the bondage of the will.[11] The doctrine of human depravity describes the matrix of reality that obtains for human beings *in statu corruptionis* (in a state of corruption).[12] The nature and radicality of this sinful condition is discerned only when fully backlit, as it were, by the nature and radicality of the outworking of salvation in Christ. Illumined by the humble self-giving unto death of the One who is the very "image of the invisible God" (Col. 1:15), Calvin discerns that God's image in the human creature has been "so vitiated and almost blotted out that nothing remains after the ruin except what is confused, mutilated and disease-ridden."[13] In and by the sin of Adam all of humanity has been estranged

10. Martyn, "Gospel Invades Philosophy," 33, emphasis added.

11. The former point is frequently and rightly made, though sometimes advanced in an effort to mitigate the intensiveness of Calvin's doctrine of sin; see, e.g., Partee, *Theology of John Calvin*, 129–36. Torrance strongly emphasizes that Calvin's account of total and radical depravation is an "inescapable inference" drawn from the total and radical judgment and salvation that God enacts, i.e., that his thinking ultimately moves from solution back to problem; see his *Calvin's Doctrine of Man*, 85–86, 89–90.

12. For concise discussion of the doctrine in close relation to early modern Reformed confessions and catechisms, see Gregory, "Presbyterian Doctrine of Total Depravity," esp. 36–37.

13. Calvin, *Institutes* 1.15.4.

completely from its proper end, its nature having been "plunged . . . into like destruction" and corrupted in "all its parts."[14] *In statu corruptionis* fallen humanity is "dead—*not sick, but dead*," such that nothing of the spiritual life remains.[15] In sermon, commentary, and treatise, Calvin's rhetorical gifts are well exercised in expressing the fact that the disruption befalling human beings with the advent of the dominion of sin is a *total* qualification:[16] "The whole man is overwhelmed—as by a deluge—from head to foot, so that no part is immune from sin and all that proceeds from him is to be imputed to sin."[17] The vision then is of the human being as a microcosm that, like the cosmos itself, is occupied and comprehensively disordered by sin. Humanity, Calvin concludes with arresting understatement, is simply in a "very different condition" from that of the state of creation.[18] The result of this "depravity by nature" is a human subject entrapped in a "most miserable necessity," the necessity of reasoning, willing, and acting in the service of sin.[19]

To speak of *necessity* in this way is to begin to grasp how, to the extent that we belong to sin, we are simply undone as moral subjects. Among the spiritual realities forfeit in the fall is "knowing how to frame our life according to the rule of [God's] law."[20] Interpreting Paul's term "flesh" holistically, Calvin conceives of the human person in toto as involved in sin and implacably inimical to God; and as with the whole, so also with all the parts. Hence the will, together with the mind, is wholly "of the flesh" such that it is "not only not subject to the law of God; *it cannot be.*"[21]

Calvin consistently argues, however, that sinners sin voluntarily and not under external compulsion. Acts of sin are voluntary—even "free" in a very narrow sense—because they are a true and unconstrained outworking and expression of fallen human nature.[22] The act of sin is *self*-determined, *self*-

14. Ibid., 2.1.3 and 6.

15. Torrance, *Calvin's Doctrine of Man*, 89.

16. The main lines of Calvin's account of the bondage of the will to sin and its liberation by grace were already established by the time he published the second edition of the *Institutes* in 1539. Calvin's later dispute with Pighius over this matter and the tract to which it gave rise, *Bondage and Liberation of the Will*, led to some further clarifications of a technical sort that can be traced in the final text of the 1559 *Institutes*. See Lane, "Influence upon Calvin of His Debate with Pighius." Lane also addresses this issue concisely in his article "Anthropology."

17. Calvin, *Institutes* 2.1.9.

18. Calvin, *Bondage and Liberation of the Will*, 156.

19. For these claims, see Calvin, *Institutes* 2.2.1; 2.3.1; Calvin, *Epistle of Paul to the Romans and to the Thessalonians*, 27 (on Rom. 1:28), 125 (on Rom. 6:6), and 147 (on Rom. 7:14): "We are, however, so addicted to sin, that we can do nothing of our own accord but sin."

20. Calvin, *Institutes* 2.2.18.

21. See Steinmetz, "Calvin and Patristic Exegesis," 131, 134, emphasis added.

22. Calvin discusses the crucial distinction between necessity and coercion at length in book 4 of his reply to Pighius, *Bondage and Liberation of the Will*, esp. 146–50 (cf. 68–70).

directed. The human is not understood to be "dragged away unwillingly into sinning" but rather, "because his will is corrupt he is held captive under the yoke of sin and therefore of necessity wills in an evil way. For where there is bondage, there is necessity. . . . We locate this necessity to sin precisely in corruption of the will, from which it follows that it is self-determined; . . . thus self-determination and necessity can be combined together."[23]

The devil may make me do it, but in every case, Calvin argues, I do so willingly as one whose nature is thoroughly conformed to the will of the lord of this age, that is, as someone whose members are fully occupied by the power of sin. The logic that Käsemann discerned at work in Paul's anthropology is operative here in Calvin: we see how the human person is ever a "piece of the world," a member of a corporate body, and fully participant in its nature, in this case a member of the Adamic body of death enacting its natural enmity toward God.[24] Fallen human will is bound to sin by an inner necessity rooted in its corruption. Calvin conceives of humans *in statu corruptionis* as fully naturalized citizens of this fallen age, true and faithful descendants of Adam.[25] The will is by definition not impotent to choose; yet it is utterly impotent to choose the good, the right, and the holy. Unmade and denatured by sin, the human moral subject has become incompetent.

It is in this connection that we ought to understand Calvin's account of the *primus usus legis*. As has been seen, the human will that has become naturally captive to sin is "not only not subject to the law of God; *it cannot be*." Under these conditions the encounter with the moral law is and can only be abortive. Even as the law reliably gives voice to the will of God, in the face of the power of sin and our corrupted nature, Calvin is bold to say, "the whole strength of the law fails and vanishes away"; it is rendered "impotent" and "useless," being of "no consequence at all in bestowing righteousness."[26] Such facts are not mere contingencies: "I am telling not only what happens *but what must happen*," Calvin explains, "for since the teaching of the law is far above human capacity, a man . . . cannot derive any benefit from it."[27] Since

---

23. Ibid., 6–70. Cf. Calvin, *Institutes* 2.3.5.

24. As above, Käsemann, "On Paul's Anthropology."

25. For this reason there is even a "perverse sense" in which sinners may be taken to be integrated subjects in view of the coherent alignment of the will with fallen nature; see Steinmetz, "Calvin and the Divided Self of Romans 7," esp. 116. Cf. Calvin, *Epistle of Paul to the Romans and to the Thessalonians*, 148: The human being "appears to sin with as free a choice as if it were in his power to govern himself." As Calvin caustically observes, this willing is "a noble 'freedom' indeed—for man not to be forced to serve sin, yet to be such a willing slave that his will is bound by the fetters of sin!" (*Institutes* 2.2.7).

26. Calvin, *Epistle of Paul to the Romans and to the Thessalonians*, 158–59 (on Rom. 8:1–4).

27. Calvin, *Institutes* 2.7.3.

the law's primary and proper work of salutary moral instruction is frustrated by human incompetence, the law's initial service is and can only be deeply alien: it serves only to condemn, to crush pretense, to expose iniquity, and thus to desolate the self before God's righteousness. In the absence of suitable hearers, as it were, the law "turns into a condition for sin and death."[28] By corrupting the will so fundamentally, sin has rendered humans strictly *unsuitable* to be addressed by the law. In the absence of a competent moral subject, genuine paraenesis is ruled out, and the encounter with the law can no longer be properly moral. If, despite "being hedged about on all sides by most miserable necessity" in virtue of the corrupting reality of sin, one "should nevertheless be instructed to aspire to a good of which he is empty, to a freedom of which he has been deprived," then this is truly and rightly a counsel of despair.[29]

Now, to say, as Calvin does, that original sin and total human corruption are "accidental" or "adventitious" realities is simply to acknowledge that they are not essential to human beings as God's good creatures: sin is an alien factor, supervening on created human nature from outside God's good design, intention, and purpose, being a "wound that clings to nature."[30] However, we ought not to imagine that these adjectives in any way mitigate the formative power of sin to shape our actual human reality.[31] This becomes clear when we notice that Calvin uses the same modifier—*adventitia*—with the same force to describe the supernatural gifts of "faith, love of God, charity toward neighbor, zeal for holiness and for righteousness."[32] That such gifts of grace are similarly adventitious or unnatural in a specific sense does nothing to lessen their decisiveness in constituting the reality and orientation of the regenerate, Christian life. So too then with sin: that sin is unnatural in the same specific sense—namely, not intrinsic to God's original creation of humanity but supervening on it—does nothing to lessen the scope or depth of

---

28. Ibid., 2.7.7.

29. Ibid., 2.2.1. Cf. also Calvin, *Bondage and Liberation of the Will*, 161: "We strongly maintain that the way is not barred in the least to exhortation and rebukes, however unable man may be to obey."

30. Calvin, *Institutes* 2.1.10–11. The *Oxford English Dictionary* defines "adventitious" as being "of the nature of an addition from without; supervenient; accidental; casua" (s.v. "adventitious").

31. This strategy is visible in Partee, *Theology of John Calvin*, 129–30, and may perhaps also be detected in Dowey, "Law in Luther and Calvin," 152–53: "For Calvin it is the fundamental alliance of law, not with the devil and his perversions, but with the created order and thus with the restoration of the image of God in redemption, that is presupposed in all his discourse about law."

32. Calvin, *Institutes* 2.2.12. In Gerhard Forde's talk of grace as an "accident," noted in chapter 1, we met a similar conception.

its power decisively to shape humanity in its Adamic history. Sin, like grace, may be adventitious, but it is no less efficacious for being so. And it is this fact that authorizes Calvin also to speak properly of humanity as "corrupt" *by nature*, "naturally depraved and faulty" and so "naturally abominable to God."[33] As we have seen, the advent of sin "so altered human nature that one can speak of the corrupted nature as if it were a new nature from which sins flowed inevitably."[34]

Although human will and reason may, in a sense, be and remain inalienably "natural," they are so only in a formal, instrumental, and so nonmoral sense. Moral theology is obliged, Calvin instructs us, to deal concretely with what becomes of such natural endowments in the history of sin and redemption, rather than abstractly with reference to creation "as such."[35] As with "nature," so talk of human "freedom" is similarly polyvalent, being fundamentally determined by the particular "state" of relation with God in which the human being is held and understood, be it *in statu integratis, corruptionis,* or *gratiae* (in an integral, corrupted, or graced state of being).[36] In view of this understanding of the radical transformation of human nature under the condition of sin and then again under the condition of grace, one might even venture to say that there is, in effect, "no unchangeable and essential human nature here."[37]

This is confirmed all the more by Calvin's account of the gracious regeneration of human being—and concomitant re-creation of the human moral agent—in the advent of salvation. Without extensively rehearsing Calvin's teaching here, we can readily see divine grace is all the more adventitious, radical, dramatic, and efficacious than even its diabolic opposite, the invasion of sin. In Calvin's view, the justification and sanctification that befall us by virtue of Christ's atoning work and the contemporary mortification and vivification effected by the Spirit do nothing less than reconstitute the human person. This saving work of God takes nothing from the old and corrupted life of sin as either cause or condition. Since *in statu corruptionis* the sinner

33. Ibid., 2.2.11. Elsewhere Paul speaks of the "children of wrath" who are "so by nature, that is, from their very origin, and from their mother's womb"; see Calvin, *Epistles of Paul the Apostle to the Galatians, Ephesians, Philippians and Colossians,* 141, glossing Eph. 2:3.

34. Engel, *John Calvin's Perspectival Anthropology,* 31n79. Cf. Calvin, *Institutes* 3.12.5.

35. While Calvin contends that certain errors—e.g., making God the author of sin—are forestalled by record of such an inalienable human nature, we might consider that the soteriological and moral significance of such "essentialist" claims is ultimately surpassed by Calvin's more "historicist" account of the transformation of human nature at the hands, as it were, of sin and grace in the outworking of redemption.

36. Scheiber, "Calvin und die Freiheit," 194. Thus "freedom" like "nature" is subjected seriatim to "varying definitions" across the history of creation, fall, redemption, and final eschatology; see Engel, *John Calvin's Perspectival Anthropology,* 31. Cf. Calvin, *Institutes* 1.15.7.

37. Boer, "John Calvin and the Paradox of Grace," 31.

is utterly incapable of divine righteousness and thus is one in whom "the life of God is extinguished," Calvin contends that the outworking of "the grace of Christ is a true resurrection from the dead."[38]

If belonging to sin unmakes moral subjectivity, then our belonging to God anew in virtue of his utterly gratuitous saving work through Christ and Spirit is our remaking as competent moral agents. But this transit is not mere restoration; it is rather a total transformation. The conversion of the sinner involves nothing less than for us "to put off ourselves and to depart from our inborn disposition"; it demands the total destruction of the flesh and so the "abolition of whatever we have from ourselves," the complete "abnegation of our own nature."[39] The saving work of God in Christ amounts to "an entirely *new creation* by which the old or what is left of it is *destroyed*."[40]

The new moral subject is therefore a gracious creation of the adventitious saving reality of God for us in Christ. For in the work of salvation, "there takes place a displacement of our humanity by the humanity of Christ" such that, as the Scots Confession states, we can and must "willingly spoil ourselves of all honour and glory of our own salvation and redemption, *as we also do of our regeneration and sanctification*."[41] In Calvin's own idiom, salvation entails that one who previously belonged to and was determined decisively by sin now belongs to and is decisively determined by Christ; the first belonging is depravity; the second is justification and regeneration.[42] As the first question of the Heidelberg Catechism puts the matter, my "only comfort in life and death" is the fact that "I am not my own, but belong with body and soul both in life and in death, to my faithful Saviour Jesus Christ" such that I am "heartily willing and ready from now on to live for him." Hans-Joachim Kraus is therefore right to identify this deliverance of the sinner from the "dominion of the devil" into a new belonging to God—*nostri non sumus, Dei sumus* (we are not our own, we are God's)—as the fundamental basis of Calvin's ethics.[43] God's gracious reclamation of captive humanity creates

---

38. Calvin, *Gospel according to St. John 1–10*, 130–31. "You may cure a wound by such treatment but you cannot restore a dead man to life. . . . A dead person can only be raised, *resurrected*, and grave sin can only be *forgiven*" (K. Barth, *Holy Spirit and the Christian Life*, 24, emphasis original).

39. Calvin, *Institutes* 3.3.8. In the earlier 1539 and related 1541 French edition, Calvin had written more strongly that conversion "involves divesting ourselves of ourselves and abandoning our own nature" by "repudiating our nature *and all our will*" (Calvin, *Institutes* [1541], 275, emphasis added). See Calvin, *Opera Selecta*, 4:63.

40. Torrance, *Calvin's Doctrine of Man*, 91, emphasis original.

41. Torrance, "Justification," 243, 237–38, emphasis added.

42. Calvin, *Institutes* 3.7.1.

43. See Kraus, "Contemporary Relevance of Calvin's Theology," 335.

a new creaturely agency that can "hear the law" beyond the contractions of the old age in a new and properly moral way.

The principal use of the law—that is, its third use—thus has an entirely soteriological foundation. Those who truly belong to God owe everything to grace and mercy, including the gift of moral competence on the basis of which they become "suitable hearers" of the law. The law is able to function properly—*in proprium*—as a life-giving moral instruction once more only because the Spirit of God "already lives and reigns in the hearts of the faithful."[44] The language that Calvin deploys of the Spirit in this regard reflects that previously used of sin and its occupation and remaking of human nature. The Spirit, who comes "not from nature but from regeneration," enlightens human minds and reforms human hearts "to live and cultivate righteousness," instilling—in conjunction with the word—a sustained desire "to seek, search for, and pursue that renewal." The Spirit casts light on darkened reason and liberates unfree wills by seizing back the human subject and breaking the necessities of its fallen nature. As Calvin goes on to explain, Christian faith "bids reason give way to, submit and subject itself to, the Holy Spirit so that the man himself may no longer live but hear Christ living and reigning within him." Only within this new belonging, only under this new lordship, only as an exercise of human freedom under the yet again "very different conditions" that obtain in virtue of the adventitious reality of God's saving grace, can there be regenerate moral agents truly addressable by the law *as law*, whose pursuit of righteousness is rightly "served" by it.[45] If, as Augustine says, "grace produces doers of the law," then this is because, in the first instance, grace itself has always also and already produced anew hearers of the law.[46]

Conclusion: Soteriology as First Moral Philosophy

We have seen that Calvin offers a historicized account of both human nature and the function of the law in the transit of the economy of salvation. In their actual encounter under the conditions of the fall, and again under the

44. Calvin, *Institutes* 2.7.11.

45. Citations in this paragraph are from Calvin, *Institutes* 2.2.27; 2.5.5; 2.2.21; 2.2.7; 3.7.1; and 2.7.12.

46. Calvin, *Bondage and Liberation of the Will*, 166, citing Augustine, *Against Two Letters of the Pelagians* 3.2.2. Calvin understands such redeemed agents to continue to be harassed and threatened by sin, as he makes plain in his exegesis of Rom. 7:14–17—where Paul "describes in his own person the weakness of the faithful, and how great it is"—and with his account of the Christian life in terms of continual repentance, vivification, and mortification; see *Institutes* 3.3.3–20.

conditions of salvation, neither the human being nor the law is any longer what it once was. Although Calvin records the notional continuity of both— for example, insisting that "the law is not injurious to us by its own nature" and that created human nature is not utterly abolished by the fall—yet in the actual outworking of the matter the serial substantive differences, rather than the formal continuities, are preeminently operative. So Calvin can say with reference to the *primus usus legis* that, in our fallen condition, "it is an accident that the law inflicts a mortal wound on us, just as if an incurable disease were rendered more acute by a healing remedy. The accident, I admit, is inseparable from the law, and for this reason the law, as compared with the Gospel, is elsewhere referred to as 'the ministration of death' [2 Cor. 3:7] . . . because our corruption provokes and draws upon us its curse."[47] Then, writing of the *tertius usus legis* (third use of the law), Calvin can remark that the law can only be said to enlighten, illumine, and minister life in as much as it is met and understood with reference to the "use it serves for the regenerate."[48] Humans thus do not engage with the law as such or according to its abiding nature; neither does the law address human moral subjects as such or according to their abiding nature. Rather, they encounter each other only according to the law's manifestation under the superintendence of sin as a "ministry of death" (2 Cor. 3:7) or under the superintendence of God's gracious Spirit as a "light to the path." In the unfolding of the actual economy of salvation, there is no law per se: rather, there is only ever the law in its varied *usus* (uses). We should not be misled to downplay the significance of this by talk of these modulations as merely "accidental" and "adventitious."

Calvin's terminology signals the historical mobility of both law and humanity in the outworking of salvation. We only have the moral law in its variegated functions *in statu corruptionis* and then again *in statu gratiae* (in the state of grace). And the moral law only has us in our variegated natures under sin and grace. Crucially, sin and grace are not only *adventitious*; they are also *efficacious*: in the course of the outworking of salvation, sin and grace fundamentally unmake and remake the reality of the human moral subject in ways that are decisive for the Christian life and thus also must be decisive for theological reflection on the nature, form, and direction of that life. I do not think it is too much to say that here Calvin thinks and speaks with an apocalyptic grammar of the kind that Martyn has discerned in the witness of Paul. Calvin would seem to have the measure of the apostle.

47. Calvin, *Epistle of Paul to the Romans and to the Thessalonians*, 145, commenting on Rom. 7:10.
48. Calvin, *Institutes* 2.7.12.

This feature of Calvin's theology suggests that we win very little purchase on the question of human moral subjectivity by reflecting directly on
the essential features of our creaturely nature as such, on reason and will
as formal structures of our enduring human essence. Set within the history
of our unmaking and remaking by the serial advents of sin and grace, such
features of human reality have very little telling moral valence.[49] It further
suggests that a Protestant Christian ethic should take its first and defining
cues from a dramatic theological account of fall and redemption. As it does
so, the putative stabilities of created order will be of less moral consequence
and interest than will the task of accounting for the inspired hearing of the
concrete commandments of the God of the gospel amid everyday life. For, as
Martyn observes, in the labor "of creating the new human agent as the new
Spirit-led community," the God who comes to save in Christ "*consistently
participates in human morality itself.*"[50] A properly evangelical theological
ethic should thus be fully suspended from soteriology, acknowledging that the
moral power of divine law as well as the moral competence of God's human
partner hangs entirely on "the establishing of a new moral life that flows from
grace," and that grace is and remains "God's sovereign realm."[51]

49. Hence Calvin's exasperation at Hilary's treatment of the human will: "But why not a
single word about the downfall of human nature, or about its restoration through the grace of
God?" (Calvin, *Bondage and Liberation of the Will*, 73).

50. Martyn, "Epilogue," 182, emphasis original.

51. Torrance, "Atonement," 252. Torrance explicitly connects this idea of the "soteriological
suspension of the ethical" with the "cosmic sweep of atoning reconciliation" attested in the
New Testament's apocalyptic idiom (254–55); the final remark is from Karl Barth, *Holy Spirit
and the Christian Life*, 20.

11

Crucified to the World

Kierkegaard's Christian Life of Humility and Gratitude

See now that I, even I, am he; there is no god besides me.
I kill and I make alive;
I wound and I heal; and no one can deliver from my hand.

—Deuteronomy 32:39

When a person is overcome by the words of divine grace, they will call him aside, where he no longer hears the secular mentality's earthly mother tongue.

—Søren Kierkegaard, "To Need God Is a
Human Being's Highest Perfection"

This chapter continues our exploration of the fundamental connection between Christian self-understanding and soteriology. More particularly, it continues to reflect on the way in which the basic grammar and substance of such an account of the Christian self might be understood to be a reduplication of the wider soteriological vision that comprehends it, being both ordered to and controlled by it. As a modern Christian thinker profoundly committed to the analysis and understanding of human

subjectivity generally, and of the distinctive subjectivity of the Christian life
in particular, Kierkegaard's writing on the Christian self and Christian life
exemplifies this claim.

In the discussion that follows I suggest that Kierkegaard's intense concentration on the negative aspects of the experience of the Christian self—
suffering, fragility, self-deception, weakness, failure, sin, and finally despair—is
a function of his no less intense commitment to a radically Pauline soteriology.
His treatment of the Christian self in these terms republishes in an anthropological register the form and consequence of the objective (and ultimately
even cosmic) reality of salvation set forth in the theology of the cross. Seen
in this way, the dialectics of death/life and divine judgment/mercy at the
heart of Paul's eschatological gospel produce an interior echo within the
life of the Christian. For this reason Kierkegaard contends that it is always
profoundly edifying to acknowledge on the one hand that even as we traverse
the world, it is utterly lost to us; and on the other hand that throughout the
life of faith, "in relation to God we are always in the wrong." In this way,
the negative form of Christian subjectivity, marked by both awareness of
sin and sacrificial dislocation within the world, attests to the deity of grace
and the radicality of its liberating work. It suggests that it is yet possible for
Christians to hear, to own, and to live from what we might call the vivifying power of the mortifying gospel of God. Precisely from this follows the
grateful and active Christian life of militant discipleship to which so many of
Kierkegaard's latter works give passionate witness. The shape of the whole
is captured concisely by Kierkegaard himself in a remark from the journals:
"Infinite humiliation and grace, and then a striving born of gratitude—this is
Christianity."[1]

The chapter unfolds in four steps. In the first, "Kierkegaard's Inverse Dialectic," I consider the contours of his distinctive treatment of Christian subjectivity with the aid of important recent work done by Sylvia Walsh and
Simon Podmore. In the second, "Infinite Humiliation and Grace," I forge
connections between this discussion and the most radical features of Paul's
soteriology, focusing on a selection of passages that illustrate the source and
logic of Kierkegaard's own edifying negativity. In the third, "Striving Born
of Gratitude," I analyze the way in which Kierkegaard conceives of the new
life that emerges from the crucible of saving divine judgment and grace to be
one of militant witness and discipleship. A fourth and final section ventures
some summary observations on our theme and its wider implications for our
thinking about the contours of an apocalyptic theology.

1. Kierkegaard, *JP* 1:434 (#993); cf. 4:711.

Kierkegaard's "Inverse Dialectic" of Christian Subjectivity

Only man is wrong; to him alone is reserved what is denied to everything else—to be in the wrong in relation to God.

—Søren Kierkegaard, *Either/Or*

The twofold ambition of Kierkegaard's second authorship is to describe Christian subjectivity "with a dialectical acuteness and a primitivity not to be found in any other literature."[2] Crucially, the first of these ambitions is ordered to the second: the value of dialectical exposition lies in its ability to help in displaying the primitive—meaning the originary—form of the Christian self. The specific dialectic Kierkegaard deploys is at once "qualitative-existential" and "inverse." It is, first, "qualitative-existential" (rather than logical) in that his account of Christian subjectivity articulates the actual living contradiction between who one now is and who one can and ought to be, or in Kierkegaard's own idiom, between the actual and the ideal. This dialectical work is relentless and radical: Kierkegaard demands that one be unhesitatingly polemical for the sake of the ideal. Second, it is "inverse" because of the specific nature of the Christian ideal in question: righteousness vis-à-vis God. The truth of the religious ideal is displayed precisely by its contradiction of the actual; further, it is this negation of the actual that properly bespeaks the character, intensity, and force of the ideal. Because it is concerned with the ideal, religious reflection generally, and specifically Christian reflection to the highest degree, "continually uses the negative as the essential form."[3] This qualitative dialectic of *Christian* existence is always negative or inverted in character because it is precisely our *un*righteousness that testifies to the infinite requirement of the righteous God, as well as God's infinite mercy.

The truth of the ideal is first suffered in existential contradiction, and only then attested by way of such dialectical inversion in thought and speech. Thus Kierkegaard claims that the "essentially Christian [thing] is always the positive that is recognizable by the negative."[4] As Sylvia Walsh's valuable recent study of Kierkegaard's account of Christian existence demonstrates so thoroughly, the positive features of the truth of Christian faith—*faith, forgiveness, new life, love, hope, joy,* and *consolation*"—are dialectically attested by four decisive negative qualifications of the Christian self: "*consciousness of sin, the possibility of offense, dying to the world* or *self-denial,* and *suffering.*"[5] By

2. Kierkegaard, *JP* 5:336 (#5914); cited by Walsh, *Living Christianly*, 6.
3. Kierkegaard, *Concluding Unscientific Postscript*, 524.
4. Kierkegaard, *JP* 4:407 (#4680); cited by Walsh, *Living Christianly*, 9.
5. Walsh, *Living Christianly*, 13–14.

lavishing "inverted attention" on these qualities, genuine Christian reflection on the self will always emphasize "the requirement in all its infinitude so that [one] rightly learns to be humbled and to rely upon grace"; indeed, he can assert (as we have already noted) that Christianity simply is "infinite humiliation and grace, and then a striving born of gratitude."[6] Crucially for our purposes here, Kierkegaard also observes that "*the apostle* always speaks out of this inverted dialectic."[7]

Note well that the apostle does not just speak *of* or even *in terms of* this inverted dialectic, but that he speaks *out of* it. The negative dialectic is itself but a late expression of the truth of the infinite contradiction one has already suffered in relation to the ideal, to the absolute, to God. All Christian subjectivity has *this* suffering as its primary, indeed apostolic, shape and source. As Kierkegaard explains, this suffering "means neither more nor less than the mark, the criterion, of my actually being involved with the absolute and of my relating myself to it" and is therefore at one and the same time also "sheer blessedness and sheer grace."[8] In short, such "suffering as the sign of the relationship to God is what Christianity is according to the New Testament."[9]

The Christian self is produced by the contradiction of one's self by God and the subsequent contradiction of the world by that same self now made angular to the world precisely in virtue of its divine contradiction: the Christian self is forged by humiliation and grace. As Simon Podmore has argued on this basis, the priority and permanence of the negative is a function of what it means for human beings to know themselves *coram deo* (in the presence of God): if true self-knowledge involves the "absolute expression" of the absolute—indeed, "infinite qualitative"—difference between humanity and God, then to pursue this truth demands that we tarry with the infinite contradiction of humanity by God in both judgment and forgiveness (again Kierkegaard's humiliation *and* grace).[10] Thus Kierkegaard himself says, as sinners, human beings are "separated from God by a yawning qualitative abyss," and "naturally when God forgives sinners he is again separated from [human beings] by the same qualitative abyss."[11]

The logic of this inverse dialectic of the Christian self runs close to that of the *primus usus legis* (first use of the law) in the Lutheran doctrine of law and

---

6. Kierkegaard, *JP* 1:434 (#993).

7. Ibid., 4:407 (#4680); cited by Walsh, *Living Christianly*, 9, some original italics removed.

8. Ibid.

9. Ibid., 4:409 (#4682). He continues, "I am far from this height, but I understand it, and I understand it to my humiliation."

10. See Podmore, *Kierkegaard and the Self before God*, xi–xxiv, 1–2.

11. Kierkegaard, *SV* 11:261; cited by Sponheim, "Kierkegaard's View of a Christian," 188.

gospel: *lex semper accusat*, the law always accuses. Yet in emphasizing that the self is negated by both divine judgment (humiliation) *and* mercy (grace), Kierkegaard wants to signal something more.[12] The older theological concept of "law" is here conceptually expanded to encompass the infinite demand that befalls human existence *coram deo*. As he once put it, "In Christianity it is not even the law which orders you to die to the world; it is love which says: Do you not love me, then? And if the answer is: Yes, then it follows as a matter of course that you must die to the world."[13] We might say that by virtue of their origin in God, both law and gospel here stand as absolute contradictions of human existence. That a human life should suffer this salutary humiliation and grace is attested "inversely" in and by Christian *consciousness of sin* and *dying to the world*.

This inverse dialectical treatment of the Christian self is represented and elaborated across the works of Kierkegaard's second and openly Christian authorship. In a longer treatment we would want to canvass specific examples drawn from texts whose very titles suggest the form: "The Gospel of Sufferings," "The Joy of It: That the Weaker You Become the Stronger God Becomes in You," and "To Need God Is a Human Being's Highest Perfection."[14] But its essential logic is concisely and programmatically set out in the first chapters of the *Philosophical Fragments*. Here the singularity, absoluteness, and eternal significance of the "moment" of the Savior's advent in truth is shown to be integrally related to the acknowledgment that those to whom he comes are in untruth, bereft of the condition of possibility for receiving the truth at all, indeed that their untruth "is not merely outside the truth but is polemical against the truth": sin is a negative position of depravity and enmity.[15] Thus divine salvation comes by way of total contradiction, effecting that break, the translation from "not to be" to "to be," what the New Testament calls *death* and *rebirth*. In this, the human owes the Savior *everything*: "that he becomes nothing and yet is not annihilated; that he owes him everything and yet becomes boldly confident; that he understands the truth, but the truth makes him free; that he grasps the guilt of untruth, and then again bold confidence triumphs in the truth."[16] *This* Christian truth about the self can be made plain only by way of the dialectics of inversion,

12. Kierkegaard can be sharply critical of Luther's own lack of dialectical sensibility at key points; see *JP* 1:192 (#486).

13. Kierkegaard, *JP* 1:219 (#538).

14. See Kierkegaard, *Christian Discourses* and for the latter *Eighteen Upbuilding Discourses*, 297–325.

15. Kierkegaard, *Philosophical Fragments*, 15. See also Hampson, *Kierkegaard*, 240–41.

16. Kierkegaard, *Philosophical Fragments*, 30–31.

the absolute need and humility of the human being serving to attest the absolute deity and graciousness of God.

In sum, Kierkegaard's account of the Christian self bespeaks the mortifying work of the gospel of God. It turns on an understanding of the pragmatics of divine grace whereby God's salutary contradiction of the human being in sin deals "a fatal blow to all his worldly thinking, aspiring, and pursuing" and turns "everything upside down."[17] To conceive of the self under the sign of this saving contradiction demands an inverse dialectic if the positive content of the gospel is to be set forth in a properly self-involving and edifying manner. For it is only the disrupted, displaced, and dislocated human self—humiliated by judgment and evacuated by grace—that attests the "moment of ultimate discontent with the world and ultimate contentment with God, . . . the moment in which is said 'now everything has become new.'"[18]

"Infinite Humiliation and Grace": Mortified unto Life at the Turning of the Ages

> For to me, living is Christ and dying is gain.
>
> —Philippians 1:21

The elements of Kierkegaard's account of the Christian self just canvassed suggest that "the becoming of a Christian is not the mild unfolding of inherent [human] possibility" but a passage brought about by the annihilating and re-creative advent of divine judgment and grace.[19] As we noticed above, Kierkegaard himself remarks that *the apostle* always speaks out of this inverted dialectic."[20] In this section of the essay we reflect briefly on some aspects of Pauline soteriology that fund Kierkegaard's own edifying negativity and apart from which it is unlikely to be properly understood.[21] The point could be demonstrated with reference to a range of Pauline texts, but for present purposes we will focus on two passages in Galatians, where Paul declares,

17. Kierkegaard, "To Need God Is a Human Being's Highest Perfection," 300.
18. Ibid., 303, citing 2 Cor. 5:17.
19. Pap. XI I A 564, cited by Sponheim, "Kierkegaard's View of a Christian," 187.
20. Kierkegaard, *JP* 4:407 (#4680), cited by Walsh, *Living Christianly*, 9, original italics removed from this quote.
21. Cyril O'Regan has recently remarked on how Kierkegaard's wider thinking about the self is "massively informed . . . by an essentially Pauline vision"; see O'Regan, "Rule of Chaos and the Perturbation of Love," 154.

"I have been crucified with Christ; it is no longer I who live, but Christ who lives in me" (2:19b–20a), and later, "May I never boast of anything except the cross of our Lord Jesus Christ, by which the world has been crucified to me, and I to the world" (6:14).[22]

In these verses Paul speaks of the consequences of the "apocalypse of Jesus Christ" (Gal. 1:12c, 16) in which God has acted redemptively on the world scene to bring a "complete and irrevocable end" to the old and passing age.[23] He understands saving divine action to be invasive and decisive: the gospel comes upon the world so as to overreach everything that has been for the sake of the new thing God is doing. As the Corinthian Letters also signal, the advent of God's salvation in Christ "destroys the wisdom of the wise" and "thwarts" all previous discernment (cf. 1 Cor. 1:19–20) by choosing "what is low and despised in the world, things that are not, to reduce to nothing things that are, so that no one might boast in the presence of God" (1 Cor. 1:28–29). This course of contradiction is the path of the "new creation" by which "everything old has passed away" (2 Cor. 5:17). The cross is, for Paul, the central act of divine rectification, the axis on which God is turning the ages and in which Christians are participating. And the "extreme language of crucifixion with Christ gives expression to one key element of such participation, the end or the permanent loss of a previous manner of life" that comes with rescue "from the present evil age" (Gal. 1:4).[24] In his gloss on Galatians 2:20, Luther calls the work of the gospel the *abolition* of the old, as the old self is displaced by the Christ whose righteousness now "lives in" one by faith.[25] Beverly Gaventa summarizes the force of the same verse: "It is the whole of the ἐγώ [*egō*, I] that is gone. . . . The gospel is singular in that it is all-consuming: there is no more ἐγώ. And the gospel is also all life giving: Christ lives in me."[26]

The point is reinforced when we reflect on the meaning of what Paul says of the double crucifixion of self to world and world to self in Galatians 6:14, "The world has been crucified to me, and I to the world." Many commentators take this subjectively: Calvin, for instance, says that here Paul speaks of

22. Other texts that invite similar reflection include 1 Cor. 1:28–31; 2 Cor. 1:12; 5:17; 11:16–12:10; Rom. 5:2–3, 11; Phil. 1:21; 3:8; etc.

23. See de Boer, *Galatians*, 159, 81–82.

24. Ibid., 161.

25. Luther on Gal. 2:20, in *Lectures on Galatians*, 238.

26. Gaventa, "Singularity of the Gospel Revisited," 193, 195. I am minded to think that it should be possible to develop an account of the Christian life conceived on the basis of the idea of the "dative self," i.e., from an account of how things come to appear when the human self is consistently understood on the grounds of its being displaced into the dative case by the divine subject and its agency (Christ *for us*, Christ *in me*, etc.).

a state of mind in which the world is despised and belittled.[27] But the kind of apocalyptic reading of the apostle we are venturing stresses that the force of this claim is much more far-reaching. To speak this way is to suggest that the entire world order, once "sacred and dependable," has been "utterly destroyed." Paul speaks of "what he takes to be an objective situation, the effect of Christ's death on an objective cross and of his own participation in that objective death"; for the apostle, the previous cosmos—the very order of things of which he was an integral part—has itself been brought to an end on the cross of Christ and has "suffered the loss of that world."[28] This reading is supported by the radical announcement of "new creation" (Gal. 6:15) as the most apt characterization of what has come about, come upon, and supplanted the passing age.

As discussed in previous chapters, Martyn also reads the passage similarly, contending that Paul speaks here of the crucifixion as a "watershed event" in which Paul has become a stranger to his previous companions "and indeed to all people who live in the world" of the old cosmic order, "as their world became a stranger to him."[29] The total contradiction and loss of the old world, and the radically disorienting birth of a new world—this is the context that demands a radically new and dialectical analysis of Christian subjectivity in which the positive is known and attested by the negative. For in the mortification of the world itself for the sake of the advent of the new, the self also is and finds itself mortified unto new life. As Paul himself says elsewhere, "I regard everything as loss because of the surpassing value of knowing Christ Jesus my Lord. For his sake I have suffered the loss of all things, and I regard them as utter rubbish, in order that I may gain Christ" (Phil. 3:8).

In sum, the human person and the world stand related as microcosm to macrocosm, but more than this: faith's "dying to the world" has as its condition of possibility and comprehensive ground the "crucifixion" of the world, which is the advent of the new creation. For this reason, the militant freedom and radical self-renunciation of Christian faith are but marks of that new humanity that, in the present time of faith, "bears the death of Jesus in the body" (cf. 2 Cor. 4:10). The unconditional ideality of Kierkegaard's inverse dialectic of the Christian self bespeaks Paul's all-consuming gospel of militant grace; it is simply a qualitative/existential implicate of the crucifixion of the Lord.

27. On Gal. 6:14–15, Calvin, *Epistles of Paul the Apostle to the Galatians, Ephesians, Philippians and Colossians,* 117.

28. De Boer, *Galatians,* 401–2.

29. Martyn, *Galatians,* 564. Cf. Luther, *Lectures on Galatians,* 404–5, remarking that "the world, not Christ, lives in men," though now Christ, not the world, lives in Paul: hence, crucifixion.

"Striving Born of Gratitude": Christian Life as Militant Discipleship

> The essentially Christian needs no defence, is not served by any defence—it is
> the attacker. . . . In Christendom, of course, it attacks from behind.[30]
>
> —Søren Kierkegaard, "Thoughts That Wound
> from Behind—For Upbuilding"

Being a creature of the crucifixion of the Lord fashioned by "humiliation and
grace," the Christian life is enacted under the lordship of the Crucified in the
form of a "striving born of gratitude." We should understand Kierkegaard's
account of the Christian life as the outworking of that "second ethics" of which
he (under the pseudonym Haufniensis) writes in *The Concept of Anxiety*.
In that text we read of a new ethics that "presupposes dogmatics," taking
as its ground the dogmatic description of the actuality of human sinfulness
and the work of divine grace on the truth of which all other ethics are simply
"shipwrecked."[31] Kierkegaard insists that the total evangelical disruption of
the old world and self must be acknowledged as the source and impetus of
the new or second life that the Christian must now live.

The watchwords of this account are provided by Matthew 6:24 and James
1:22: "No one can serve two masters" and "Be doers of the word, and not
merely hearers."[32] Following the master exclusively and doing the Word obediently specify the nature of Christian "striving" as he envisages it. Here the
inverse dialectic of Christian existence continues to hold: the Christian life is
manifest only in and through suffering permanent antinomy with the world
as it is set "in opposition to the immediate and universal forms of existence."[33]
Rooted in the New Testament witness, as just discussed, Kierkegaard understands the Christian of "the present age" to be situated even more fundamentally in the contested overlap of the old and new ages. In this eschatological
location, "the world is going neither forward nor backward" but rather is "the
element that can provide the test of being a Christian, who in this world is
always a member of the church militant."[34] In this way individual Christian
lives reiterate the macrocosmic confrontation of the new and old worlds.

---

30. From the epigraph to Kierkegaard, "Thoughts That Wound from Behind—For Upbuilding," 162.

31. "Sin, then, belongs to ethics only insofar as upon this concept it is shipwrecked with the
aid of repentance" (Kierkegaard, *Concept of Anxiety*, 17; cf. 18–24).

32. Kierkegaard, *For Self-Examination / Judge for Yourself!*, 13–51 and 145–209. On the
importance of the latter in Kierkegaard's work, see Bauckham, "Kierkegaard and the Epistle
of James," 39–54.

33. Walsh, *Living Christianly*, 150.

34. Kierkegaard, *PC* 232.

The existence that takes shape in faith's grateful struggle to serve Christ and obey the Word is permanently *repentant*, heeding the summons "You all must become different and do otherwise" in response to the commanding gift of grace.[35] In reliance on God, it entails venturing a life of "unalloyed divine service" whose "hymn of praise is in the obedience," a life at once joyful, ascetic, agonistic, and marked by suffering.[36]

The Christian life is *militant* and essentially so; it simply is "militant piety."[37] In the first place, the militancy of the Christian life is a function of the fact that it is lived out where a "kingdom not from this world" (John 18:36) has erupted into a world marked by "mutinous untruth," not least concerning Christianity and the true shape of the life of faith.[38] In this context and in disruptive ways, all forms of Christian existence that "witness to the truth" cut across the settled conventions of the environment, including those of Christendom.[39] This is what occasions the *offense* of which Kierkegaard speaks so often in the later works. The Christian appears in this world as an alarmingly unnatural creature whose very existence calls into question natural life because his "love of God is hatred of the world."[40] As Kierkegaard explains, "Christianity, and being a true Christian must to the highest degree be an offense to the natural man, that he must regard Christianity as the greatest treason and the true Christian as the meanest traitor to being a human being."[41] One of the fundamental reasons this is so is that the Christian life is "drawn to Christ *in lowliness*," and in tracing this downward or kenotic movement, Kierkegaard insists on the ideality of humble striving in a world of achievement.[42]

35. Luther, Smalcald Articles 3.3, in *Triglot Concordia*, 481.

36. Kierkegaard, *Christian Discourses*, 84, 86. Louis Dupré considers this one of Kierkegaard's most important contributions to theology, namely, "the reintegration of Christian asceticism in the *sola fide* doctrine of the Reformation" (*Kierkegaard as Theologian*, xi). George Pattison, less positively, observes the "sombre shadow of a world-denying form of religiosity" that "constantly grows in intensity and depth as the authorship continues" (*Kierkegaard and the Crisis of Faith*, 114–15). The idea of the Christian life as "venturing in reliance upon God" comes from Kierkegaard, *For Self-Examination / Judge for Yourself!*, 100, 102.

37. Kierkegaard, *Point of View*, 130.

38. Kierkegaard, *For Self-Examination / Judge for Yourself!*, 19; *PC* 211. True "Christianity is a militant teaching, is a polemic, that . . . posits eternal enmity between God and the world"; *JP* 1:200 (#499).

39. Kierkegaard, *For Self-Examination / Judge for Yourself!*, 193, where the phrase is applied to Luther. Elsewhere he stresses that it is precisely in confessing Christianity in the world that the church is militant (*PC* 217; cf. 212).

40. Kierkegaard, *PC* 224.

41. Kierkegaard, *For Self-Examination / Judge for Yourself!*, 140. Cf. "All human wisdom consists in this glorious or golden principle: to a certain degree, there is a limit, or in the 'both-and,' 'also'; the unconditional is madness" (154).

42. Kierkegaard, *PC* 209.

Hence "militant" in Kierkegaard's account of the Christian life designates the dynamic and offensive form the life of faith adopts in its collision with the world as a result of its tenacious positive commitment to the ideal and unconditional character of the Christian claim. As Kierkegaard said of his own witness, "It is not polemical against any particular person, is not finitely polemical against anything finite but is infinitely polemical only in order to throw light on the ideal" because "the true Christian perspective for every Christian qualification is polemical within or away from finitude toward the eternal."[43] This is key: Christian militancy is indexed to truth, being a function of it and tethered to its service. Kierkegaard can assert that "the church militant is truth" only because it is the nature of divine truth to enjoin faith's militancy.[44] The advent of the truth wrestles its human witnesses free from their ignorant complicity in the untruth of the world, including that of Christendom, and thereby sets them permanently at odds with it. "There may be quite a number of true Christians in Christendom," Kierkegaard remarks, "but every such one is also militant."[45]

The Christian life offends precisely as it attests the truth of the unconditional grace and claim that creates and sustains it. But this way of putting that matter is too abstract. Better and more concretely, Christian life offends to the extent that it actually follows after the one who is "the way, and the truth, and the life" (John 14:6). Crucially, the truth from which the militancy of faith derives is not a proposition but *a life*. In a key passage Kierkegaard elaborates the import of this claim: "Thus Christ is the truth in the sense that to *be* the truth is the only true explanation of what truth is. . . . The being of truth is the redoubling of truth within yourself, within me, within him, that your life, my life, his life expresses the truth approximately in the striving for it, that your life, my life, his life is approximately the being of the truth in the striving for it just as the truth was in Christ a *life*, for he was the truth."[46] For this reason, a Christian offers a militant testimony *only* in the form of a life of faithful striving to imitate Christ, who himself became "unconditionally heterogeneous with everyone" and yet remained in the world for their sake "in order to suffer."[47] The true Christian is Christ's imitator, not his admirer.[48] Kierkegaard envisages such imitation

---

43. Kierkegaard, *Point of View*, 133, 130.
44. Kierkegaard, PC 219.
45. Kierkegaard, *Christian Discourses*, 229.
46. Kierkegaard, PC 205.
47. Kierkegaard, *For Self-Examination / Judge for Yourself!*, 168. Cf. PC 219.
48. Kierkegaard, PC 254. Cf. Kierkegaard, *For Self-Examination / Judge for Yourself!*, 198–99: "Christ wants admirers no more now than he did then, to say nothing of drivellers; he wants only disciples."

as a nonidentical repetition of the movement and shape of Christ's own existence, which is the prototype of all Christian lives.[49] It is "nonidentical" because Christ is "also much more than the prototype," for at the same time he is the Redeemer and the "object of faith."[50] The prototypical work of Christ in his self-abasement and lowliness is to propel and to beckon and to leave traces—"footprints," Kierkegaard calls them at one point—to direct those who would follow after him as imitators.[51] He at once announces and enacts the unconditional divine requirement even as he himself fulfills it *for us*.[52] But this *for us* includes his unconditional summons to follow him. So the concept of imitation is best filled out with the idea of discipleship (*Efterfølgelsen*, following after), with which it keeps close company in Kierkegaard's late works.

Along with his radical self-abasement, Kierkegaard stresses Christ's prototypical heterogeneity and eschatological freedom vis-à-vis the world. Of this he writes, "Just like a straight line that touches the circle at only one point, so was he in the world and yet outside the world, serving only one master."[53] Christ's life and way is the life and way of one who is out of phase with and angular to the old world precisely because he inhabits and acts from the new before us and "for us." Drawn into this same heterogeneity and freedom by grace, the essentially Christian form of life comes to share in Christ's own abasement. In collision with the world, Christian difference or alterity is manifest in persistent self-denial and suffering.[54]

The struggle to serve one master, to do the word—this militant discipleship—is "born of gratitude."[55] Arising from thankfulness, Christian striving after the prototype is also the authentic *expression* of gratitude to God for the difficult gift of salvation: "Christ," he writes, "has desired only one kind of gratitude: from the individual, and as practically as possible in the form of imitation."[56] To be drawn actively to follow after the prototype is not to suffer "the law's

49. The idea of Christ as "prototype" is developed at several points, including Kierkegaard, PC 238–43, and most extensively in Kierkegaard, *For Self-Examination / Judge for Yourself!*, 147–213.

50. Kierkegaard, *Point of View*, 131. In PC he writes that "Christ came to the world with the purpose of saving the world, also with the purpose—this in turn is implicit in his first purpose—of being *the prototype*" (238). Cf. Kierkegaard, *For Self-Examination / Judge for Yourself!*, 159; and JP 2:235 (#1862).

51. Kierkegaard, PC 238.

52. Kierkegaard, *For Self-Examination / Judge for Yourself!*, 159.

53. Kierkegaard, *For Self-Examination / Judge for Yourself!*, 167.

54. Kierkegaard, *Works of Love*, 56.

55. "Imitation or discipleship does not come first, but 'grace'; *then* imitation follows as a fruit of gratitude"; Kierkegaard, JP 2:338 (#1886).

56. Ibid., 2:190 (#1518).

demand that a poor wretch of a man must torture himself"[57] with impossible burdens; rather, it is the living worship of the redeemed: "So also with the believer in relation to God—expressing his gratitude in words, perhaps even in more elegant and artistically chosen words (and this is an utterly wrong direction), he will finally reach a point where he must say: I cannot stand it, this no longer satisfies my need; you must, O God, permit me a far stronger expression for my gratitude—works."[58] Such works are works of self-giving love. And precisely as such they are also so many occasions for suffering and forms of suffering, an inalienable aspect of the Christian's militant collision with the environing world for the sake of the truth. Indeed, Kierkegaard can summarize the true ambition of love's striving in just these terms, as he writes, "Your only desire must be to suffer for the truth in order to express some gratitude for what Christ is for you. This, you see, is Christianity."[59] Once again, the inverse dialectic provides the fundamental grammar of Kierkegaard's theology of the Christian life: here joy is found in the suffering that bespeaks the truth of a disciple's grateful life of service. Indeed, such suffering itself provides renewed occasions for gratitude to God, as Kierkegaard explains: "And when everything seems to storm in upon us, when everything totters, when all depends on bending without breaking, he who from a full heart can say: All God's gifts are good when they are received with gratitude—in this gratitude and by this gratitude he has overcome the world."[60] The gratitude that strives in discipleship against the world subjectively reduplicates the objectivity of the divine striving in the abasement of the cross that has already overcome the world.

Concluding Remarks: A Fully Soteriological Account of the Christian Life

> To need God is nothing to be ashamed of but is perfection itself.
>
> —Søren Kierkegaard, "To Need God Is a
> Human Being's Highest Perfection"

Allow me to venture four remarks by way of conclusion. The first is simply to observe that—as I hope to have shown—with its radical account of salvation

57. Ibid., 2:340 (#1892).
58. Ibid., 4:335 (#4524).
59. Ibid., 4:495 (#4867).
60. Ibid., 2:186 (#1507). On the importance of this theme, see Gouwens, *Kierkegaard as Religious Thinker*, 139–40, and esp. 153–85.

by an absolute, gracious divine contradiction of the world in Christ for the sake of the world, Kierkegaard's inverse dialectic of Christian existence should be understood as a reiteration in a focused anthropological register of the contours of Pauline soteriology. Christian subjectivity rightly offers an interior echo of the cosmic revolution wrought by the apocalypse of the gospel of God. Both the deity of God and the graciousness of grace, we might say, provide the fundamental logic of salvation and so also of the saved self, which finds itself brought to naught in order to be made alive, and being made anew, knows itself to be dislocated, wrenched out of phase with the "form of this world," which "is passing away" (1 Cor. 7:31). The kind of self and the sort of subjectivity at issue in the gospel seems to be one in which the self is always utterly dependent on the gift of divine saving truth, a truth that, because it is divine, "kills to make alive" and that can never be digested or possessed by the actual but that always cuts across the actual in the invasion of the ideal on the actual. Kierkegaard offers a fully soteriological account of the Christian life as a "micro-cosmic apocalyptic."[61]

Second, and more to the matter of the discourse of theology itself: one might entertain the awkward thought—already canvassed in the immediately preceding chapters—that on such grounds there is little that is really Christianly interesting about the "natural" human self and subjectivity as such. Such interest as there is in theological anthropology more generally is a consequence of a real, pressing, and abiding interest in the saving reality of God and its effects, and so is always a function of soteriology. Soteriology must increase; anthropology as such must decrease, we might say.[62] Cyril O'Regan has observed that Kierkegaard's thinking about the human moves on the basis of a "Reformation axiom" that theology and not philosophy has "the necessary vocabulary to deal with radical change," in particular the most radical of changes involved in the drastic "perturbation" of the self in its encounter with "God as given definitively in Christ." The heart of his concern is, O'Regan contends, the inauguration of a "new and a redeemed stream of temporality, a new order of self-relation" that "forever bears the mark of a wound for which no pre-eschatological cure can be provided."[63] Perhaps Kierkegaard's example invites the thought that serious Christian thinking about human life in the world remade by the gospel can and must be fully soteriological, without remainder.

61. The phrase "micro-cosmic apocalyptic," already cited above, comes from Jones, "Apocalyptic Luther," 312, where it is used of Luther's own soteriology.
62. Cf. John 3:29–30. Kierkegaard, "He Must Increase; I Must Decrease," 275–96.
63. O'Regan, "Rule of Chaos and the Perturbation of Love," 144, 136.

If, as Kierkegaard holds, Christianity is nothing if not a "radical cure" that "transforms everything fundamental in a person," then Christian talk of the self is fundamentally and inescapably soteriological in both content and aim, as has just been suggested.[64] But more than this—and here is our third point—the *edifying character* of such discourse also becomes important.[65] Kierkegaard's practice suggests that the discourse of the Christian self is always confessional, always a provocation and invitation, and so always at least indirectly *kerygmatic*. In calling to mind the fundamental difference it makes to think of the human *coram deo*, it calls to mind truths about human subjectivity in which subjectivity itself (including one's own) is at stake; this discourse can never just speak *about* subjectivity; it must always also speak *to* it, seeking acknowledgment and assent. It is an "existence communication," never properly second-order discourse but always also first-order discourse of witness and devotion, inviting, permitting, and demanding its "reduplication" in life: in short, a call to discipleship.

Fourth and finally, Christian theology has long been anxious about any tendency to reduce theological anthropology to a doctrine of sin, denouncing such a prospect in the service of the philanthropy of theology, and more broadly the humanity of Christianity. But perhaps Kierkegaard's inverse dialectics of the Christian self—understood, as I have argued here, as a subjective reiteration of Paul's apocalyptic gospel—might tempt us to reconsider this anxiety. Could admission of our "being in untruth" be the only properly edifying anthropological fact that really matters in light of salvation? Acknowledging the fate of the self fully at the mercy of divine judgment and grace, could we perhaps discover the joy of losing a world that is, in fact, already well lost? And might we espy a depth of freedom and love in a life whose angularity to the world itself suffers, honors, and so attests the fundamental and salutary angularity of that new creation in which, as Paul has it, "neither circumcision nor uncircumcision is anything" (Gal. 6:15)? Could we come to hear, to know, and thus to live fully and freely from the liberating fact that "in relation to God we are always in the wrong" and so strive militantly in gratitude to follow Christ in this world made strange?

64. See Thulstrup, "Kierkegaard as an Edifying Christian Author," 181. Cf. "*Christianity is a radical cure*" (Kierkegaard, Journal AA 18 [1835], in *Kierkegaard's Journals*, 29). Kierkegaard writes elsewhere that "Christianity or becoming a Christian is like any radical cure: one puts it off as long as possible" (Pap. I A 89, quoted in *Kierkegaard's Journals*, 335).

65. In the theme of "edification" more generally, see Thulstrup, "Kierkegaard as an Edifying Christian Author," 179–82; Müller, "Der Begriff 'das Erbauliche' bei Sören Kierkegaard"; as well as Pattison, "Dialogical Approach."

Perhaps. But only if we, like Kierkegaard, are convinced that in relation to God we are always in the wrong, and this is not "a truth you must acknowledge, not a consolation that alleviates your pain, not a compensation for something better, but it is a joy in which you win a victory over yourself and over the world, your delight, your song of praise, your adoration, a demonstration that your love is happy, as only that love can be with which one loves God."[66]

66. Kierkegaard, *Either/Or*, 2:351.

12

A Theological Ethics
of God's Apocalypse

Dietrich Bonhoeffer

The suspension of all things human within an unqualified apocalyptic—
a suspension which is unqualified because it is apocalyptic—is perhaps
the possibility glimpsed by the Theology of Crisis.

—Walter Lowe, "Prospects
for a Postmodern Christian Theology"

Is Bonhoeffer's moral theology *apocalyptic*? This question is unsettled from
front to back. The texts that constitute Bonhoeffer's *Ethics* are unsteady
though well-worked fragments of the actual theological ethics he hoped to
write. More unsettled still is the meaning of "apocalyptic," whose popular
and scholarly valences are as many as they are divergent and contested. Even if
one could steady the question, prospects for a positive answer appear remote.
Readers of the *Ethics* have not been led to the idea of "apocalyptic": quite
the opposite. One possible exception here is Larry Rasmussen, who does associate Bonhoeffer with apocalyptic eschatology.[1] Yet even he considers the
association forced: turning to apocalyptic means *diverging* from Bonhoeffer,
who was "almost immunized" against such an eschatological perspective by
Lutheran confessional and German academic traditions, says Rasmussen.[2]

1. Rasmussen, *Dietrich Bonhoeffer*, 75–88.
2. Ibid., 75–76.

169

Reviewing Rasmussen's work, Charles West critically concurred: "This is not Bonhoeffer's eschatology or social ethic. Rasmussen realizes this, although he finds some quotations that could be stretched in this direction. . . . Rasmussen's thrusts in the direction of a revolutionary eschatology and an Anabaptist ecclesiology are ones Bonhoeffer could not have followed."[3]

If as able a commentator as Rasmussen has gone looking for apocalyptic in Bonhoeffer and come up short, why attempt to ask and to answer the question again? I do so because, as I aim to demonstrate, when Bonhoeffer's *Ethics* is read in light of the recent studies of Pauline apocalyptic we have been concerned to engage in this book, it becomes clear that such judgments should be revised. In fact, in key sections of his *Ethics*, Bonhoeffer was pushing against just those ecclesial and academic conventions of German neo-Lutheranism that obscured the apocalyptic cast of Paul's discursive world.[4] In this chapter I want to argue that in draft upon draft of his *Ethics* manuscript, Bonhoeffer is definitely working out a theological ethic whose intent is to conform to the contours of Paul's apocalyptic gospel.

Recent reconsideration of Pauline apocalyptic by de Boer, Martyn, before them also J. Christiaan Beker, and others has discerned with renewed clarity, as we have seen, that in Paul's gospel "revelation" (*apocalypsis*) denotes God's redemptive invasion of the fallen order of things such that reality itself is decisively remade in the event. God's advent in Christ utterly disrupts and displaces previous patterns of thought and action and gives rise to new ones that better comport with the reality of a world actively reconciled to God. This is particularly true of theology and ethics in their interconnection, as I have labored to show in previous chapters treating questions of law and Christian moral subjectivity. The gospel of inescapable judgment and inordinate forgiveness constitutes the world anew; hence new, apocalyptic antinomies displace those antinomies that have previously structured theological and ethical reflection and judgment. Apocalyptic, on this view, is more than a literary genre or a form of extreme ancient rhetoric; it is a mode of theological discourse fit to give voice to the radical ontological and epistemological consequences of the gospel, consequences intensely relevant to doing Christian ethics. The basic moral question that Paul's apocalyptic gospel demands to be asked and answered is this: "What has *paraenesis* to do with *apocalypsis*?"[5]

3. Charles West, review of *Dietrich Bonhoeffer: His Significance for North Americans*, by Larry Rasmussen.

4. See the characterization of neo-Lutheranism provided by the German editors in their "Afterword," in Bonhoeffer, *Ethics*, 417–18.

5. This phrasing is that of Meeks, "Apocalyptic Discourse," 462.

In his work of the 1930s and 1940s, including the *Ethics*, it seems plain to me that Bonhoeffer is laboring to ask and to answer just this question. The ethical works from this period can and should be read, I think, as a series of experimental attempts to orient Christian morals in face of the evangelical fact that "the incursion of a new world" in Christ "renders ancient good uncouth."[6] What shape can theological ethics take once one acknowledges that keeping abreast of the devastatingly gracious and dynamic character of God's reworked reality demands that Christian theology "attack the underlying assumptions" of all other ethics in order to overreach them, to the point of making it questionable that one should still speak of "ethics" at all?[7] How can ethics reflect the real and relentless criticism that befalls the Christian community—together with all humanity—from the gracious incursion of the Word of God, recognition of which is the hallmark of all truly Protestant thinking as Bonhoeffer understands it?[8] In Christian life and thought, just what exactly does penultimate worldly justice have to do with the ultimate justification of sinners, which comes from above?

Substantiating the claim that Bonhoeffer is preoccupied with just this line of questioning, and exploring its significance, requires that we first and concisely rehearse some of the most salient aspects of Paul's apocalyptic gospel; it requires, second, that we examine the aspects of Bonhoeffer's *Ethics* that correspond to this peculiar evangelical apocalyptic; and third, it demands that we think on the possible consequences of such a correspondence for understanding both Bonhoeffer and the business of theological ethics as whole.

The Marks of Pauline Apocalyptic

> One does not correctly interpret a Pauline doctrinal text if one transmits it as a piece of genuine theology, as *pura doctrina*; instead, one must make this theology comprehensible as the witness to the living Christ.
>
> —Dietrich Bonhoeffer, "Lecture on Contemporizing New Testament Texts"

As we have already gleaned from our thinking about recent discussions of Paul's apocalyptic gospel in earlier chapters, the term "apocalyptic" in this

---

6. Ibid.

7. Bonhoeffer, *Ethics*, 299.

8. See Bonhoeffer's essay "Protestantism without Reformation," 459: "God did not grant a Reformation to American Christendom. . . . American theology and the churches as a whole have never really understood what 'critique' by God's word means in its entirety. That God's 'critique' is also meant for religion, for the churches' Christianity, even the sanctification of Christians, all that is ultimately not understood . . . because the sole foundation for God's radical judgment and radical grace is at this point not recognized."

context designates neither a literary genre nor a class of speculative or visionary imaginings regarding "how it all ends."[9] Rather, it denotes an understanding of Christ as "the effective and definitive disclosure of God's rectifying action" whereby the old "world or age is destroyed and brought to an end."[10] Indeed, as we have emphasized time and again in this regard, "apocalypse" in this context is shorthand for a distinctive acknowledgment of the divine identity and eschatological importance of Jesus Christ.[11] Paul's witness is that what takes place in Christ is the incursion of God's power into the world *with effect*. Revelation is "no mere disclosure of previously hidden secrets, nor is it simply information about future events." For revelation itself is an event that *initiates*, even as it *discloses*, a new state of affairs; not simply "a making known," revelation is also "a making way for," involving God's conclusive "activity and movement, an invasion of the world below from heaven above."[12] The event in which God is made known as Savior, the coming of the Christ, is the very event that saves. We might say concisely: divine revelation *is* redemption.

As such, revelation is not exclusively or even chiefly a cognitive affair, a matter of teaching believers to "consider the world differently." For the achievement of reconciliation is the inauguration of a wholly new human situation. Paul's talk of the human situation overturned and set to rights by God (2 Cor. 5:17) signals the radical discontinuity between human captivity to sin and the gift of a restored relationship with God, something manifest in those distinctive "apocalyptic antinomies" of spirit and flesh, light and dark, old and new that populate the New Testament.[13]

As an advocate for this new age, the gospel is not mere reportage but brings to bear "the power of God for salvation" (Rom. 1:16; 1 Cor. 1:18). Yet it is testimony: a telling of the "good news" that human captivity to sin is ended by God's graciously powerful rescue. It is the declaration that God has vindicated his name "for in [Christ] every one of God's promises is a 'Yes'" (2 Cor. 1:20). As such, the gospel involves knowledge of God's self-disclosure in Christ, albeit knowledge made strange by its being implicated

9. For a concise but thorough summation, see Martyn, "Apocalyptic Gospel in Galatians." Cf. Beker: "Paul's apocalyptic gospel is constituted by certain apocalyptic components that he derives from his Jewish apocalyptic world and that he radically modifies because of his encounter with Christ and the Christian tradition that he inherits" (*Paul's Apocalyptic Gospel*, 30). Beker's dense summary of the marks of Paul's apocalyptic thought follows on 30–53.

10. De Boer, "Paul, Theologian of God's Apocalypse," 25.

11. Harink, *Paul among the Postliberals*, 68.

12. De Boer, "Paul, Theologian of God's Apocalypse," 25. Cf. Morse, *Not Every Spirit*, 243–44.

13. On this see Scholer, "'God of Peace,'" 57.

in salvation. As Paul says, he no longer knows of Christ in terms of the old situation ("according to the flesh") but only in light of the new ("according to the cross").[14] Yet he does *know*. Again, we might say concisely: thus, divine redemption *is* revelation.

If the identification of revelation and redemption in this way is a first hallmark of Paul's apocalyptic discourse, a second is its claim that evangelical talk is talk of *reality*. The gospel speaks of what has taken place and of the state of affairs that God's "incursion" or "invasion" for sinners' sake has *actually* brought about.[15] We have already noted that what matters supremely in this gospel is "God's decision and deed in Jesus Christ," the uncontingent gift of the new life. Now we are alerted to the fact that those who hear its message are always already implicated in that of which it speaks. The logic of the apocalyptic gospel is thus never one of *possibility*. It does not take the form "if . . . then," and it is not an offer to be realized only on its acceptance.[16] Neither is it an abstract *idea* subsequently in need of concrete embodiment in the world. Even when put in the mode of promise, accent falls on the reality of God's saving activity deciding the day (cf. Phil. 1:6). So, for example, Martyn restates the primary message of Galatians simply as "'*God has done it!*' . . . [And] there are two echoes: 'You are to live it out!' and 'You are to live it out *because* God has done it *and* because God will do it!'"[17] Such a gospel, as de Boer says, "has little or nothing to do with a decision human beings must make, but everything to do with a decision God has already made on their behalf," which is identified with God's enactment of salvation in Christ.[18] Reconciliation is real, and so God's gracious justification establishes our "true position in the world" without awaiting our permission.[19] The Christian community together with the world as a whole now exists in the time between God's "having done" and "will do," between God's saving apocalypse in Christ and the final parousia.

In sum, the apocalyptic gospel announces the vindication of God in the wayward world by the decisive incursion of his gracious and powerful presence to judge and so to save. Jesus Christ *is* this advent and saving act of God. The scope of this act encompasses all things: there is "no reserve of

---

14. On this see Martyn, "Epistemology at the Turn of the Ages," 107–10.

15. Martyn, "Apocalyptic Gospel in Galatians," 260.

16. As in the "two ways" of the *Didache* 1.1, 5.1. Cf. Martyn, "Apocalyptic Gospel in Galatians," 247–51; Duff, "Significance of Pauline Apocalyptic for Ethics," 279–80. Both Martyn and Duff speak of this as "the two-step dance."

17. Martyn, *Galatians*, 103.

18. De Boer, "Paul, Theologian of God's Apocalypse," 33.

19. Lehmann, "Toward a Protestant Analysis of the Ethical Problem," 3. Cf. Calvin, *Institutes* 3.6.7.

space or time or concept or aspect of creation outside of, beyond or undetermined by the critical, decisive and final action of God in Jesus Christ."[20] So, all Christian life and thought can and must know that it takes place firmly in the wake of "*God's* crisis which has overtaken and overturned the world as it is."[21]

The Apocalyptic Shape of Bonhoeffer's Ethics of Justification

> A community that sets itself apart [is] a community that also hears the apocalypse.
>
> —Dietrich Bonhoeffer, "Lecture on Contemporizing New Testament Texts"[22]

The intrinsic interest and importance of some of Bonhoeffer's distinctive ethical categories—for example, responsibility, vicarious representation, the penultimate, worldliness—can and do readily eclipse the fact that Bonhoeffer's work in ethics is essentially a series of "beautiful iterations of doctrine" written in close proximity to the Scriptures and consistently concerned to orient a peculiarly Christian life in the modern world.[23] And his ethics, as Paul Lehmann contends, "can only be understood when it is recognized to be a new . . . interpretation of the doctrine of justification."[24] Interestingly, when Bonhoeffer wrote to Karl Barth in 1936 that his own work *Nachfolge* (*Discipleship*) was basically an "interpretation of the Sermon on the Mount and the Pauline doctrine of justification and sanctification" worked out in "an ongoing silent dispute" with Barth's work,[25] Barth replied that while he was "very anxious to hear the results," he was "not without some concern." What worried him was the ease with which those who work on these doctrines resign "the original christological and eschatological approach in favour of (in fact, increasingly abstract!) actualizations in a specifically human sphere."[26] It seems to me that Bonhoeffer took Barth's cautionary word to heart, and that the apocalyptic character of his thought shows his deep and ongoing concern for the integrity of the "christological-eschatological beginning" of

---

20. Harink, *Paul among the Postliberals*, 69.

21. Kay, "Word of the Cross at the Turn of the Ages," 55.

22. Bonhoeffer, "Lecture on Contemporizing New Testament Texts," 432, alt. The corresponding German text reads, "Gemeinde, die sich abgrenzt. . . . Gemeinde, die auch Apokalypse hört."

23. The phrase is from Robinson, "Dietrich Bonhoeffer," 115. Cf. the afterword by the editors of the German edition of the *Ethics*, 431. I consider this matter further in "'Completely within God's Doing.'"

24. Pfeifer, "Die Gestalten der Rechtfertigung," 178.

25. Bonhoeffer in a letter to Karl Barth dated September 19, 1936, in DBWE 14:252–53.

26. K. Barth, in letter to Bonhoeffer dated October 14, 1936, in DBWE 14:266–67.

the Christian life. As such it is close to the heart of Bonhoeffer's extended effort to rid justification of "cheap verbalism" and to "restore to it its full value."[27]

What Bonhoeffer said of *Discipleship* is no less true of the *Ethics* that followed it. Here too justification shows itself to be central to the proceedings. Bonhoeffer distinctly expounds the doctrine through the interplay of three central categories: *revelation, reconciliation*, and *reality*.[28] And these categories are freighted with the logic of Pauline apocalyptic. This can be discerned most sharply in the two claims that structure all of Bonhoeffer's theological ethics: first, that *revelation is reconciliation*, and second, that the event of reconciliation in Jesus Christ is *constitutive of reality*.

Revelation Is Reconciliation

What takes place in the self-disclosure of God in Jesus Christ, Bonhoeffer says, is nothing less than an eruption of "the reality of God . . . into the reality of this world"[29] for the sake of its salvation. Bonhoeffer's God comes to the world freely and martially to secure a "victory over [human] unrighteousness" on the cross.[30] If this gospel is not mere folly, then it is the humane incursion of God's *power*.[31] As God's revelation, Christ is "God's Word personally addressed to the human being," and forgiveness is a reality in this world solely because the One who declares it effectually is "in his person, the Word of God."[32]

Bonhoeffer's talk of the "Word of God" respects the apocalyptic grammar that identifies God's self-disclosure and its saving effect. For example, we read that when "the ultimate word" of grace is spoken, God's judgment effectively befalls men and women.[33] Or again that "the event of justification of a sinner is something ultimate. . . . There is no word of God that goes beyond God's

---

27. Bethge, *Dietrich Bonhoeffer*, 372.

28. Clifford Green, editor of the critical English edition of the *Ethics*, confirms this: "In Jesus Christ God creates a new reality in Christ; it is a reality, not merely a potentiality. . . . This reconciliation functions as an axiom in the *Ethics*." "From the perspective of God, so to speak, the reconciliation of God and world, God and humanity, is in Jesus Christ, an ontological reality. At the same time the reconciliation of God and the world is a reality by which human beings are transformed; they are con-formed to this reconciliation, and it thereby forms them." See Bonhoeffer, *Ethics*, 9, 7.

29. Ibid., 49, 54.

30. Bonhoeffer, *Discipleship*, 257.

31. "It is power, not knowledge or wisdom, that stands over against foolishness" (in DBWE 14:351n80, alt.); "*Der 'Torheit' gegenüber steht die 'Kraft' und nicht die Erkenntnis order Weisheit*" (Bonhoeffer, "Zu I Korinther 1,18," 332n77).

32. Bonhoeffer, "Lectures on Christology," in DBWE 12:317.

33. Bonhoeffer, *Ethics*, 146.

grace."[34] God's Word is a conclusive act that saves (reconciliation) *and* discloses this act as God's own (revelation). For Bonhoeffer, the Word of God is always an eschatological performative utterance whose saying, as it were, makes it so.

Further, in keeping with the apocalyptic Pauline gospel, Bonhoeffer stresses that God's humble advent to set things right in Christ is entirely uncontingent, even a kind of "gracious violence"[35] upon the precincts of human sin. Unexpected and unbidden, God's sovereign entry onto the field of human affairs questions—nay, *assails*—the putative rule of human reasoning, ways, and means. The Word of God "bursts in" on women and men, and their situation is "powerfully torn open" as "the labyrinth of their lives collapses."[36] As Bonhoeffer explained to an American audience in 1932, "In Christ all men are respectively condemned or resuscitated. . . . Justification is pure self-revelation, pure way of God to man. No religion, no ethics, no metaphysical knowledge may serve man to approach God. They are all under the judgment of God, they are works of man. Only the acknowledgment that God's word alone helps and that every other attempt is and remains sinful, only this acknowledgment receives God."[37] Hence human reasons and God's reasons, human ways and God's ways, all come to blows, first in conversation and then in act: "Let us ask again what happens if the claim of the counter Logos is questioned. The human logos kills the Logos of God, the Word become human, which it has just questioned. Because the human logos does not want to die itself, the Logos of God, which is death to the human logos, must die instead. The Word become human must be hung on the cross and killed by the human logos."[38] Yet the resurrection, for Bonhoeffer, is a profound rejoinder rooted in God's unshakable will to save, wherein God, having accomplished human salvation on the cross, makes it known that his mercy is sovereign, asking the human creature, in a manner akin to Job's God: "Who are you, you who can only ask about me because you have been justified and received grace through me?"[39]

The world is a *different* place as a result of the Word that justifies the ungodly, and in this new world nothing is as it once was thought to be.

34. Ibid., 149.

35. Martyn, in relation to the novels of Flannery O'Connor, speaks of the "violent action of grace invading territory largely held by the devil" and of "*gracious* violence" ("Apocalyptic Gospel in Galatians," 262, esp. 262n43).

36. Bonhoeffer, *Ethics*, 146.

37. Bonhoeffer, "Concerning the Christian Idea of God," in DBWE 10:451–61, esp. 460–61. The essay was originally published in *Journal of Religion* 12 (1932).

38. Bonhoeffer, "Lectures on Christology," in DBWE 12:305. That reconciliation is achieved via the most intense conflict is made clear in Bonhoeffer's description of this event as the salutary clash of the human logos and what he calls the divine *Counter* Logos (302–4).

39. Bonhoeffer, "Lectures on Christology," in DBWE 12:305.

"Knowing Jesus Christ as the reconciler," Bonhoeffer writes, Christians find that they are "chosen, and thus no longer able to choose at all" and so "are thus filled with a *new* knowledge in which the knowledge of good and evil has been overcome."[40] Because this is so, Bonhoeffer can only take up the question of ethics Christianly by admitting at the outset a vertiginous disorientation. He says, "Those who wish to focus on the problem of a Christian ethics are faced with an outrageous demand—from the outset they must give up as inappropriate to this topic, the very two questions that led them to deal with the ethical problem: 'How can I be good?' and 'How can I do something good?' Instead they must ask the wholly other, completely different question: what is the will of God?"[41] Or, again he observes even more starkly, "The knowledge of good and evil appears to be the goal of all ethical reflection. The first task of Christian ethics is to supersede that knowledge. This attack on the presuppositions of all other ethics is so unique that it is questionable whether it even makes sense to speak of Christian ethics at all."[42]

An apocalyptic sensibility is to the fore in passages like this, the very ones in which Bonhoeffer programmatically stages his theological ethics as a whole. The onset of salvation unsettles the most settled of schemes—such as that of "good and evil," "sacred and secular"—and gives rise to "wholly other" and "completely different questions" because of the "act of God which tears man out of this reflection into an *actus directus* [immediate and unreflective act] toward God."[43] The utter dissolution and remaking of their situation strips believers of a whole world of discourse. Apocalyptic interpretation of Paul, as we have noticed, points out the central place of just such an "epistemic crisis" in the gospel: God's saving act "crucifies the world" to the believer (cf. Gal. 6:14); God's world-dissolving judgment and world-constituting forgiveness result in a "*loss of cosmos*," a shattering of the whole world of discourse, dissolving fixed antinomies and throwing hitherto meaningful construals of reality into "new and confusing patterns" (as evidenced in Gal. 3:27–28).[44] This is exactly what Bonhoeffer holds to take place when language and thought suffer "participation in the encounter of Christ with the world."[45]

40. Bonhoeffer, *Ethics*, 316–17.
41. Ibid., 47.
42. Ibid., 299. Here the term "supersede" renders the German *aufheben*, an important philosophical term of art.
43. Bonhoeffer, "Theology of Crisis," in DBWE 10:474.
44. Martyn, "Apocalyptic Gospel in Galatians," 256.
45. Bethge, *Dietrich Bonhoeffer*, 623.

Reconciliation in Jesus Christ Is Constitutive of Reality

Bonhoeffer's theology wears a further apocalyptic mark on its sleeve. It is his firm contention that God's reconciling act is constitutive of the reality of the Christian life. Of this he writes, "The origin and essence of all Christian life are consummated in the one event that the Reformation has called the justification of the sinner by grace alone. It is not what a person is per se, but what a person is in this event, that gives us insight into the Christian life. Here the length and breadth of human life are concentrated in one moment, one point."[46] But this is certainly not all. As Marilynne Robinson has artfully remarked, for Bonhoeffer, Christian talk of salvation "functions not as ornament but *as ontology*," making "the most essential account that can be made of Being itself."[47] We see this clearly when Bonhoeffer declares: "In Jesus Christ the reality of God has entered into the reality of this world. The place where the questions about the reality of God and about the reality of the world are answered at the same time is characterized solely by the name: Jesus Christ. God and the world are enclosed in this name. In Christ all things exist (Col. 1:17). From now on we cannot speak rightly of either God or the world without speaking of Jesus Christ. All concepts of reality that ignore Jesus Christ are abstractions."[48] From here Bonhoeffer goes on to reject any notion that the world can be thought of as an "autonomous sector" in relation to God because such a view "denies *the fact* of the world's *being accepted* in Christ, the grounding of the reality of the world in revelational reality."[49] Rather, Christians must think differently of the world as justified by God since, as he explains, "this very world that has been condemned in Jesus Christ is, in Christ, also accepted and loved and is promised a new heaven and a new earth. The world that is passing away has been claimed by God. We must therefore continue to reckon with the world's worldliness but at the same time reckon with God's rule over it."[50] God's ultimate act, the sovereign act of reconciliation, is "truth and reality" in Christ and not mere possibility or idea. For Bonhoeffer, this is simply a transcendent and irrefragable fact that "constitute[s] the real outside" of all human beings.[51]

Claims such as these led Jürgen Moltmann, in his 1959 study of Bonhoeffer's *Ethics*, to characterize his ethical thought as "theocratic" or "christocratic."[52]

---

46. Bonhoeffer, *Ethics*, 146.
47. Robinson, "Dietrich Bonhoeffer," 118.
48. Bonhoeffer, *Ethics*, 54.
49. Ibid., 60, emphasis added.
50. Ibid., 224.
51. Ibid., 149; Bonhoeffer, "Theology of Crisis," in DBWE 10:467.
52. Moltmann, *Herrschaft Christi und soziale Wirklichkeit nach Dietrich Bonhoeffer*, 34–38.

With this broad characterization, Moltmann rightly stressed Bonhoeffer's unbending assertion of the *cosmic* scope and significance of God's saving action in Christ. As Bonhoeffer himself contends, both Christ's "exclusive claim" ("Whoever is not for me is against me," Matt. 12:30) and his "all-encompassing claim" ("Whoever is not against us is for us," Mark 9:40) must be upheld together: "The more exclusive, the more free and open. Isolated from each other, however, the exclusive claim leads to fanaticism and sectarianism, the all-encompassing claim to the secularization and capitulation of the church. The more exclusively we recognize and confess Christ as our Lord, the more will be disclosed to us the breadth of Christ's lordship."[53] Acknowledging that the sovereign apocalypse of God in Christ remakes reality *as a whole* demands that Bonhoeffer forswear both sectarian and *volkskirchliche* ecclesiologies. Neither Pietism—"a last effort to maintain Protestant Christianity as a religion"—nor the civil religion of the established church as an "institution of salvation" comports with *this* gospel.[54]

Such emphasis on the exclusive and encompassing nature of God's claim in Christ is not restricted to Bonhoeffer's later, wartime writing. Lecturing in Potsdam-Hermannswerder in the autumn of 1932, Bonhoeffer took as his theme the congregation's prayer that God's Kingdom should come on earth and began accusingly:[55] "We are otherworldly or we are secularists, but in either case this means we no longer believe in God's kingdom. We are hostile to the Earth, because we want to be better than it, or we are hostile to God, because God robs us of the Earth, our mother. . . . Otherworldliness and secularism are simply two sides of the same coin—*namely, the lack of belief in God's kingdom.*"[56] Religious flight from the world is robbed of its future when God in Christ returns human beings to their status as true children of the earth; so too our varied secular self-assertions are brought to naught, as we never "thereby elude God," who always acts to bring women and men "back under God's dominion."[57] This exercise of

---

53. Bonhoeffer, *Ethics*, 344.

54. This remark about Pietism is cited in the introduction to Bonhoeffer, *True Patriotism*, 14. The second remark on the church is from Bonhoeffer, "Lecture on Contemporizing New Testament Texts," in DBWE 14:433. Cf. also Beker, *Paul's Apocalyptic Gospel*, 41, where writing of Paul's gospel, he explains that "the church, then, lives in continuous tension between being *against the world* and being *for the world*. If it emphasizes too strongly withdrawal from the world in a dualistic fashion, it threatens to become a purely sectarian apocalyptic movement that betrays the death and resurrection of Christ as God's redemptive plan for the world; but if it exclusively emphasizes participation in the world, it threatens to become another 'worldly' phenomenon, accommodating itself to whatever the world will buy and so becoming part of the world."

55. Bonhoeffer, "Thy Kingdom Come!," in DBWE 12:285–97.

56. Ibid., 285–86, 288.

57. Ibid., 286–87.

lordship is rooted in the apocalyptic vindication of the Son—"The king-dom of God is the *kingdom of resurrection* on Earth"[58]—and once again is strictly a matter of reality. As Bonhoeffer concludes, it is "not what *God* could do and what *we* could do that forms the basis of our prayer for the coming of the kingdom, but what God *does* for us and what God will do for us again and again."[59]

As Bonhoeffer comes to argue in the *Ethics*, only trust that reality has in fact been decisively constituted by God's apocalypse in Christ underwrites "serious" grappling with moral life in the world. Against abstract "sectarian" and "compromise" postures toward the world, he says this:

> Neither the idea of a pure Christianity as such nor the idea of the human being as such is serious, but only God's reality and human reality as they have become one in Jesus Christ. What is serious is not some kind of Christianity, but Jesus Christ himself. In Jesus Christ God's reality and human reality take the place of radicalism and compromise. There is no Christianity as such; if there were, it would destroy the world. There is no human being as such; if there were, God would be excluded. Both are ideas. There is only the God-man Jesus Christ who is real, through whom the world will be preserved until it is ripe for its end.[60]

The realism that Bonhoeffer sets over against all idealism in church and theology is thus apocalyptic. Since "revelation gives itself without precondi-tion and is alone able to place one into reality," he says, serious theological ethics, no less than dogmatics, must struggle for forms of thinking appropri-ate to God's apocalypse in Christ Jesus.[61] The ages having turned, Christians are alert to the fact that they stand together with all others in a world whose reality has been both taken apart and put back together *with effect* by God's redemptive triumph through the cross: it has become Christ-reality.

Consequences and Conclusions

Is it possible, then, that Pauline apocalyptic affords us an important inter-pretative key to Bonhoeffer's theological ethics? And if so, just how and in what respects is our understanding of these ethics affected? To conclude this chapter, let me to venture some remarks on these and related questions.

58. Ibid., 291.
59. Ibid.
60. Bonhoeffer, *Ethics*, 155.
61. Bonhoeffer, *Act and Being*, 89. See also the editors' remarks on 162.

An Ethic of God's Apocalypse?

Charles West argued that Bonhoeffer's theological ethics could never be thought of as apocalyptic for this stated reason:

> The difference lies between the words "ultimate" and "new." There is much language in Bonhoeffer, as there is in the Bible, about conversion, from Pharisaism to Christ, from law to gospel, from bondage to freedom. There is in this sense a new creation. But for Bonhoeffer the ultimate is the origin as well as the end of human life. Grace is not new. It has accompanied the history of the world from the beginning. Criticism and resistance are not the only expressions, therefore, of a Christ-centered hope. Participation, preservation, and building of structures of relative justice in a sinful world are also part of it.[62]

I think West somewhat misjudged Bonhoeffer's understanding of God's salutary advent and its effects. Nothing in the *Ethics* rescinds Bonhoeffer's earlier judgment that "man's continuity is always continuity in sin" such that "God's first word is the radical breaking of all continuity with man in His radical judgment upon man as sinner, and His act of grace is the creation of a new man with whom God remains in continuity."[63] Bonhoeffer's own idiom consistently stresses the *disjunction* between old and new, the *crisis* in all registers of creaturely existence (moral, epistemic, ontological) brought about by God in Christ, even as it also emphasizes the incursion of God's *new* creation as the establishment of the total relevant and crucially *dynamic* context for human life and thought. What we then find in Bonhoeffer's work, including the *Ethics*, are not merely "some quotations that could be stretched" (as West put it) in the direction of apocalyptic but rather a whole way of thinking whose organizing logic is very closely aligned with that of Paul's apocalyptic gospel.[64]

---

62. West, review of *Dietrich Bonhoeffer: His Significance for North Americans*, 472–73.

63. Bonhoeffer, "Theology of Crisis," in DBWE 10:467.

64. The significance of eschatology in Bonhoeffer's theology has not gone entirely unnoticed, of course, and one quite recent work in particular appreciates this aspect of his ethics. See Prüller-Jagenteufel, *Befreit zur Verantwortung*, 277, 280–81, 282. The author argues that Bonhoeffer upholds an "eschatological dynamic," by which he means that Bonhoeffer "does not hold the thesis that God *is* the Lord of the world, but rather that he *becomes* such; not that the reality of God's revelation *is* real in the world, but rather that it *becomes* such. Responsible action thus means nothing more, but also nothing less, than having a hand in Christ *becoming in the penultimate* what he already *is in the ultimate*—Redeemer and Lord of *all* human beings and the *whole* world" (91–92). Here, "eschatology" serves as a qualifier to soften reality claims, while in the reading of Bonhoeffer that I am advancing, "eschatology" or "apocalyptic" are terms that denote the effective dynamism and theological seriousness of such reality claims. I have made a case for the importance of eschatology to understanding the prison letters elsewhere; see my "Secularity and Eschatology in Bonhoeffer's Late Work."

The cardinal importance of the doctrine of justification for Bonhoeffer's theological ethic is further indication of all this. For in Bonhoeffer's hands, this doctrine *does* bespeak "the onset of something radically new" rather than offer mere consolation and "rescue in the face of recurring failure."[65] Its role in Bonhoeffer's theological ethics is to republish with dogmatic density the form and force of Paul's apocalyptic gospel.[66]

If this is so, then some of Bonhoeffer's distinctive themes receive a new and different cast. Take, for example, the *promeity* of God in Christ. "Promeity" is a term by which Bonhoeffer records that for God *to exist* and *to exist to save* are inseparable,[67] in keeping with the identity of revelation and reconciliation. This identity in fact makes it "godless"—as Bonhoeffer says in appealing directly to Luther—to think of God's presence apart from the divine saving activity *pro-me* in Christ.[68] Inflected apocalyptically, *promeity* expresses not so much a static disposition of God, as is often thought, as it does the relentless *dynamism* of God's unbidden saving agency. It reiterates that God's apocalypse in Christ is, like the hound of heaven, a "force of forgiveness [that humans] cannot weary, or diminish or evade."[69] There is movement and scope in Bonhoeffer's concept of *promeity*. Where God is, God is actively intruding to judge and so to save.

Bonhoeffer's sense that Christian engagement with the world should be shot through with confident hope and *not* the anxiety ingredient in missionary logics of "if/then" or "offer/realization"—such a sense also flows from the face that *these contingent possibilities have already been surpassed by the uncontingent reality of reconciliation*. Pauline apocalyptic locates the life and service of the Christian community firmly within the widest possible view of God's agency and endeavor. Engaging the world in this way within the exclusive *and* encompassing work of Christ testifies to both their common reality and dynamic difference-in-unity. There is freedom to be about the penultimate and worldly things of human life, not in spite of what is ultimate but because

65. Rasmussen, *Dietrich Bonhoeffer*, 78. Yet Bonhoeffer says, "Justification is the new creation of the new human being" (Bonhoeffer, *Discipleship*, 260). Cf. also Prüller-Jagenteufel, *Befreit zur Verantwortung*, 280.

66. Recently Bruce McCormack reminded recalcitrant Protestant theology of precisely this same claim. The doctrine of justification is "deeply ontological" because at its root "lies recognition that human *being*" is a function of God's decisive act in Jesus Christ to justify the ungodly. See McCormack, "What's at Stake in Current Debates over Justification?," 115.

67. Bonhoeffer, "Lectures on Christology," in DBWE 12:314: "The being of Christ's person is essentially relatedness to me. His being-Christ is his being-for-me. . . . The very core of his person is *pro-me*. This is not a historical, factual or ontic statement, but rather an ontological one."

68. Ibid. For more reflection on this, see my essay "Christ for Us Today," 25–41.

69. Robinson, "Dietrich Bonhoeffer," 110.

of it and for its sake.[70] As Ernst Wolf rightly observed of the *Ethics* already during the early years of its reception, we must not overlook the fact that, "for Bonhoeffer, 'worldly ethics' is possible finally only as 'Christian ethics' in which apprehension of the 'penultimate' is made possible by that which is 'ultimate.' For him what was at issue throughout was life in 'the ultimate,' 'the self-evident character of such a life.'"[71] The "church for others," then, denotes a church whose existence comports with the encompassing and exclusive truth of God's saving apocalypse in Christ.

All this also changes the way we might take the remarks in the late prison writing about "the world come of age," "religionless Christianity," and the "nonreligious interpretation of biblical concepts." Bonhoeffer's turn to these ideas can be seen as a provocative if staccato reiteration of the theme of the ultimate and penultimate developed at some length in the *Ethics*. Since "the achieved rescue of creation brings the whole of it under grace," whatever these phrases mean in detail, their responsible interpretation will always honor Bonhoeffer's denial of false autonomy to the "secular."[72] It is the advent of the reality of reconciliation, much more than the simple advance of secularization, that has dissolved, for Bonhoeffer, the old antinomy of religious and secular. In the wake of God's epoch-making incursion in Christ, the categories "religious" and "secular" no longer map onto reality as it has been remade. Genuine worldliness is creaturely life unhinged and rehinged by the grace that invades the fallen world in Christ. Still in the 1940s, Bonhoeffer's critique of religion has under it largely apocalyptic mainsprings: the Christian way forward in a "world come of age" reflects first and foremost the relentless and decisively formative pressure of the "world to come." As Bonhoeffer remarked in 1935 in a slightly different idiom, "The present is determined primarily not by the past but by the *future*, and this future is Christ, is the Holy Spirit. . . . The criterion of the authentic present resides outside that present itself, resides in the future, in Scripture and in the word

70. God's justification by grace makes the Christian's way in the world strange: it is shaped by the fact that the penultimate things of the world are "completely superseded by the ultimate and . . . no longer in force" so that "we must also speak of penultimate things, not as if they had some value of their own, but so as to make clear their relation to the ultimate. For the sake of the ultimate we must speak of the penultimate" (Bonhoeffer, *Ethics*, 151).

71. Wolf, "Das Letze und das Vorletze," 32.

72. Robinson, "Dietrich Bonhoeffer," 122. Indicative of this are claims made in the prison letters that we do not meet Christ "on the boundaries" but at the center or "in the midst of our lives" (Bonhoeffer, *Letters and Papers from Prison*, DBWE 8:367). Even more stringently denied is any reading that takes these categories as attempts to jostle for the *relevance* of faith and theology in a modern world. See Bonhoeffer, "Lecture on Contemporizing New Testament Texts," in DBWE 14:414–18.

of Christ attested there."[73] It is possible for Christians to embrace the dissolution of religion as a historical development finally because human religion has already been abolished prospectively by God's eschatological act
of justifying the ungodly.

Pauline Apocalyptic and the Continuity of Bonhoeffer's Corpus

Discerning the formative power of Pauline apocalyptic on Bonhoeffer's
theological ethics may also cast some light on the disputed question of the
continuity of Bonhoeffer's corpus. Recognizing the prominence of Pauline
apocalyptic thought forms in texts from across the 1930s as well as so clearly
in the *Ethics* seems to call into question any notion that the later work in
ethics and the prison writings represent a marked departure from what has
gone before. Further, if this biblical *Denkform* (pattern of thought) is an
important aspect of Bonhoeffer's own theological constitution, then can
the question of continuity and development be properly assessed without
attending *in particular* to the wide array of scriptural expositions authored
as sermons, letters, lectures, and so forth during these years?[74] And if texts
such as these—rather than, say, the earlier dissertations or the final *Letters
and Papers from Prison*—were adjudged to represent the center of gravity in the whole corpus, how might our understanding of the whole be
affected?

The architectonic presence of Pauline apocalyptic motifs in Bonhoeffer's
Ethics also raises afresh the question of Bonhoeffer's abiding relation to dialectical theology. Perhaps we are now able to see something that can readily
be elided by intense focus on the philosophical entanglements of Bonhoeffer's
earliest work, and the *geisteswissenschaftliche* (scholarly humanistic) valences
of themes in the prison correspondence:[75] that in the whole of his theological
existence, "Bonhoeffer showed himself to be a decisive adherent of the new
theology of the Word of God."[76] Ought we not to take seriously the claim of
the author of the *Ethics* that he expressly desires to "stand in the tradition of

73. Bonhoeffer, "Lecture on Contemporizing New Testament Texts," in DBWE 14:418.

74. On the significance of straightforward biblical exposition in Bonhoeffer's corpus, see
Webster, "Reading the Bible."

75. For the former, see, e.g., C. Marsh, *Reclaiming Dietrich Bonhoeffer*. And as indicative
of the latter, see Würstenberg, "Bonhoeffer Revisited." Here as elsewhere, Würstenberg argues
that the thought of Ortega y Gasset and Dilthey, rather than the "theology of crisis," provides
the decisive context within which to understand the provocative themes of the prison letters,
such as nonreligious interpretation and Christian worldliness. For the reasons canvassed here,
I am not so persuaded.

76. Editor's afterword, Bonhoeffer, *Act and Being*, 163.

Paul, Luther, Kierkegaard, in the tradition of genuine Christian thinking"?[77] Are the thought forms of Pauline apocalyptic perhaps those that Bonhoeffer believed could resist and lead beyond the "revelatory positivism" that troubled him latterly, and make good on the promise of the renewed theology of the Word under which he himself labored?

Bonhoeffer: Theologian of the Word of God

There is, of course, a great deal else to be said, both about the apocalyptic account of the gospel and about its capacity to illumine further both these and other aspects of Bonhoeffer's work. A more comprehensive study is needed to explore in detail the place of both the *cross* and the *social and political forms* brought about by the incursion of grace onto the human scene in both Paul's apocalyptic gospel and Bonhoeffer's theological ethics. The theme of representative suffering, for instance, as well as Bonhoeffer's ecclesiology and the significance of his ecumenical engagement, will undoubtedly have further light shed on them by careful consideration of their apocalyptic valences.[78] So too within the *Ethics* itself, all this should influence the way we approach the interrelation of the dual account of ethics as obedience to the concrete divine command on the one hand, and ethics as formation on the other. This interpretive direction looks to be fruitful in disclosing how much more *dynamic*, more *dialectical*, and more *immediately Pauline* the theological ethics of Bonhoeffer may be, and also fruitful in shifting our appreciation of some of its most interesting and important themes. The permanently revolutionary character of Bonhoeffer's thought is less a reflection of his theological genius (which was real) than it is of his saturation in the "strange new world of the Bible." What the prominence of Pauline apocalyptic in Bonhoeffer's *Ethics* makes plain is his abiding commitment to practice Christian dogmatics and ethics so as to "yield some place to the Word of God," a Word that faith knows to be both eloquent and militant in the world for whose sake the church exists.[79]

---

77. Bonhoeffer, "Theology of Crisis," in DBWE 10:463.

78. Reconciliation as an act of divine power and "gracious violence" finds concrete form in the cross of Christ, since it is "the word of the cross that is . . . the power of God" (1 Cor. 1:18 RSV); the notion of the formative reality of the new creation finds concrete human expression in the life of the Christian community, where there arise forms of human life that honor the breach that God has opened between the old and new worlds, and bear witness to the uncontingent grace of God in its disciplines (arcane as they may be) as well as in "prayer and righteous action." On both these themes, see Bonhoeffer, *Letters and Papers from Prison*, DBWE 8:364–65, 373, 389–90, 475–83.

79. The phrase is from John Calvin, *Institutes* 3.4.29.

And perhaps the compelling power of the *Ethics* flows from Bonhoeffer's own firm grasp of the uncontingent, prevenient, invading, and humanizing power of God's grace and his keen discernment, together with the apostle Paul, that the acting in congruity with that reality is the fundamental freedom and responsibility of a Christian under the eschatological lordship of Christ.[80]

---

80. For two distinctive contemporary projects inspired by this vision of Bonhoeffer's, see McBride, *Church for the World*, and Harvey, *Taking Hold of the Real*.

13

Discipleship

Militant Love in the Time That Remains

They have been redeemed from humankind . . . [and] follow the
Lamb wherever he goes.

—Revelation 14:4

Discipleship and Its Discontents

Discipleship is a category with which theology denotes the dynamic form
of Christian life that results from the gift of God's gracious salvation in and
through Jesus Christ. Its semantic range encompasses much of what traditional accounts of the *ordo salutis* (order of salvation) consider variously
under the rubrics of sanctification, regeneration, mortification, vivification,
and perseverance. Distinctively, in our talk of discipleship we necessarily consider how the shape and direction of the Christian life may be illuminated
by specific reflection on the patterned relations between Jesus and those he
gathered to himself during his ministry, as this is depicted in the biblical witness. Such talk sets the question of Christian life in particular relief against
the backdrop of Jesus's preaching and teaching, his summons and service, and
requires that we reckon with the significance of all this in substantiating our
understanding of holiness and that freedom for whose sake Christ sets people
free (Gal. 5:1). At stake in an account of discipleship is thus recognition of

the designs that saving divine grace has on those it overtakes, the nature and claim of the "better righteousness" that befits the advent of God's reign on and among his people (cf. Matt. 5:20), and the contours of that "newness of life" into which Christians are raised on the other side of their participation in Christ's death (Rom. 6:4). As such, discipleship can also recommend itself as a watchword beneath which to articulate the lineaments of a distinctly *Christian* ethic. In short, when we make discipleship our theme, we ask, How ought we to characterize a human life that, having been justified, redeemed, and reconciled to God *by* Jesus Christ, is now given time and place in which to live anew *in* and *with* Christ?

The Christian tradition displays many and varied answers to this question, not all of which explicitly adopt the idiom of "discipleship." In teaching about the cultivation of the Christian life, early apologists and theologians readily spoke of Christianity as a *philosophia*, adapting the tradition in pagan antiquity that conceived of philosophy as a set of intellectual and physical practices aimed at attaining to a distinctive way of being in the world, a way of life keyed ever more perfectly to guiding truths.[1]

Such pedagogical emphases were extended in later centuries, finding particular expression within medieval monastic rules—paradigmatically, that of Benedict—charters of order, piety, and discipline for communities whose very purpose was education into exemplary religious life. Recurrent medieval monastic reforms consciously sought renewed forms of Christian existence that more immediately reflected the evangelical summons to poverty and purity of life in conformity with Christ.[2] Out of this history arises the traditional Catholic delineation of "evangelical counsels of perfection," poverty, chastity, and obedience, into which religious life is especially consecrated above and beyond the precepts of the "new law," which are binding on all Christians. By the practice of these counsels, monastic Christians may "devote themselves in a special way to the Lord" and "spend themselves increasingly for Christ" as they strive to "follow Christ more freely and imitate him more nearly" within their religious life.[3] As such, the vocation of ordered religious life has long been understood to be a distinctive, and perhaps even exclusive, site of Christian discipleship. The emergence of the popular lay spirituality movement

1. See Hadot, *Philosophy as a Way of Life*, 126–43. On the adoption of the discourse of *paideia* (education as formation) into Christian self-descriptions, see Jaeger, *Early Christianity and Greek Paideia*, 86–102, where the example of Gregory of Nyssa is concisely discussed.

2. See Köpf, s.v. "Mendicant Orders," in *Religion Past and Present*.

3. From *Perfectae Caritatis* (decree on the renewal of religious life), §1, in *Documents of Vatican II*, 466–67. Cf. Thomas Aquinas, *Summa Theologia* I-II, q. 108, art. 4, II-II, q. 184, art. 3, and q. 186.

Devotio Moderna during the fifteenth century sought to extend the franchise of such discipleship—to conceive of Christendom as "*a single monastery, as it were*," as Erasmus once put it[4]—by reconnecting lay existence with the dispositions and practices of *sequela Christi*, that exceptional striving to follow Christ. This spirit is paradigmatically distilled in the opening lines of the fifteenth-century work *The Imitation of Christ*, by Thomas à Kempis: "'*He who follows me, walks not in darkness*,' says the Lord [John 8:12]. By these words of Christ we are advised to imitate his life and habits if we wish to be truly enlightened and freed from all blindness of heart. Let our chief effort, therefore, be to study the life of Jesus Christ."[5]

Zealous for the evangelical truths of *sola gratia* and *sola fide* (salvation by grace and faith alone), and eager to reform ecclesiastical traditions *sola scriptura* (by Scripture alone), the magisterial Reformers repudiated the notion that the discipleship represented by pursuit of the "counsels of perfection" was elective and supererogatory. They argued that all Christians are "commonly bound" by a single rule of life "committed by God to the whole Church," and called to perfect an existence marked by a faith that stirs fervent love expressed in service, and a freedom that fears nothing of this world, including death.[6] These Protestants commended as normative a single pattern of Christian life, characterized as the free and priestly service of all believers in the power of the Spirit (Lutheran), or Spirit-afforded grateful obedience to the law of grace (Reformed).[7] Such accounts—variously developed and amplified in particular by later Puritan and pietistic theologies during following centuries—typically emphasized the conformity of Christian life to the shape of Christ's own humility and self-giving by stressing motifs such as self-denial, neighbor love, cross bearing, and submission to Christ "living and reigning within."[8] Yet they rarely spoke of "discipleship."

4. Erasmus, *Correspondence of Erasmus*, 297.

5. Thomas à Kempis, *Imitation of Christ*, 5. For other examples, see Van Engen, *Devotio Moderna*.

6. The quotation is from Calvin, *Institutes* 4.8.12 (cf. 2.8.56 and 4.8.11). A paradigmatic presentation of this position is given by Luther, "Judgment of Martin Luther on Monastic Vows" (1521), in *Luther's Works* 44:243–400.

7. Calvin's characterization of the positive function of the biblical law within the Christian life as its third, principal, and proper use (*Institutes* 2.7.12) became a Reformed commonplace. Lutheran teaching formalized a distinction between the "works of the law" and those "fruits of the Spirit," which Christians perform "as if they knew no command, threat, or reward" and only thereby "walk according to the law of God" as "children of God" (Formula of Concord, art. 6, in Lutheran Church, *Book of Concord*, 503).

8. The last phrase is from Calvin, *Institutes* 3.7.1. This whole passage (3.6–7) is indicative of the Reformed approach. On the Lutheran view, see Luther, "Freedom of a Christian," 9–53. Here we see the basis for Max Weber's observation that a consequence of the Reformation was

Indeed, as they developed, these lines of thinking increasingly emphasized that while Christ's own self-giving and love may provide a distinct measure for conduct within the various orders, relations, and stations of life, these creaturely givens themselves constitute a "primeval divine order that shapes human life" and continues to provide the primary points of reference for a Christian ethic. Discipleship occurs fully "within the household of the world," in sober recognition of the overriding claims of the orders of creation and preservation as creaturely conditions of possibility, as it were, for Christian life.[9] Most radically, it became possible to identify without remainder the content of Christian discipleship with the fulfillment of the duties of natural creaturely life.[10] In any case, leading Protestant accounts settled on the understanding that the Christian life cannot be solely one of evangelical discipleship but must always somehow combine discipleship *and* the prudential ethics suited to negotiating life in the world that is. The alternatives—either "homeless discipleship or a home without discipleship"—were adjudged unthinkable and unworkable, overzealous or impious.[11]

Historically, Anabaptists have also opposed any two-tier vision of Christian discipleship, but they were also impatient with compromises between the gospel and the current order of things. Their distinctive commitment to recover an apostolic church marked by public conversion, visible holiness, and voluntary membership drew fire from other Protestants as a "new monasticism" whose "angelic zeal" imposed baptism as a fresh "monastic constraint" rather than a "friendly exhortation to the Christian life."[12] While repudiating such criticisms, Menno Simons could grant the analogy with monasticism since as "children of God and disciples of Christ," they acknowledge Jesus as the sole "Abbot" and "Prior" over the assembly of the saints called out from

---

to make "every man a monk" in whatever state of life; see M. Weber; *Protestant Ethic and the Spirit of Capitalism*, 121. For examples of pietistic developments, see Law, *Serious Call to a Devout and Holy Life*; and Whaling, *John and Charles Wesley: Selected Writings and Hymns*.

9. The phrase is from Bayer, *Freedom in Response—Lutheran Ethics*, 117. Cf. Wenz, "Natural Law and the Orders of Creation," 91–93.

10. See Wingren, *Flight from Creation*, 52–53, where the life of faith is a life returned fully to the "natural duties" of creaturely existence.

11. Bayer, *Freedom in Response*, 129; cf. 136. Bayer discusses how Luther "walks a tightrope" in his efforts to coordinate the ethos of creaturely life with the claims of the new life of Christian freedom: "Our thought must reckon with a radical ethic of discipleship and a sapiential code of household duties, with wisdom and the cross. *That* tension is not resolved so long as we are on our pilgrimage!" (115). The abiding role of natural law or its surrogates in Protestant ethics is one of the marks of this tension.

12. The phrases are from Calvin, *Institutes* 4.12.12; and Zwingli, "Of Baptism," 152. Friesen, "Anabaptism and Monasticism," 174–97, provides an informative historical investigation of these charges and their substance.

the world.[13] It has been suggested that discipleship, with special emphasis on the immediacy of the example and leadership of Jesus and its social consequences, is *the* chief identifier of the distinctively Anabaptist vision.[14] For this reason, Anabaptist theologies of the Christian life have been key in bringing the discourse of discipleship into wider ecumenical theological discussion during the past century.

Starting with these compressed historical remarks in mind, we must reckon with the thought that the doctrine of the Christian life, and perhaps especially the discourse of discipleship within it, is potentially one of the most "seductive" and "dangerous" dogmatic loci.[15] Why is this so? As Gerhard Forde has observed, it is sorely tempting to think of discipleship, and of sanctification generally, as the finally pressing and "serious business" of reflecting on our own role and contributions to salvation on the far side of God's justifying grace. He identifies the twin dangers of *moralism* and *unreality*, which attend every anxious effort to demonstrate that the Christian life is "different, vital, relevant, abundant, and obviously superior to every other kind of life."[16] Regarding *moralism*, extended discussions of the active life of Christians can, whether by design or by drift, corrode our grasp of the permanent priority and prevenience of gracious divine agency, entangling us in the perverse business of trying to become "work-saints" off in pursuit of an "ethical adventure."[17] Regarding *unreality*, in a manner akin to what Nicholas Healy has called "blueprint ecclesiologies," normative accounts of discipleship can foster paralyzing disjunctions between reality and ideality; while such accounts may stir up ardor at times, they can also entrap Christian life in a desultory oscillation between hypocrisy and despair.[18] Other theologians untroubled by such worries, or even anxious that cautions such as these threaten to deflate properly extensive treatment of Christian discipline and holiness, contend that the only thing dangerous about discipleship is its pervasive *neglect*. They consider discipleship to be the long neglected "stepchild" of Protestant theology and ethics,

13. Menno Simons, as quoted in Friesen, "Anabaptism and Monasticism," 187, 193.

14. Bender, "Anabaptist Vision"; and Burkholder, "Anabaptist Vision of Discipleship." Cf. Bender, "Anabaptist Theology of Discipleship."

15. For what follows see Forde, "Christian Life," 395. Cf. Forde, "Lutheran View," 15–17.

16. Forde, "Christian Life," 395.

17. Luther, "Freedom of a Christian," 31; Bonhoeffer, *Discipleship*, 73. Writing from prison in 1944, Bonhoeffer worried that the struggle to "acquire faith by trying to live a holy life"—to which he dedicated his own work *Discipleship*—could be co-opted by an aspirant religiosity alien to the gospel and so undermine the proper immersion of the Christian life in and for the world for which Christ suffered. See Bonhoeffer, *Letters and Papers from Prison*, DBWE 8:485. Yet importantly, he also says: "I stand by what I wrote in that volume."

18. Healy, *Church, World and the Christian Life*, 26–27.

whose ongoing disregard within contemporary Christian proclamation and self-understanding constitutes a "great omission" that effectively renders much contemporary Christianity merely nominal.[19] They charge that the church's balking at the rigors of discipleship has to answer for the apparent dissolution of "real" Christianity within a decadent, compromised, and disintegrating Christendom; what is needed, they suggest, are renewal programs aimed to recover the authenticity, purposefulness, and integrity of Christian life.[20]

I suggest that if we are to discern the promise of discipleship while forestalling the attendant perils, we need a clear assertion and tenacious defense of the fact that the form and substance of discipleship is entirely derivative of the identity and saving work of the living Lord Jesus Christ. Discipleship is a practical reflex of Christology, the persistent work of registering what it means here and now that "we are the ones who are reached and affected by the existence of the Son of Man Jesus Christ, . . . that we are recipients of the direction of this Lord."[21] The dynamism involved is not provided by the movement between theory and praxis, and neither is it a function of the fact that the discourse of Christology "emerges from Christian living and leads into Christian living," however true that may be.[22] More than any methodological commitment, what proves singularly decisive here is the real dynamic presence and activity of the living Lord Jesus Christ himself, eloquent in the power of the Spirit to announce with effect the forgiveness and sovereign claim of God, the advent of the Kingdom. Whether there is discipleship in the church, and in what such discipleship will consist, will be answered by attending to the reality of Christ's sovereign presence to faith, or not at all. The hope for avoiding debilitating abstraction and moralism in a theology of discipleship, as well as for repudiating any illegitimate curtailment of the freedom of the Christian life, similarly rests here. As Bonhoeffer put it, discipleship "has no other content than Jesus Christ himself, being bound to him, in community with him."[23]

To Heed the Call of the One Who Goes On Before

The function of the discourse of discipleship is to recollect the living lordship of Jesus Christ—crucified, risen, and ascended—as the principal matter

---

19. Wolf, *Sozialethik*, 150; Willard, *Great Omission*; and concisely in Willard, "Discipleship."
20. To echo Kierkegaard, *PC* 228–31.
21. K. Barth, *CD* IV/2:266. Cf. Webster, "Imitation of Christ," 116: "To talk of human 'correspondences' to Jesus Christ is to make a *Christological* statement."
22. Moltmann, *Way of Jesus Christ*, 43.
23. Bonhoeffer, *Discipleship*, 74.

of the Christian life, and thus to ensure that such a life is suffused with and animated by the militancy of the eschatological gospel of God. Christians are disciples of Christ inasmuch as they serve and attest his lordship in the present time, during which "he must reign until he has put all his enemies under his feet" (1 Cor. 15:25). The relationship between the Christian and Jesus Christ is profoundly asymmetrical, far exceeding the ordering of the relations between teachers and pupils generally. The nature of this excess is displayed in the paradigmatic Gospel stories of Jesus's calling of the first disciples.[24] Shorn and abrupt as they are, these narratives emphasize the absolute authority and liberty of Jesus's summons to follow him; they signal that his call inaugurates something urgent and unanticipated, something radically new; they also make plain that the call disrupts and dislocates the disciple from the world as he has known it; finally, they show that the call of Jesus issues a writ of allegiance to him and seeks to secure service for him: from the very first, there is an intimate relation between the call to discipleship and commission to service: "I will make you fish for people" (Matt. 4:19); "The harvest is plentiful, but the laborers are few" (Luke 10:2). Those who fall in with this master are not being schooled for as long as it takes for them to train up as religious teachers in their own right, as was commonly the case with the pedagogical relationship of teachers and pupils in antiquity. Rather, they are recruited to a permanent position as a follower of Jesus and enter into an "unqualified community of life and destiny" with him as a saved servant in his train.[25] For Christ's disciples "have but one master, the Messiah [Christ]" (Matt. 23:10 NABRE).

Jesus calls his disciples, then, not finally as an exemplar, a religious sage or teacher of the law, but in accordance with his unique and unsubstitutable identity as the Son and Christ of God.[26] This reality places any naive notion of discipleship as "imitation" under rather severe strain. In order to characterize the "fit" between Christ and disciple, we need to conceive of it in ways that register the abiding "conspicuous discontinuity" between the identity and activity of Jesus and that of his disciples. The metaphorical extension of the language of "following" is well suited to do so. First, it acknowledges that the identity of Christian disciples is conferred *ad extra* (from outside

24. See Mark 1:16–20; 2:14; and parallels.
25. Hengel, *Charismatic Leader and His Followers*, 86, 87. Walter Brueggemann sees this pattern closely reflected in the pattern of the Lord's call to Israel; see Brueggemann, "Evangelism and Discipleship."
26. For discussion of this, see E. Schweitzer, *Lordship and Discipleship*, 11–21; cf. Marcus, *Mark 1–8*, 179–86, 224–32; and the important study of Hengel, *Charismatic Leader and His Followers*, esp. 38–83.

themselves) by the call of Jesus as eschatological Lord and Savior: the disciple is drafted into service. Second, it makes patent that Christ's disciples must ever "follow at a distance" as it were: always subject to his active governance, always displaying in their own lives the consequences of his singular salutary life and lordship.[27] The disciple is not in pursuit of an ideal, not even of an embodied ideal. Instead, disciples are laboring in the Spirit to remain in the wake of Jesus's own singular work and way, with an eye on the difference that the dawning of the reign of God makes to their reality. To be seized by divine grace in this way is to be bound in solidarity to Christ, to track his course, and to serve his cause in the world. The essential business of the life of the congregation—listening incessantly for the Word in Scripture and sermon, honoring the dominical ordinances of baptism and the Lord's Supper, the worship and praise of God's goodness, invocation of God's mercy and salvation on the community and the world, and taking responsibility for all for which we pray in humane practical action—can rightly be thought of as the "easy yoke" (cf. Matt. 11:30), which tethers Christians to their living Lord, aids us in discerning his governing presence, and directs our movement on the way.

We may further specify the nature of this discipleship by considering another suggestive valence of the biblical language of "following." The semantic range of the biblical concept of "following" used in connection with the call of Jesus includes reference to the movement of warriors who have been called up to accompany their leader into the fray, an image also extended into the depiction of Israel "go[ing out] after the Lord" (e.g., Hos. 11:10).[28] Suggestively, the same language of following (*akoloutheō*), rarely used in relation to Jesus outside the Gospels, appears in the Apocalypse (Rev. 14:4), where the Lamb of God is depicted as "Christ the King . . . on the move, marching out to meet his enemies" together with his followers, who are "utterly available to the Lord."[29] This text provides an amplified apocalyptic echo of both the risen Christ's "going ahead of" his disciples into Galilee (Mark 16:7) and the scenario of the act of gathering the first disciples. The Gospels closely connect this first call with Christ's own royal struggle against anti-God powers (beginning with the Satan in the wilderness), who plainly see that Jesus has "come to destroy" them (Mark 1:24). In this context, we are compelled to understand Jesus's promise to make the disciples "fish for people" (Mark 1:17) in light of its eschatological and explicitly martial meanings from the background

27. Outka, "Following at a Distance," 149, 154. Bultmann stresses that the farewell discourses in John's Gospel serve to establish precisely this difference and so, as James Kay puts it, forefend any "mawkish eagerness to fraternize with Jesus" (Kay, *Christus Praesens*, 80–81).
28. Hengel, *Charismatic Leader and His Followers*, 18–20; cf. Marcus, *Mark 1–8*, 183–84.
29. Mangina, *Revelation*, 173.

literature of the Old Testament: as Joel Marcus observes, this image casts all the disciples' future endeavors "as a participation in God's eschatological war against demonic forces," a contest that, moreover, "recapitulates God's redemption of Israel from Egyptian bondage."[30] This is because in the advent of the Son, "God has turned the world into hotly contested territory," and "those enslaving powers do not peacefully yield their turf to God, as every parish minister knows well."[31]

This suggests that an account of Christian discipleship would do well to emphasize the reality of the royal office of Jesus Christ and to call out those characterizations of Christian existence that comport with the reality of our redemption by his sovereign victory.[32] To this end, we might usefully rehabilitate the figure of Christ as "captain" as essential to the discourse of discipleship. Taking his cue from texts of Hebrews—which speak of Jesus as "the pioneer of [our] salvation" (2:10) and call on the faithful to be "looking to Jesus the pioneer and perfecter of our faith" (12:2)—Swiss reformer Huldrych Zwingli frequently spoke of Christ as both "the captain and the ensign under which we serve [*militamus*]."[33] Overreaching Erasmus's humanistic appropriation of the image of the Christian life as *militia Christi*, Zwingli's figure of the captaincy of Christ has as its central concern the public significance of the lordship of Christ in the midst of life.[34] The soubriquet connects with and helps to concentrate much of what we have discerned of discipleship to this point. Disciples are those "enlisted" into Christ's service and standing at his disposal, rallied to him in the cause of his reign; faith in the captain takes the form of loyalty to his direction amid the fray; and the order and movement of the Christian community, like the order of a troop of combatants, arises from the commanding presence of their captain in their midst. In sum, "here we have it—graphically portrayed in a picture that comes alive for every hearer and reader—still the same living Christ, and everything in the Christian warfare relates to him—believing and living, trusting, obeying and dying, finding comfort and serving. In all these things . . . our captain, Christ Jesus, never leaves us comfortless."[35] The overarching fact that the life of discipleship is

---

30. Marcus, *Mark 1–8*, 184–85. The illustrative texts in view are Jer. 16:16; Amos 4:2; Ezek. 19:2–5; Hab. 1:14–17.

31. Martyn, "World without End or Twice-Invaded World?," 125.

32. For valuable discussion of Christ's royal office, see Sherman, *King, Priest, and Prophet*, 116–68. Sherman also contends that the royal account of Christ's saving work should govern systematic discussion of soteriology; see 158–62. This is a point we argued above, in chap. 4.

33. *Christus et dux et signum est, sub quo militamus*. See Locher, *Zwingli's Thought*, 72–86.

34. For the text of Erasmus's influential *Enchiridion militia christiani*, see Rummel, *Erasmus Reader*.

35. Locher, *Zwingli's Thought*, 85.

permanently dependent on the living call and command of Christ is sharply displayed here: Christians are recruited "to a condition in which the disciples walk in the wake of Jesus, pulled along by his movement, set in motion by him but always *unlike* him and so *behind* him."[36]

Crucially, however, Zwingli's figuration of Christ as captain drives time and again to a single point: Christ is our captain because he "demands that we should risk our life in his battle," and he is our captain "because Christianity is something for which one must be prepared to die."[37] The turning point in the eschatological contest to which Christ recruits is undoubtedly the cross. This fact is made patent time and again in the Gospel narratives when the meaning of discipleship is inseparably welded to the advent of the kingdom of God *and* the passion of Christ. The cross thus provides one of the essential coordinates of discipleship: it represents the defining norm of the meaning and course of Christ's captaincy, and thus also the shape of any disciplined following, even "at a distance."[38] The Gospels relentlessly link Jesus's teaching about his fate, in which the reality of the cross features starkly, to his instruction concerning the nature of discipleship. Mark once again provides a particularly sharp instance, embedding Jesus's most concentrated teaching on what solidarity with him as one of his company involves within a threefold series of passion predictions (Mark 8:31–10:45). Drawn together finally under the culminating rubric of "taking up the cross" (Matt. 10:38, 16:24; Mark 8:34; Luke 9:23), the evangelists make plain that discipleship shares in the movement of the Savior to the cross: the existence of every believer is to be conformed to the life of the Crucified, to own him.[39] It does so inasmuch as it takes shape in lives of service, lives of humble self-giving for others, and as such lives marked by suffering. For in the service of the Master who is the servant of all, and whose life is given over for all, the epitome of faithful following can only take the shape of self-dispossession for the sake of others (Mark 10:42–45). As concepts of kingship and captaincy are here subjected to radical redefinition in view of the actuality of the cross, so too is the meaning of that martial struggle into which the Christian is drawn.[40]

The substantive pattern of this witness is at once distilled and expanded in the early Christian hymn Paul cites in Philippians in a passage (2:5–11) that

36. Webster, "Discipleship and Calling," 141.
37. Locher, *Zwingli's Thought*, 84–85. Cf. 84: "We notice that Zwingli only speaks of 'Captain Christ' when it is a question of dying; or, to be more precise, of being ready to die—of martyrdom."
38. Hays, *Moral Vision of the New Testament*, 84.
39. Harrisville, "Christian Life in Light of the Cross," 228.
40. On the thoroughgoing redefinition of "kingship" here, see Sherman, *King, Priest, and Prophet*, 142–51.

proves a touchstone for any account of the Christian life as discipleship. There are good reasons to be wary of a reading of the passage as a straightforward invitation to *imitatio Christi* (imitation of Christ) (cf. 1 Cor. 11:1; Col. 1:24).[41] This does not hinder the point to be made here: Christ's singular movement of *exinanitio* (humiliation, self-emptying; cf. Phil. 2:7, Vulgate) is a movement of utter gratuity, the magnitude of which catches up those it unseats from the situation of sin and leads them to purpose (φρονέω, *phroneō*; Phil. 2:5) only that which Christ purposes, to submit to Christ's own purpose as their decisive context. In conformity with the *exinanitio* of the Son of God for us—the apocalypse of the Father's limitless love—discipleship takes the form of loving self-giving for the neighbor in the dizzying freedom of the gospel. In binding us to himself, Christ binds us to go with him where he goes and to those to whom he goes: the hopeless, outcasts, and sinners, whom he makes our brothers and sisters. We do well to acknowledge that the humiliation of following Christ, the cost of discipleship, is not an end in itself. Rather, as Jesus's own way in the world is not the denial but the affirmation and progress of eschatological life, correspondingly the humility and sacrifice of the Christian life is but the shape freedom takes for those who live by grace, as they serve and live for others.[42] Just as the suffering of Jesus is the form that divine *promeity* takes onto the cross, so too the manifold and varied "sharing in the suffering of God in Christ" (cf. Rom. 8:17; 1 Cor. 12:26; Col. 1:24) that discipleship involves is but the form assumed as our own, now radically eccentric existence for others.[43] As Luther summarized the matter, explicitly glossing Philippians 2:5–8, a Christian, "like Christ his head, . . . should be content with this form of God which he obtained by faith" and in evangelical liberty "take upon himself the form of a servant, . . . serve, help, and in every way deal with his neighbor as he sees that God through Christ has dealt and still deals with him."[44]

For this reason, as we speak of the holiness or sanctity of the band of Christian disciples, we confess that in conformity with the movement of its lord, its very life lies in its "openness to the street and even the alley, in its turning to the profanity of all human life."[45] Only in such active service and openness to the world for whose sake Christ came low to save does the life of the Christian church tell the truth about the way things actually are. Only in

41. For concise discussion of this matter, see Hawthorne, "Imitation of Christ."
42. On this point, see K. Barth, *Ethics*, 328–30. David Kelsey discusses reconciled human life under this very rubric in the second volume of his *Eccentric Existence*.
43. Bonhoeffer, *Letters and Papers from Prison*, DBWE 8:48.
44. Luther, "Freedom of a Christian," 42.
45. K. Barth, *CD* IV/1:725.

such ways do Christ's disciples own him before the world, in the power of the Spirit refusing to repeat Peter's denial. By exercising the alarming evangelical freedom of a disciple in discrete times and places, we herald the advent of the kingdom. The life of discipleship is a pragmatic answer to the question "Who is lord of the world?" Such a life, moved by the Spirit to live in freedom *from* sin and *for* both God and neighbor, thus represents a powerful "practical commentary" on the proclamation of the gospel of God.[46] The credibility of this witness is intrinsic to the structure of discipleship: as one follows Christ "without trying to become Christ, at a distance rather than from too nearby," one thereby manifests what Hans Frei has styled an "intimacy of total contrast which is paradoxically one with total identity."[47] Following Jesus is no rigid mimicry. It is rather a "participation in the quality that characterized his political being."[48] But this is so only because it is already a form of life, like Jesus's own, made possible by and conformed to the humiliation of the Son of God, who in coming low to save brings the very reign of heaven with him.

Conscripted to Service

By reflecting on the Christian life qua Christian, we consider a human existence as it "stands in a particular relationship to Jesus Christ, and to that extent with the subjective realisation of the atonement."[49] In this, as we have endeavored to show, both the identity of Jesus Christ and the distinctive relation—the character of salvation—that he establishes with us prove decisive. Precisely because the advent of God in Christ involves the eruption of the Kingdom of God, the apocalypse of rampant divine grace, the provision of new life through faith in Christ "does not aim at passivity but, on the contrary, at activity."[50] The sterile opposition between understandings of Christian righteousness as a "legal fiction" and as the achievement of "work-saints" is surmounted only where salvation is seen in an eschatological perspective, where the invasion of divine grace in Christ does not merely "remove" sin while leaving the person intact but rather removes the person from the sin-ruled world and translates him or her into the Christ-governed world.[51] One may rightly speak of the

---

46. Ibid., 4:270. The life of discipleship thus hopes to offer a "persistent and joyful witness concerning Christ's present lordship in all realms of life" (Visser 't Hooft, *Kingship of Christ*, 17).

47. Frei, *Identity of Jesus Christ*, 80. For discussion of Frei's contributions to understanding the "Christological governance" of ethics, see Outka, "Following at a Distance," 144–60.

48. Yoder, *War of the Lamb*, 80.

49. K. Barth, *CD* IV/1:644.

50. Gollwitzer, *Introduction to Protestant Theology*, 151, 168.

51. Forde, "Christian Life," 436.

permanent relocation of disciples effected by Christ's eschatological claim and summons.[52] To be drafted into the company of Jesus's followers is to have been made, as Paul attests, a veritable "new creation" (2 Cor. 5:17). Thus the summons of Jesus—because it is the summons of the Christ, the harbinger of the reign of God—does not just instruct or inspire. Rather, it brings about a radically new situation, a place beyond the "enmity between law and gospel"; the overwhelming assault of grace dislocates the disciple from the old world, such that Christ, as it were, becomes one's very context.[53]

Because this is so, the life of discipleship is marked by a distinctive evangelical militancy. Indeed, by characterizing the Christian life as a life of discipleship, we specifically recall that it is lived out only and ever as one is a "member of the Church militant."[54] The Spirit-driven struggle of discipleship embraces both an inward mortification of the old Adam and an outward insurgency against the powers of the age. Enlisted by Christ, and thus also always instructed and directed afresh by his word, his disciples may exercise their evangelical freedom "in an active dedication of their lives to [Christ's] service, and to preparation for it"; in so doing, they heed a particular call "to engage in a specific uprising" against the perverse and unrighteous disorder that still besets and disrupts human life, the wreckage caused by the lordlessness of the anti-God powers of sin and death unleashed in the order of the fall.[55] Although defeat of these powers is the very work of Christ himself, he graciously constitutes his company of disciples an *ecclesia militans*, a body gathered, upheld, and commissioned to "act for the dawning of the rule of God," a struggle in which they must "rebel and fight *for* all, . . . even, and in the last resort precisely, for those with whom they may clash."[56] Here as ever, the character of their lord and captain decides the identity and activity of his followers: "If Christians were not the *militia Christi*, the *ecclesia militans*, engaged in a struggle with the human plight," it would "not be Christianity

---

52. Cf. Webster, "Discipleship and Calling," 134, where he speaks of an abiding "dislocation."

53. Bonhoeffer, *Discipleship*, 59, 62–63; Yoder, *Politics of Jesus*, 228, contends that the accent in the Pauline "in Christ" falls "not on transforming the ontology of the person (to say nothing of transforming his psychological or neurological equipment) but on transforming the perspective of the one who has accepted Christ as his context." The claim is ecumenically acknowledged—see Balthasar, *Theo-drama*, 3:385: "Thus the 'sphere' in which the Christian lives . . . is summed up by the term *en Christō* [in Christ]."

54. Kierkegaard, *PC* 232.

55. K. Barth, *CD* IV/4:211–13. The treatment of the "lordless powers" that follows (213–33) must be read in connection with Barth's earlier discussion of the strange unreality of "nothingness" that arises and empowers sin and evil in God's good creation, in *CD* III/3:289–368. Cf. Krötke, *Sin and Nothingness in the Theology of Karl Barth*.

56. Hengel, *Charismatic Leader and His Followers*, 88; K. Barth, *CD* IV/4:208–10.

or the church of Jesus Christ."[57] In the service of the "man for others," disciples know a kind of spiritual insomnia, a patient and sleepless attention to the movements of their Lord, the insurgency of divine love. To "watch" with Christ and so to remain alert to his ceaseless salutary movement and direction, to accompany his royal progress with *prayer* (Matt. 26:41), that is the essential labor of those he has recruited to his service.

In sum, the Christian life knows the governance and direction of the risen and ascended Christ, the blessing of his captaincy. As we have seen, key to any account of Christian discipleship is full appreciation of Christ's lordship, his unique and exclusive claim on the life of each Christian en route to that time when everything yet arrayed against God's graciousness will be trampled and put under foot and, like Christians themselves, will have been killed and made alive. Recognizing the eschatological character of the kingdom as that which is *coming upon us* (rather than our bringing it about) makes possible a distinctive understanding of the "progress" of our discipleship. Whatever faithfulness we know in the matter of discipleship is a function of our being ever more fully shaped by the grace that is coming upon us in the form of Christ's love and lordship, as we are overrun by "the steady invasion of the new."[58] In another biblical idiom, we can speak of discipleship arising only from our communion with Christ, the head who directs the body, the vine who supplies life to the branches. As Yoder wrote: "Following Jesus really means basing our action on our participation in Christ's very being. . . . We are already part of his body; we do not become so through following him. Following Jesus is the result, not the means, of our fellowship with Christ."[59] In any case the theological reality is but one: discipleship is and remains solely an eschatological possibility arising from the gracious call and command of Christ the Lord. As such, it is the shape of the human life of faith now militant in love during the time that remains.

57. K. Barth, CD IV/4:211.
58. Forde, "Lutheran View," 39.
59. Yoder, *Discipleship as Political Responsibility*, 61.

Bibliography

Adams, Edward. *Constructing the World: A Study in Paul's Cosmological Language.* London: T&T Clark, 2000.

Adams, Jens, Hans-Joachim Eckstein, and Hermann Lichtenberger, eds. *Dienst in Freiheit: Ernst Käsemann zum 100. Geburtstag.* Neukirchener-Vluyn: Neukirchener Verlag, 2008.

Adams, Sam. *The Reality of God and Historical Method: Apocalyptic Theology in Encounter with N. T. Wright.* Downers Grove, IL: IVP Academic, 2017.

Allison, Dale C. *The Sermon on the Mount: Inspiring the Moral Imagination.* New York: Crossroad, 1999.

Altizer, Thomas J. J. *The Call to Radical Theology.* Edited by L. McCullough. Albany, NY: SUNY Press, 2012.

Anderson, Pamela Sue. *Kant and Theology.* London: T&T Clark, 2010.

Anselm. *Cur Deus Homo.* In *Anselm of Canterbury: The Major Works*, edited and translated by B. Davies and G. R. Evans, 260–356. Oxford: Oxford University Press, 1998.

Augustine. *De natura et gratia.* PL 44. Edited by Jacques-Paul Migne. Paris, 1865.

Aulén, Gustaf. "Chaos and Cosmos: The Drama of Atonement." *Interpretation* 4, no. 2 (1950): 156–67.

———. *Christus Victor: An Historical Study of the Three Main Types of the Idea of the Atonement.* Translated by A. G. Herbert. London: SCM, 1970.

———. *The Faith of the Christian Church.* Translated by E. H. Wahlstrom. Philadelphia: Fortress, 1960.

Bal, Mieke. "Postmodern Theology as Cultural Analysis." In *The Blackwell Companion to Postmodern Theology*, edited by G. Ward, 3–23. New ed. Oxford: Blackwell, 2004.

Balthasar, Hans Urs von. *Origen, Spirit and Fire: A Thematic Anthology of His Writings.* Translated by R. J. Daly. Washington, DC: Catholic University Press of America, 1984.

———. *Theo-drama.* Vol. 3. San Francisco: Ignatius, 1992.

Barclay, John. "Paul and the Philosophers: Alain Badiou and the Event." *New Blackfriars* 91, no. 1032 (March 2010): 171–84.

———. "Under Grace: The Christ-Gift and the Construction of a Christian *Habitus.*" In *Apocalyptic Paul: Cosmos and Anthropos in Romans 5–8,* edited by Beverly Roberts Gaventa, 59–76. Waco: Baylor University Press, 2013.

Barrett, C. K. *Commentary on the First Epistle to the Corinthians.* 2nd ed. London: A&C Black, 1971.

Barth, Karl. *Christ and Adam: Man and Humanity in Romans 5.* Translated by T. A. Smail. New York: Harper, 1956.

———. "The Christian in Society (1919)." In *The Word of God and Theology,* translated by A. Marga, 31–70. London: T&T Clark, 2011.

———. "Christian Prayer according to the Reformers." In *Prayer and Preaching,* translated by B. E. Hooke, edited by A. Roulin, 9–63. London: SCM, 1964.

———. "The Christian's Place in Society." In *The Word of God and the Word of Man,* translated by D. Horton. New York: Harper & Bros., 1928.

———. *Church Dogmatics.* 4 vols. Edinburgh: T&T Clark, 1956–75.

———. "Der Christ in der Gesellschaft." In *Anfänge der dialektischen Theologie,* edited by J. Moltmann, 1:3–37. Munich: Christian Kaiser, 1962.

———. *The Epistle to the Romans.* Translated by E. Hoskyns. London: Oxford University Press, 1933.

———. *Ethics.* Translated by G. W. Bromiley. New York: Seabury Press, 1981.

———. *The Holy Spirit and the Christian Life: The Theological Basis of Ethics.* Translated by R. Birch Hoyle. Louisville: Westminster John Knox, 1993.

———. "The Interpretation of the Lord's Prayer according to the Reformers." In *Prayer and Preaching,* translated by B. E. Hooke, edited by A. Roulin, 24–63. London: SCM, 1964.

———. "Prayer in the Reformation." In *Prayer and Preaching,* translated by B. E. Hooke, edited by A. Roulin, 9–63. London: SCM, 1964.

———. *Romans: A Shorter Commentary.* Translated by D. H. van Daalen. London: SCM, 1963.

———. *Römerbrief.* Munich: Christian Kaiser, 1922.

Barth, Markus. *Justification.* Translated by A. M. Woodruff III. Grand Rapids: Eerdmans, 1971.

Bauckham, Richard. "The Divinity of Jesus in the Letter to the Hebrews." In *Jesus and the God of Israel,* 233–53. Grand Rapids: Eerdmans, 2008.

———. "Kierkegaard and the Epistle of James." In *Kierkegaard and Christian Faith*, edited by Paul Martens and C. Stephen Evans, 39–54. Waco: Baylor University Press, 2016.

Bavinck, Herman. *Saved by Grace: The Holy Spirit's Work in Calling and Regeneration.* Translated by N. D. Kloosterman. Grand Rapids: Reformation Heritage, 2008.

Bayer, Oswald. *Freedom in Response—Lutheran Ethics: Sources and Controversies.* Translated by J. F. Cayzer. Oxford: Oxford University Press, 2007.

———. "Theses on the Doctrine of Justification." *Lutheran Quarterly* 22 (2008): 72–75.

Beker, J. Christiaan. *Paul's Apocalyptic Gospel: The Coming Triumph of God.* Philadelphia: Fortress, 1982.

———. *Paul the Apostle: The Triumph of God in Life and Thought.* Philadelphia: Fortress, 1984.

Bender, Harold S. "The Anabaptist Theology of Discipleship." *Mennonite Quarterly Review* 24 (1950): 25–32.

———. "The Anabaptist Vision." In *The Recovery of the Anabaptist Vision*, edited by G. F. Hershberger, 29–56. Scottdale, PA: Herald Press, 1957.

Berkhof, Hendrikus. *Christian Faith: An Introduction to the Study of the Faith.* Grand Rapids: Eerdmans, 1991.

Berkouwer, G. C. *Faith and Sanctification.* Grand Rapids: Eerdmans, 1952.

———. *The Triumph of Grace in the Theology of Karl Barth.* Translated by H. R. Boer. Grand Rapids: Eerdmans, 1956.

———. *The Work of Christ.* Translated by C. Lambregtse. Grand Rapids: Eerdmans, 1965.

Bethge, Eberhard. *Bonhoeffer: Eine Biographie.* Gütersloh: Gütersloher Verlagshaus, 1994.

———. *Dietrich Bonhoeffer: Theologian, Christian, Contemporary.* Translated by E. Mosbacher et al. London: Collins, 1970.

Betz, Hans Dieter. *The Sermon on the Mount.* Minneapolis: Fortress, 1995.

Beyerle, Stefan. "Von der Löwengrube ins himmlische Jerusalem: Erwägungen zur jüdischen Apokalyptik." *Glaube und Lernen* 14 (1999): 23–34.

Blackwell, Ben C., John K. Goodrich, and Jason Maston, eds. *Paul and the Apocalyptic Imagination.* Minneapolis: Fortress, 2016.

Boer, Roland. "John Calvin and the Paradox of Grace." *Colloquium* 41, no. 1 (2009): 22–40.

Bonhoeffer, Dietrich. *Act and Being.* Translated by H. M. Rumscheidt. DBWE 2. Minneapolis: Fortress, 1996.

———. "Christ, Reality and the Good." In *Ethics*, 47–75.

———. "Concerning the Christian Idea of God." In *Barcelona, Berlin, New York: 1928–1931*, translated by D. Stott, edited by C. J. Green, 451–61. DBWE 10.

Minneapolis: Fortress, 2008. Originally published in *Journal of Religion* 12, no. 2 (1932): 177–85.

———. *Creation and Fall*. Edited by John W. de Gruchy. Translated by Douglas S. Bax. DBWE 3. Minneapolis: Fortress, 1997.

———. *Discipleship*. Translated by B. Green and R. Krause. DBWE 4. Minneapolis: Fortress, 2002.

———. *Ethics*. Translated by I. Tödt et al. DBWE 6. Minneapolis: Fortress, 2005.

———. "Lecture on Contemporizing New Testament Texts." In *Theological Education at Finkenwalde, 1935–1937*, edited by M. Brocker and H. G. Barker, translated by D. W. Stott, 413–32. DBWE 14. Minneapolis: Fortress, 2013.

———. "Lectures on Christology." In *Berlin: 1932–1933*, edited by L. Rasmussen, translated by I. Best and D. Higgins, 299–360. DBWE 12. Minneapolis: Fortress, 2009.

———. *Letters and Papers from Prison*. Edited by J. de Gruchy. Translated by I. Best et al. DBWE 8. Minneapolis: Fortress, 2010.

———. "Protestantism without Reformation." In *Theological Education Underground: 1937–1940*, edited by V. J. Barnett, translated by V. J. Barnett et al., 438–62. DBWE 15. Minneapolis: Fortress, 2012.

———. "The Theology of Crisis." In *Barcelona, Berlin, New York: 1928–1931*, translated by D. Stott, edited by C. J. Green, 462–76. DBWE 10. Minneapolis: Fortress, 2008.

———. "Thy Kingdom Come! The Prayer of the Church-Community for God's Kingdom on Earth." In *Berlin, 1932–1933*, edited by L. Rasmussen, translated by I. Best, D. Higgins, and D. W. Stott, 285–97. DBWE 12. Minneapolis: Fortress, 2009.

———. *True Patriotism: Letters, Lectures and Notes, 1939–1945*. Edited by E. H. Robertson. Translated by E. H. Robertson and J. Bowden. London: Collins, 1973.

———. "Zu I Korinther 1,18." In *Illegale Theologenausbildung: Finkenwalde, 1935–1937*, edited by O. Dudzus and J. Henkys, with S. Bobert-Stützely, D. Schulz, and I. Tödt, 329–33. Dietrich Bonhoeffer Werke 14. Munich: Christian Kaiser, 1996.

Bornkamm, Karin. "Amt Christi." In *Religion in Geschichte und Gegenwart*, edited by Hans D. Betz et al., 1:439–40. 4th ed. Tübingen: Mohr Siebeck, 1998.

———. *Christus—König und Priester: Das Amt Christi bei Luther im Verhältnis zur Var- und Nachgeschicte*. Tübingen: Mohr Siebeck, 1998.

Bosc, Jean. *The Kingly Office of the Lord Jesus Christ*. Translated by J. K. S. Reid. Edinburgh: Oliver & Boyd, 1959.

Bovon, François. *Luke*. Vol. 2, *A Commentary on the Gospel of Luke 9:51–19:27*. Translated by D. S. Deer. Edited by H. Koester. Minneapolis: Fortress, 2013.

Braaten, Carl E. *Christ and Counter-Christ: Apocalyptic Themes in Theology and Culture*. Philadelphia: Fortress, 1972.

———. "Protestants and Natural Law." *First Things* 19 (January 1992): 20–26.

———. "The Recovery of Apocalyptic Imagination." In *The Last Things: Biblical and Theological Perspectives on Eschatology*, edited by C. E. Braaten and R. W. Jenson, 14–32. Grand Rapids: Eerdmans, 2002.

———. "The Significance of Apocalypticism for Systematic Theology." *Interpretation* 25, no. 4 (1971): 480–99.

Brown, Delwin, Sheila Greeve Davaney, and Kathryn Tanner, eds. *Converging on Culture: Theologians in Dialogue with Cultural Analysis and Criticism*. Oxford: Oxford University Press, 2001.

Brown, Raymond E. "The Pater Noster as an Eschatological Prayer." *Theological Studies* 22 (1961): 175–208.

Brueggemann, Walter. "Evangelism and Discipleship: The God Who Calls, the God Who Sends." *Word & World* 24, no. 2 (2004): 121–35.

Brümmer, Vincent. *What Are We Doing When We Pray? On Prayer and the Nature of Faith*. Aldershot, UK: Ashgate, 2008.

Brunner, Emil. *The Christian Doctrine of Creation and Redemption*. Translated by O. Wyon. London: Lutterworth, 1952.

Burkholder, J. Lawrence. "The Anabaptist Vision of Discipleship." In *The Recovery of the Anabaptist Vision*, edited by G. F. Hershberger, 135–51. Scottdale, PA: Herald Press, 1957.

Burrows, Millar. "Thy Kingdom Come." *Journal of Biblical Literature* 74, no. 1 (1955): 1–8.

Busch, Eberhard. *Drawn to Freedom: Christian Faith Today in Conversation with the Heidelberg Catechism*. Translated by W. H. Rader. Grand Rapids: Eerdmans, 2010.

Cady, Linnell. *Religion, Theology, and American Public Life*. Albany, NY: SUNY Press, 1993.

Caird, G. B. *Principalities and Powers*. Oxford: Clarendon, 1956.

Calvin, John. *The Bondage and Liberation of the Will: A Defence of the Orthodox Doctrine of Human Choice against Pighius*. Edited by A. N. S. Lane. Translated by G. I. Davies. Grand Rapids: Baker Academic, 1996.

———. *The Commentaries of John Calvin on the Old Testament*. Vol. 1, *Genesis*. Edinburgh: Calvin Translation Society, 1843–48.

———. *The Epistle of Paul the Apostle to the Romans and to the Thessalonians*. Translated by R. Mackenzie. Edited by D. W. Torrance and T. F. Torrance. Grand Rapids: Eerdmans, 1995.

———. *The Epistles of Paul the Apostle to the Galatians, Ephesians, Philippians and Colossians*. Edited by D. W. Torrance and T. F. Torrance. Translated by T. H. L. Parker. Grand Rapids: Eerdmans, 1996.

———. *The Gospel according to St. John 1–10*. Translated by T. H. L. Parker. Edited by D. W. Torrance and T. F. Torrance. Grand Rapids: Eerdmans, 1995.

———. *A Harmony of the Gospels. Matthew, Mark and Luke*. Vol. 1 of *Calvin's Commentaries*, edited by D. W. Torrance and T. F. Torrance, translated by A. W. Morrison. Grand Rapids: Eerdmans, 1995.

———. *Institutes of the Christian Religion* (1536). Translated by Ford Lewis Battles. Grand Rapids: Eerdmans, 1995.

———. *Institutes of the Christian Religion* (1541 French ed.). Translated by E. A. McKee. Grand Rapids: Eerdmans, 2009.

———. *Institutes of the Christian Religion* (1559). Edited by J. T. McNeil. Translated by Ford Lewis Battles. Philadelphia: Westminster, 1960.

———. *Opera Selecta*. Vol. 4, *Institutionis christianae religionis*. Edited by P. Barth and G. Niesel. Munich: Christian Kaiser, 1931.

Campbell, Douglas A. *The Quest for Paul's Gospel: A Suggested Strategy*. London: T&T Clark, 2005.

Catechism of the Council of Trent. Translated by J. Donovan. Baltimore: James Myres, 1833.

Chapman, Mark D. *Ernst Troeltsch and Liberal Theology*. Oxford: Oxford University Press, 2001.

Charles, J. Daryl. *Retrieving the Natural Law: A Return to Moral First Things*. Grand Rapids: Eerdmans, 2008.

Charlesworth, James H. "Jewish Prayers at the Time of Jesus." In *The Lord's Prayer: Perspectives for Reclaiming Christian Prayer*, edited by D. L. Migliore, 36–55. Grand Rapids: Eerdmans, 1993.

Clemo, Jack. "The Awakening." In *The Awakening: Poems Newly Found*, edited by J. Hurst, A. M. Kent, and A. C. Symons, 68–69. London: Francis Boutle, 2003.

Collins, John J., Bernard McGinn, and Stephen J. Stein, eds. *The Encyclopedia of Apocalypticism*. 3 vols. London: Continuum, 1998.

Collins Winn, Christian T. *"Jesus Is Victor!" The Significance of the Blumhardts for the Theology of Karl Barth*. Eugene, OR: Pickwick: 2009.

Conzelmann, Hans. *1 Corinthians*. Translated by J. W. Leitch. Philadelphia: Fortress, 1975.

Crisp, Oliver, ed. "Reformed Accounts of Free Will." Special issue, *Journal of Reformed Theology* 8, no. 3 (2014).

Critchley, Simon. *The Faith of the Faithless: Experiments in Political Theology*. London: Verso, 2012.

Cullmann, Oscar. *The Earliest Christian Confessions*. Translated by J. K. S. Reid. London: Lutterworth, 1949.

———. "The Kingship of Christ and the Church in the New Testament." In *The Early Church*, translated by A. J. B. Higgins, 103–37. London: SCM, 1956.

Cupitt, Donald. *Life, Life*. Santa Rosa, CA: Polebridge, 2003.

Dalferth, Ingolf U. "Karl Barth's Eschatological Realism." In *Karl Barth: Centenary Essays*, edited by S. Sykes, 14–45. Cambridge: Cambridge University Press, 1989.

Danker, Frederick W., Walter Bauer, William F. Arndt, and F. Wilbur Gingrich. *Greek-English Lexicon of the New Testament and Other Early Christian Literature*. 3rd ed. Chicago: University of Chicago Press, 2000.

Dantine, Wilhelm. "Creation and Redemption: Attempt at a Theological Understanding in the Light of the Contemporary Understanding of the World." *Scottish Journal of Theology* 18 (June 1965): 129–47.

———. "*Regnum Christi—Gubernatio Dei*. Dogmatische Überlegungen zum Begriff der 'Herrschaft.'" *Theologische Zeitung* 15 (1959): 195–208.

Davaney, Sheila Greeve. *Historicism: The Once and Future Challenge for Theology*. Minneapolis: Fortress, 2006.

———. *Pragmatic Historicism: A Theology for the Twenty-First Century*. Albany, NY: SUNY Press, 2000.

Davies, J. P. *Paul among the Apocalypses*. London: T&T Clark, 2016.

Davies, W. D., and Dale C. Allison. *The Gospel according to Saint Matthew*. Vol. 1. London: T&T Clark, 1988.

Davis, Joshua B. "The Challenge of Apocalyptic to Modern Theology." In Davis and Harink, *Apocalyptic and the Future of Theology*, 1–50.

Davis, Joshua B., and Douglas Harink, eds. *Apocalyptic and the Future of Theology: With and beyond J. Louis Martyn*. Eugene, OR: Cascade, 2012.

Dean, William. "The Challenge of the New Historicism." *Journal of Religion* 66, no. 3 (1986): 261–81.

de Boer, Martinus C. "Apocalyptic as God's Eschatological Activity in Paul's Theology." In *Paul and the Apocalyptic Imagination*, edited by Ben C. Blackwell, John K. Goodrich, and Jason Maston, 45–63. Minneapolis: Fortress, 2016.

———. *The Defeat of Death: Apocalyptic Eschatology in 1 Corinthians and Romans 5*. Sheffield: Sheffield Academic, 1988.

———. *Galatians*. Louisville: Westminster John Knox, 2011.

———. "Paul and Apocalyptic Eschatology." In *The Continuum History of Apocalypticism*, edited by B. McGinn et al., 166–94. New York: Continuum, 2003.

———. "Paul, Theologian of God's Apocalypse." *Interpretation* 55, no. 1 (2002): 21–33.

Deines, Roland. "God's Role in History as a Methodological Problem for Exegesis." In *Acts of God in History: Studies towards Recovering a Theological Historiography*, 1–26. Tübingen: Mohr Siebeck, 2013.

Derrida, Jacques. "Of an Apocalyptic Tone Recently Adopted in Philosophy." *Oxford Literary Review* 6, no. 2 (1984): 3–37.

Division of Studies of the World Council of Churches. "The Lordship of Christ over the Church and the World." *Ecumenical Review* 11, no. 4 (1959): 437–49.

Documents of Vatican II. Edited by W. M. Abbott. Translated by J. Gallagher. Piscataway, NJ: America, 1966.

Douglas, R. Conrad. "A Jesus Tradition Prayer." In *Prayer from Alexander to Constantine: A Critical Anthology*, edited by Mark Kiley et al., 211–16. London: Routledge, 1997.

Dowey, Edward A. "Law in Luther and Calvin." *Theology Today* 41, no. 2 (1984): 146–53.

Duff, Nancy. "Pauline Apocalyptic and Theological Ethics." In *Apocalyptic and the New Testament: Essays in Honor of J. Louis Martyn*, edited by J. Marcus and M. L. Soards, 279–96. Sheffield: Sheffield Academic, 1989.

———. "The Significance of Pauline Apocalyptic for Ethics." In *Apocalyptic and the New Testament: Essays in Honor of J. Louis Martyn*, edited by J. Marcus and M. L. Soards. Sheffield: Sheffield Academic, 1989.

Dunn, James. *Jesus and the Spirit*. Grand Rapids: Eerdmans, 1975.

Dupré, Louis. *Kierkegaard as Theologian*. London: Sheed & Ward, 1964.

Eastman, Susan. "The Lord's Prayer." In *Prayer: Christian and Muslim Perspectives*, edited by D. Marshall and L. Mosher, 79–90. Georgetown: Georgetown University Press, 2013.

Ebeling, Gerhard. *Dogmatik des christlichen Glaubens*. Vol. 3. 3rd ed. Tübingen: Mohr Siebeck, 1983.

Einstein, Albert. "Geometry and Experience." In *Ideas and Opinions*, 232–46. New York: Souvenir, 1973.

Ellul, Jacques. *Prayer and Modern Man*. Translated by C. E. Hopkin. New York: Seabury, 1970.

Engel, Mary Potter. *John Calvin's Perspectival Anthropology*. Eugene, OR: Wipf & Stock, 2002.

Erasmus, Desiderius. *The Correspondence of Erasmus*. Vol. 2. Translated by R. A. B. Mynors and D. F. S. Thomson. Toronto: University of Toronto Press, 1975.

Feuerbach, Ludwig. *The Essence of Christianity*. Translated by M. Evans from the 2nd German ed. London: J. Chapman, 1853.

Firestone, Chris, and Nathan Jacobs. *In Defense of Kant's Religion*. Bloomington: Indiana University Press, 2008.

Fitzmyer, J. A. *First Corinthians*. Anchor Yale Bible 32. New Haven: Yale University Press, 2008.

Forde, Gerhard. *Captivation of the Will*. Edited by Steven Paulson. Grand Rapids: Eerdmans, 2005.

———. "Christian Life." In *Christian Dogmatics*, edited by Carl Braaten and Robert Jenson, 2:391–465. Philadelphia: Fortress, 1984.

———. *Justification by Faith: A Matter of Death and Life*. Mifflintown, PA: Sigler, 1990.

———. *The Law-Gospel Debate*. Minneapolis: Augsburg, 1969.

———. "The Lutheran View." In *Christian Spirituality: Five Views of Sanctification*, ed. D. L. Alexander, 13–32. Downers Grove, IL: InterVarsity, 1988.

———. *A More Radical Gospel: Essays on Eschatology, Authority, Atonement, and Ecumenism*. Edited by M. C. Mattes and S. Paulson. Grand Rapids: Eerdmans, 2004.

———. *The Preached God: Proclamation in Word and Sacrament*. Edited by M. C. Mattes and S. Paulson. Grand Rapids: Eerdmans, 2007.

———. *Theology Is for Proclamation*. Minneapolis: Fortress, 1990.

———. *Where God Meets Man: Luther's Down-to-Earth Approach to the Gospel*. Minneapolis: Augsburg, 1972. Reprint, 1991.

———. "The Work of Christ." In *Christian Dogmatics*, edited by C. E. Braaten and R. Jenson, 2:5–103. Philadelphia: Fortress, 1984.

Fox, George. *The Great Mystery of the Great Whore Unfolded*. Reprint ed. State College, PA: New Foundation, 1990.

Frei, Hans. *The Identity of Jesus Christ: The Hermeneutical Bases of Dogmatic Theology*. Philadelphia: Fortress, 1975.

Frey, Christofer. "Eschatology and Ethics." In *Eschatology in the Bible and in Jewish and Christian Tradition*, edited by H. Graf Reventlow, 62–74. Sheffield: Sheffield Academic, 1997.

Frey, Jörg. "Demythologizing Apocalyptic? On N. T. Wright's Paul, Apocalyptic Interpretation, and the Constraints of Construction." In *God and the Faithfulness of Paul: A Critical Examination of the Pauline Theology of N. T. Wright*, edited by C. Heilig, J. T. Hewitt, and M. F. Bird, 489–531. Tübingen: Mohr Siebeck, 2016.

Friesen, Abraham. "Anabaptism and Monasticism: A Study in the Development of Parallel Historical Patterns." *Journal of Mennonite Studies* 6 (1988): 174–97.

Funk, R. W., ed. *Apocalypticism*. Special issue, *Journal for Theology and the Church* 6 (1969).

Gathercole, Simon. "Sin in God's Economy: Agencies in Romans 1 and 7." In *Divine and Human Agency in Paul and His Cultural Environment*, edited by J. M. Barclay and S. J. Gathercole, 158–72. London: T&T Clark, 2008.

Gaventa, Beverly Roberts. *Apocalyptic Paul: Cosmos and Anthropos in Romans 5–8*. Waco: Baylor University Press, 2013.

———. "The Cosmic Power of Sin in Paul's Letter to the Romans." In Gaventa, *Our Mother Saint Paul*, 125–36.

———. "God Handed Them Over." In Gaventa, *Our Mother Saint Paul*, 113–23.

———. "'Neither Height nor Depth'—Cosmos and Soteriology in Paul's Letter to the Romans." In *Apocalyptic and the Future of Theology: With and beyond J. Louis Martyn*, edited by J. B. Davis and D. Harink, 183–99. Eugene, OR: Cascade, 2012.

———. "Neither Height nor Depth: Discerning the Cosmology of Romans." *Scottish Journal of Theology* 64 (2011): 265–78.

———. *Our Mother Saint Paul*. Louisville: Westminster John Knox, 2007.

———. "The Singularity of the Gospel Revisited." In *Galatians and Christian Theology: Justification, the Gospel, and Ethics in Paul's Letter*, edited by M. W. Elliott, S. J. Hafemann, N. T. Wright, and J. Frederick, 187–99. Grand Rapids: Baker Academic, 2014.

Genderen, J. van, and W. H. Velema. *Concise Reformed Dogmatics*. Translated by G. Bilkes and E. M. van der Maas. Phillipsburg, NJ: P&R, 2008.

Gillespie, Thomas W. "Studying Theology in Apocalyptic Times." *Princeton Seminary Bulletin* 23, no. 1 (2002): 1–10.

Gollwitzer, Helmut. *Introduction to Protestant Theology*. Translated by D. Cairns. Philadelphia: Westminster, 1982.

Gorringe, Timothy. *Karl Barth: Against Hegemony*. Oxford: Oxford University Press, 1999.

Gouwens, David J. *Kierkegaard as Religious Thinker*. Cambridge: Cambridge University Press, 1996.

Grab, Wilhelm, and Ulrich Barth, eds. *Gott im Selbstbewußtsein der Moderne: Zum neuzeitlichen Begriff der Religion*. Gütersloh: Gütersloher Verlaghaus, 1993.

Grabill, Stephen J. *Rediscovering the Natural Law in Reformed Theological Ethics*. Grand Rapids: Eerdmans, 2006.

Gray, John. *The Immortality Commission*. London: Penguin, 2012.

Gregory, Thomas M. "The Presbyterian Doctrine of Total Depravity." In *Soli Deo Gloria: Essays in Reformed Theology*, edited by R. C. Sproul, 36–53. Nutley, NJ: P&R, 1976.

Guggenheimer, Heinrich. *The Scholars' Haggadah: Ashkenazic, Sephardic, and Oriental Versions*. London: Jason Aronson, 1998.

Gunton, Colin. *The Actuality of Atonement: A Study of Metaphor, Rationality, and the Christian Tradition*. Edinburgh: T&T Clark, 1989.

Hadot, Pierre. *Philosophy as a Way of Life*. Translated by M. Chase. Oxford: Blackwell, 1995.

Hailsham, Lord. *Elective Dictatorship*. London: British Broadcasting Corporation, 1976.

Hampson, Daphne. *Kierkegaard: Exposition and Critique*. Oxford: Oxford University Press, 2013.

Hardy, Dan. "Created and Redeemed Sociality." In *God's Ways with the World: Thinking and Practicing Christian Faith*, 188–205. Edinburgh: T&T Clark, 1996.

Harink, Douglas. *Paul among the Postliberals: Pauline Theology beyond Christendom and Modernity*. Grand Rapids: Brazos, 2003.

―――. "Paul and Israel: An Apocalyptic Reading." *Pro Ecclesia* 16, no. 4 (2007): 359–80.

Harnack, Adolf von. *What Is Christianity?* Translated by T. B. Saunders. London: Williams and Norgate, 1901.

Harrisville, Roy A. "Christian Life in Light of the Cross." *Lutheran Quarterly* 23 (2009): 218–32.

Harvey, Barry. *Taking Hold of the Real: Dietrich Bonhoeffer and the Profound Worldliness of Christianity.* Eugene, OR: Cascade, 2015.

Harvie, Timothy. "Living the Future: The Kingdom of God in the Theologies of Jürgen Moltmann and Wolfhart Pannenberg." *International Journal of Systematic Theology* 10, no. 2 (2008): 149–64.

Hasselmann, Niels. "The Lordship of Christ in Ecumenical Discussion." *Lutheran Forum* 14 (1967): 93–101.

Hawthorne, Gerald F. "The Imitation of Christ: Discipleship in Philippians." In *Patterns of Discipleship in the New Testament*, edited by R. N. Longenecker, 163–79. Grand Rapids: Eerdmans, 1996.

Hayek, Friedrich A. *Law, Legislation and Liberty.* Rev. ed. 3 vols. London: Routledge, 1982.

Hays, Richard. *First Corinthians.* Interpretation. Louisville: John Knox, 1997.

―――. *The Moral Vision of the New Testament.* New York: HarperCollins, 1996.

―――. "'Why Do You Stand Looking Up toward Heaven?' New Testament Eschatology at the Turn of the Millennium." *Modern Theology* 16, no. 1 (2000): 115–35.

Healy, Nicholas M. *Church, World and the Christian Life.* Cambridge: Cambridge University Press, 2000.

Heinemann, Joseph. "The Background of Jesus' Prayer in the Jewish Liturgical Tradition." In *The Lord's Prayer and Jewish Liturgy*, edited by J. J. Petuchowski and M. Brocke, 81–92. London: Burns & Oates, 1978.

Hengel, Martin. *The Charismatic Leader and His Followers.* Translated by J. C. G. Greig. Edinburgh: T&T Clark, 1981.

Heppe, Heinrich. *Reformed Dogmatics.* Edited by E. Bizer. Translated by G. T. Thomson. London: Allen & Unwin, 1950.

Hoye, William. *The Emergence of Eternal Life.* Cambridge: Cambridge University Press, 2014.

Jaeger, Werner. *Early Christianity and Greek Paideia.* Cambridge, MA: Harvard University Press, 1961.

Jennings, Theodore W., Jr. "Apocalyptic and Contemporary Theology." *Quarterly Review* 4, no. 3 (1984): 54–68.

Jenson, Robert. "Apocalypticism and Messianism in Twentieth Century German Theology." In *Messianism, Apocalypse and Redemption in Twentieth Century*

German Thought, edited by W. Cristaudo and W. Baker, 3–12. Adelaide: ATF Press, 2006.

Jeremias, Joachim. "The Lord's Prayer in Modern Research." *Expository Times* 71, no. 5 (1960): 141–46.

Jewett, Robert. *Romans: A Commentary*. Minneapolis: Fortress, 2007.

Jones, Ken Sundet. "The Apocalyptic Luther." *Word & World* 25, no. 3 (2005): 308–16.

Jüngel, Eberhard. *Death, the Riddle and the Mystery*. Translated by I. Nicol and U. Nicol. Philadelphia: Fortress, 1975.

———. "The Emergence of the New." In *Theological Essays II*, 35–58.

———. "Die Ewigkeit des ewigen Lebens." In *Ganz Werden: Theologische Erörterungen V*, 345–53. Tübingen: Mohr Siebeck, 2003.

———. *The Freedom of a Christian: Luther's Significance for Contemporary Theology*. Translated by R. A. Harrisville. Minneapolis: Augsburg, 1988.

———. *God as the Mystery of the World*. Translated by D. Guder. Edinburgh: T&T Clark, 1983.

———. *Justification: The Heart of the Christian Faith*. Translated by John Webster. Edinburgh: T&T Clark, 2001.

———. "Der königliche Mensch: Eine christologische Reflexion auf die Würde des Menschen in der Theologie Karl Barths." In *Barth Studien*, 233–45. Gütersloh: Gütersloher Verlaghaus, 1982.

———. "The Last Judgment as an Act of Grace." *Louvain Studies* 15 (1990): 389–405.

———. "On the Dogmatic Significance of the Historical Jesus." In *Theological Essays II*, 82–119.

———. *Theological Essays II*. Edited by John Webster. Translated by Arnold Neufeldt-Fast. Edinburgh: T&T Clark, 1995.

———. "Value-Free Truth: The Christian Experience of Truth in the Struggle against the 'Tyranny of Values.'" In *Theological Essays II*, 191–215.

Kant, Immanuel. *Critique of Practical Reason*. In *Practical Philosophy*, edited and translated by M. J. Gregor, 133–272. Cambridge: Cambridge University Press, 1996.

———. *Religion within the Boundaries of Mere Reason*. In *Religion and Rational Theology*, edited and translated by A. Wood and G. di Giovanni, 55–215. Cambridge: Cambridge University Press, 1996.

———. *Religion within the Limits of Reason Alone*. Translated by T. M. Greene and H. H. Hudson. New York: Harper, 1960.

Käsemann, Ernst. "The Beginning of the Gospel: The Message of the Kingdom of God." In Käsemann, *On Being a Disciple of the Crucified Nazarene*, 3–14.

———. *Commentary on Romans*. Translated by G. W. Bromiley. London: SCM, 1980.

———. "God's Image and Sinners." In *On Being a Disciple of the Crucified Nazarene*, 108–19.

———. "Healing the Possessed." In *On Being a Disciple of the Crucified Nazarene*, 195–205.

———. "Justice for the Unjust." In *On Being a Disciple of the Crucified Nazarene*, 226–34.

———. *Kirchliche Konflikte*. Vol. 1. Gottingen: Vandenhoeck & Ruprecht, 1982.

———. *New Testament Questions of Today*. Translated by W. J. Monague. London: SCM, 1969.

———. *On Being a Disciple of the Crucified Nazarene*. Translated by R. A. Harrisville. Grand Rapids: Eerdmans, 2010.

———. "One Lord Alone." *Expository Times* 110 (1999): 249–51.

———. "On Paul's Anthropology." In *Perspectives on Paul*, translated by M. Kohl, 1–31. Philadelphia: Fortress, 1971.

———. "On the Subject of Primitive Christian Apocalyptic." In *New Testament Questions of Today*, 108–37.

———. "The Righteousness of God in an Unrighteous World." In *On Being a Disciple of the Crucified Nazarene*, 181–94.

———. "Righteousness of God in Paul." In *New Testament Questions of Today*, 168–82.

———. "Some Thoughts on the Theme 'Doctrine of Reconciliation in the New Testament.'" In *The Future of Our Religious Past: Essays in Honour of Rudolf Bultmann*, translated by C. E. Carlston and R. P. Scharlemann, edited by J. M. Robinson, 49–64. London: SCM, 1971.

———. "Theologians and the Laity." In *New Testament Questions of Today*, 286–300.

———. "A Theological Review." In *On Being a Disciple of the Crucified Nazarene*, xii–xxi.

———. *The Wandering People of God*. Translated by R. A. Harrisville and I. L. Sandberg. Philadelphia: Augsburg, 1984.

———. "What I Have Unlearned in 50 Years as a German Theologian." *Currents in Theology and Mission* 15 (1988): 325–35.

Kaufman, Gordon D. *Systematic Theology: A Historicist Perspective*. New York: Charles Scribner's Sons, 1968.

Kay, James F. *Christus Praesens: A Reconsideration of Rudolf Bultmann's Christology*. Grand Rapids: Eerdmans, 1994.

———. Review of *Paul among the Postliberals*, by Douglas Harink. *Union Seminary Quarterly Review* 56, nos. 3–4 (2002): 203–5.

———. "The Word of the Cross at the Turn of the Ages." *Interpretation* 53, no. 1 (1999): 44–56.

Keck, Leander. "Justification of the Ungodly and Ethics." In *Rechtfertigung: Festschrift für Ernst Käsemann*, edited by J. Friedrich et al., 199–209. Munich: J. C. B. Mohr, 1976.

———. "Paul and Apocalyptic Theology." *Interpretation* 38 (1984): 229–41.

————. *Paul and His Letters*. Rev. ed. Minneapolis: Fortress, 1988.

Keller, Catherine. *Apocalypse Then and Now: A Feminist Guide to the End of the World*. Boston: Beacon, 1996.

————. *God and Power: Counter-Apocalyptic Journeys*. Minneapolis: Fortress, 2005.

Kelsey, David. *Eccentric Existence: A Theological Anthropology*. 2 vols. Louisville: Westminster John Knox, 2009.

Kerr, Nathan R. *Christ, History and Apocalyptic: The Politics of Christian Mission*. London: SCM, 2008.

Kierkegaard, Søren. *Christian Discourses*. Edited and translated by H. V. Hong and E. H. Hong. Princeton: Princeton University Press, 1997.

————. *The Concept of Anxiety*. Edited and translated by R. Thomte and A. B. Anderson. Princeton: Princeton University Press, 1980.

————. *Concluding Unscientific Postscript*. Edited and translated by H. V. Hong and E. H. Hong. Princeton: Princeton University Press, 1992.

————. *Eighteen Upbuilding Discourses*. Edited and translated by H. V. Hong and E. H. Hong. Princeton: Princeton University Press, 1990.

————. *Either/Or*. 2 vols. Edited and translated by H. V. Hong and E. H. Hong. Princeton: Princeton University Press, 1987.

————. *For Self-Examination / Judge for Yourself!* Edited and translated by H. V. Hong and E. H. Hong. Princeton: Princeton University Press, 1990.

————. "He Must Increase; I Must Decrease." In *Eighteen Upbuilding Discourses*, 275–89.

————. "Journal AA 18 (1835)." In *Kierkegaard's Journals and Notebooks*, vol. 1, translated by H. V. Hong and E. H. Hong, edited by N. J. Cappelcørn et al., 29–31. Princeton: Princeton University Press, 2007.

————. *Journals and Papers*. 4 volumes. Translated and edited by H. V. Hong and E. H. Hong. Bloomington: Indiana University Press, 1967–78.

————. *Philosophical Fragments, Johannes Climacus*. Translated by H. V. Hong and E. H. Hong. Princeton: Princeton University Press, 1985.

————. *The Point of View*. Edited and translated by H. V. Hong and E. H. Hong. Princeton: Princeton University Press, 1998.

————. "Thoughts That Wound from Behind—For Upbuilding." In *Christian Discourses*, 161–62.

————. "To Need God Is a Human Being's Highest Perfection." In *Eighteen Upbuilding Discourses*, 297–326.

————. *Works of Love*. Edited and translated by H. V. Hong and E. H. Hong. Princeton: Princeton University Press, 1995.

Koch, Klaus. *Ratlos vor der Apokalyptik*. Gütersloh: Gütersloher Verlaghaus, 1970. Translated into English by M. Kohl as *The Rediscovery of Apocalyptic*. London: SCM, 1972.

Köpf, Ulrich. "Mendicant Orders." In *Religion Past and Present*, edited by H. D. Betz, D. S. Browning, B. Janowski, and E. Jüngel, vol. 8, s.v. Leiden: Brill, 2012.

Kraus, Hans-Joachim. "The Contemporary Relevance of Calvin's Theology." In *Toward the Future of Reformed Theology: Tasks, Topics, Traditions*, edited by D. Willis and M. Welker, 323–38. Grand Rapids: Eerdmans, 1999.

———. *Systematische Theologie*. Neukirchener: Neukirchener Verlag, 1983.

Kreck, Walter. *Die Zukunft des Gekommenen: Grundprobleme der Eschatologie*. Berlin: Evangelische Verlagsanstalt, 1961.

Krötke, Wolf. "Hope in the Last Judgment and Human Dignity." *International Journal of Systematic Theology* 2, no. 3 (2000): 270–82.

———. *Sin and Nothingness in the Theology of Karl Barth*. Translated by P. G. Ziegler and C.-M. Bammel. Princeton: Princeton Theological Seminary, 2005.

———. *Die Universalität des offenbaren Gottes: Gesammelte Aufsätze*. Munich: Christian Kaiser, 1985.

Ladd, George Eldon. *Jesus and the Kingdom: The Eschatology of Biblical Realism*. London: SPCK, 1966.

Lane, Anthony. "Anthropology." In *The Calvin Handbook*, translated by H. J. Baron et al., edited by H. J. Selderhuis, 276–85. Grand Rapids: Eerdmans, 2009.

———. "The Influence upon Calvin of His Debate with Pighius." In *John Calvin: Student of the Church Fathers*, 179–90. Edinburgh: T&T Clark, 1999.

Law, William. *A Serious Call to a Devout and Holy Life*. Mahwah, NJ: Paulist Press, 1978.

Lehmann, Paul L. "A Christian Alternative to Natural Law." In *Die moderne Demokratie und ihr Recht: Festschrift für Gerhard Leibholz zum 65. Geburtstag*, edited by K. D. Bracher et al., 517–49. Tübingen: Mohr Siebeck, 1966.

———. *Christologie und Politik: Eine theologische Hermeneutik des Politischen*. Gottingen: Vandenhoeck & Ruprecht, 1987.

———. *The Decalogue and a Human Future*. Grand Rapids: Eerdmans, 1995.

———. *Ethics in a Christian Context*. New York: Harper & Row, 1963.

———. "Faith and Worldliness in Bonhoeffer's Thought." In *Bonhoeffer in a World Come of Age*, edited by P. Vorkink II, 25–45. Philadelphia: Fortress, 1968.

———. "Karl Barth, Theologian of Permanent Revolution." *Union Seminary Quarterly Review* 28, no. 1 (1972): 67–81.

———. "Law." In *A Handbook of Christian Theology*, edited by M. Halverston and A. C. Cohen, 203–7. New York: Living Age Books, 1958.

———. "Law as a Function of Forgiveness." *Oklahoma Law Review* 12, no. 1 (1959): 102–12.

———. "The Metaphorical Reciprocity between Theology and Law." *Journal of Law and Religion* 3, no. 1 (1985): 179–92.

———. "Toward a Protestant Analysis of the Ethical Problem." In *Journal of Religion* 24, no. 1 (1944): 1–16.

———. *The Transfiguration of Politics.* New York: Harper & Row, 1975.

Levering, Matthew. *Biblical Natural Law.* Oxford: Oxford University Press, 2008.

Lewis, Scott M. *What Are They Saying about New Testament Apocalyptic?* New York: Paulist Press, 2004.

Locher, Gottfried W. *Zwingli's Thought: New Perspectives.* Leiden: Brill, 1981.

Lochman, Jan Milič. *The Lord's Prayer.* Translated by G. W. Bromiley. Grand Rapids: Eerdmans, 1990.

Locke, John. *Second Treatise of Government.* Translated by C. B. Macpherson. Indianapolis: Hackett, 1980.

Lohmeyer, Ernst. *The Lord's Prayer.* Translated by J. Bowden. London: Collins, 1965.

Long, D. Stephen. *Hebrews.* Louisville: Westminster John Knox, 2011.

Lowe, Walter. "Prospects for a Postmodern Christian Theology: Apocalyptic without Reserve." *Modern Theology* 15, no. 1 (January 1999): 17–24.

———. "Why We Need Apocalyptic." *Scottish Journal of Theology* 63, no. 1 (2010): 41–53.

Luther, Martin. "Babylonian Captivity of the Church" (1520). In *Word and Sacrament II*, translated by A. T. W. Steinhäuser, edited by A. R. Wentz, 1–126. Luther's Works 36. St. Louis: Concordia, 1959.

———. *The Bondage of the Will.* Translated by J. I Packer and O. R. Johnston. Westwood: Revel, 1959.

———. "The Freedom of a Christian." In *Selected Writings of Martin Luther*, edited by G. Tappert, 9–53. Minneapolis: Fortress, 2007.

———. "The Judgment of Martin Luther on Monastic Vows" (1521). In *The Christian in Society I*, edited and translated by M. Atkinson, 243–400. Luther's Works 44. Philadelphia: Fortress, 1966.

———. *Lectures on Galatians.* Luther's Works 27. Philadelphia: Concordia, 1963.

———. *Paul's Epistle to the Galatians.* New York: R. Carter, 1856.

———. Smalcald Articles. In *Triglot Concordia: The Symbolical Books of the Evangelical Lutheran Church.* St. Louis: Concordia, 1921.

Lutheran Church, Evangelical. *Book of Concord: The Confessions of the Evangelical Lutheran Church.* Edited by R. Kolb and T. J. Wengert. Translated by C. P. Arand et al. Minneapolis: Fortress, 2000.

Luz, Ulrich. *Matthew 1–7.* Translated by W. C. Linss. Minneapolis: Augsburg Fortress, 1989.

MacKinnon, Donald M. "Prayer, Worship, and Life." In *Christian Faith and Communist Faith*, edited by D. M. MacKinnon, 242–56. London: Macmillan, 1953.

Mangina, Joseph. *Karl Barth: Theologian of Christian Witness.* Louisville: Westminster John Knox, 2004.

———. *Revelation.* Grand Rapids: Brazos, 2010.

Marcus, Joel. *Mark 1–8*. New York: Doubleday, 1999.

Marsh, Charles. *Reclaiming Dietrich Bonhoeffer: The Promise of His Theology*. Oxford: Oxford University Press, 1994.

Marsh, John. *The Gospel of St. John*. London: Penguin, 1991.

Martyn, J. Louis. "Afterword: The Human Moral Drama." In *Apocalyptic Paul: Cosmos and Anthropos in Romans 5–8*, edited by Beverly Gaventa, 157–66. Waco: Baylor University Press, 2013.

———. "Apocalyptic Antinomies." In *Theological Issues in the Letters of Paul*, 111–24.

———. "The Apocalyptic Gospel in Galatians." *Interpretation* 54, no. 3 (2000): 246–66.

———. "The Church's Everyday Life." In *Theological Issues in the Letters of Paul*, 231–97.

———. "De-apocalypticizing Paul: An Essay Focused on *Paul and the Stoics* by Troels Engberg-Pedersen." *Journal for the Study of the New Testament* 24 (2002): 61–102.

———. "Epilogue: An Essay in Pauline Meta-ethics." In *Divine and Human Agency in Paul and His Cultural Environment*, edited by J. M. Barclay and S. J. Gathercole, 173–83. London: T&T Clark, 2008.

———. "Epistemology at the Turn of the Ages." In *Theological Issues in the Letters of Paul*, 89–110.

———. "From Paul to Flannery O'Connor with the Power of Grace." In *Theological Issues in the Letters of Paul*, 279–97.

———. *Galatians*. Anchor Bible 33A. New York: Doubleday, 1997.

———. "God's Way of Making Right What Is Wrong." In *Theological Issues in the Letters of Paul*, 141–56.

———. "The Gospel Invades Philosophy." In *Paul, Philosophy, and the Theopolitical Vision*, edited by Douglas Harink, 13–33. Eugene, OR: Cascade, 2010.

———. *History and Theology in the Fourth Gospel*. 2nd ed. Nashville: Abingdon, 1978.

———. "Listening to John and Paul on Gospel and Scripture." *Word & World* 12, no. 1 (1992): 68–81.

———. "*Nomos* plus Genitive Noun in Paul: The History of God's Law." In *Early Christianity and Classical Culture: Comparative Studies in Honor of Abraham J. Malherbe*, edited by J. T. Fitzgerald and T. H. Oldbricht, 575–87. Leiden: Brill, 2003.

———. "Paul and His Jewish Christian Interpreters." *Union Seminary Quarterly Review* 42 (1987–88): 1–15.

———. Review of *New Testament Questions of Today*, by Ernst Käsemann. *Union Seminary Quarterly Review* 25, no. 4 (1970): 556–58.

———. *Theological Issues in the Letters of Paul*. Edited by J. Barclay, J. Marcus, and J. Riches. Edinburgh: T&T Clark, 1997.

———. "World without End or Twice-Invaded World?" In *Shaking Heaven and Earth*, edited by C. Roy Yoder et al., 117–32. Louisville: Westminster John Knox, 2005.

Matlock, R. Barry. *Unveiling the Apocalyptic Paul*. London: T&T Clark, 1996.

Mattes, Mark. "Gerhard Forde on Revisioning Theology in Light of the Gospel." *Lutheran Quarterly* 13, no. 4 (2006): 373–93.

Mazaheri, John H. "Calvin's Interpretation of 'Thy Kingdom Come.'" *Zwingliana* 40 (2013): 101–11.

McBride, Jennifer. *The Church for the World: A Theology of Public Witness*. Oxford: Oxford University Press, 2014.

McCormack, Bruce L. "Can We Still Speak of 'Justification by Faith'? An In-House Debate with Apocalyptic Readings of Paul." In *Galatians and Christian Theology: Justification, the Gospel, and Ethics in Paul's Letter*, edited by M. W. Elliott, S. J. Hafemann, N. T. Wright, and J. Frederick, 159–84. Grand Rapids: Baker Academic, 2014.

———. "Longing for a New World: On Socialism, Eschatology and Apocalyptic in Barth's Early Dialectical Theology." In *Theologie im Umbruch der Moderne: Karl Barths frühe Dialektische Theologie*, edited by G. Pfleiderer and H. Matern, 135–49. Zurich: Theologischer Verlag, 2014.

———. "What's at Stake in Current Debates over Justification? The Crisis of Protestantism in the West." In *Justification: What's at Stake in the Current Debates?*, edited by M. Husbands and D. Trier, 81–117. Downers Grove, IL: InterVarsity, 2004.

McKee, Elsie Anne. "John Calvin's Teaching on the Lord's Prayer." In *The Lord's Prayer: Perspectives for Reclaiming Christian Prayer*, edited by D. L. Migliore, 88–106. Grand Rapids: Eerdmans, 1993.

McKim, Donald K. "Karl Barth on the Lord's Prayer." In Karl Barth, *Prayer: 50th Anniversary Edition*, 124–31. Louisville: Westminster John Knox, 2002.

McNeil, John T. "Natural Law in the Teaching of the Reformers." *Journal of Religion* 26, no. 3 (1946): 168–82.

Meeks, Wayne. "Apocalyptic Discourse and Strategies of Goodness." *Journal of Religion* 80, no. 3 (2000): 461–75.

Meyer, Paul. *The Word in the World*. Louisville: Westminster John Knox, 2004.

Milbank, John. "Invocations of Clio: A Response." *Journal of Religious Ethics* 33 (2005): 3–44.

Minear, Paul S. *The Bible and the Historian: Breaking the Silence about God in Biblical Studies*. Nashville: Abingdon, 2002.

———. *The Kingdom and the Power*. Philadelphia: Westminster, 1950.

Moltmann, Jürgen. *The Coming of God: Christian Eschatology*. Translated by M. Kohl. London: SCM, 1996.

———. "The Final Judgment: Sunrise of Christ's Liberating Justice." *Anglican Theological Review* 89, no. 4 (2007): 565–76.

———. *Herrschaft Christi und soziale Wirklichkeit nach Dietrich Bonhoeffer*. Theologische Existenz heute 71. Munich: Christian Kaiser, 1959.

————. "Sun of Righteousness: The Gospel about Judgment and the New Creation of All Things." In *Sun of Righteousness, Arise! God's Future for Humanity and the Earth*, translated by M. Kohl, 127–48. London: SCM, 2010.

————. *Theologie der Hoffnung*. Munich: Christian Kaiser, 1965.

————. *The Theology of Hope*. Translated by J. W. Leitch. London: SCM, 1967.

————. "Trends in Eschatology." In *The Future of Creation*, translated by M. Kohl, 18–40. Philadelphia: Fortress, 1979.

————. *The Way of Jesus Christ: Christology in Messianic Dimensions*. Translated by M. Kohl. London: SCM, 2000.

Moo, Douglas. *The Epistle to the Romans*. Grand Rapids: Eerdmans, 1996.

Morse, Christopher. *The Difference Heaven Makes: Rehearing the Gospel as News*. London: T&T Clark, 2010.

————. "'If Johannes Weiss Is Right . . .': A Brief Retrospective on Apocalyptic Theology." In *Apocalyptic and the Future of Theology: With and beyond J. Louis Martyn*, edited by J. B. Davis and D. Harink, 137–53. Eugene, OR: Cascade, 2012.

————. *Not Every Spirit: A Dogmatics of Christian Disbelief*. Valley Forge, PA: Trinity Press International, 1994.

Müller, E. R. Karl. "Jesus Christ, Threefold Office of." In *New Schaff-Herzog Encyclopedia of Religious Knowledge*, vol. 6, edited by S. Macauley Jackson, s.v. Grand Rapids: Baker, 1953.

Müller, Paul. "Der Begriff 'das Erbauliche' bei Sören Kierkegaard." *Kerygma und Dogma* 31, no. 2 (1985): 116–34.

Neufeld, Vernon H. *The Earliest Christian Confessions*. Leiden: Brill, 1963.

Neusner, W. H. "*Exercitum Pietatis*—Calvin's Interpretation of the Lord's Prayer." In Supplement 10, *Acta Theologica* 28, no. 2 (2008): 95–107.

Niebuhr, Reinhold. *The Nature and Destiny of Man*. Vol. 2. New York: Charles Scribner's Sons, 1964.

Niederwimmer, Kurt. *The Didache*. Edited by H. W. Attridge. Translated by L. M. Maloney. Minneapolis: Fortress, 1998.

Niesel, Wilhelm. *Reformed Symbolics: A Comparison of Catholicism, Orthodoxy, and Protestantism*. Translated by D. Lewis. London: Oliver & Boyd, 1962.

O'Connor, Flannery. *Mystery and Manners*. Edited by S. Fitzgerald and R. Fitzgerald. New York: Farrar, Straus & Giroux, 1961.

O'Regan, Cyril. "The Rule of Chaos and the Perturbation of Love." In *Kierkegaard and Christian Faith*, edited by Paul Martens and C. Stephen Evans, 131–56. Waco: Baylor University Press, 2016.

————. *Theology and the Spaces of Apocalyptic*. Milwaukee: Marquette University Press, 2009.

Origen. *Commentariis in evangelium Matthaei*. In *Origenes Werke*. Vol. 12. Edited by E. Klostermann and E. Benz, 13–235. Leipzig: Teubner, 1941.

Orr, William F., and James A. Walther. *1 Corinthians*. Anchor Bible 32. Garden City, NY: Doubleday, 1976.

Outka, Gene. "Following at a Distance: Ethics and the Identity of Jesus." In *Scriptural Authority and Narrative Interpretation*, edited by G. Green, 144–60. Philadelphia: Fortress, 1987.

Overbeck, Franz. *On the Christianity of Theology*. Edited and translated by J. Wilson. San Jose: Pickwick, 2002.

Ovey, Michael J. "Appropriating Aulén? Employing *Christus Victor* Models of the Atonement." *Churchman* 124, no. 4 (2010): 297–330.

Paige, Terrence. "1 Corinthians 12:2—A Pagan *Pompe?*" *Journal for the Study of the New Testament* 44 (1991): 57–65.

Pannenberg, Wolfhart. *Jesus-God-Man*. Translated by L. L. Wilkins and D. A. Priebe. Philadelphia: Westminster, 1976.

———. *Offenbarung als Geschichte*. Gottingen: Vandenhoeck & Ruprecht, 1963.

———. "On the Theology of Law." In *Ethics*, translated by K. Crim, 23–56. London: Search, 1981.

———. *Systematic Theology*. Translated by G. W. Bromiley. 3 vols. Grand Rapids: Eerdmans; London: T&T Clark, 1991–98. Electronic book, London: Continuum, 2004.

Partee, Charles. *The Theology of John Calvin*. Louisville: Westminster John Knox, 2008.

Pattison, George. "A Dialogical Approach to Kierkegaard's *Upbuilding Discourses*." *Zeitschrift für neuere Theologiegeschichte* 3, no. 2 (1996): 185–202.

———. *Kierkegaard and the Crisis of Faith*. London: SPCK, 1997.

Paulson, Steven. "The Place of Eschatology in Modern Theology." *Lutheran Quarterly* 12, no. 3 (1998): 327–53.

Pearson, Lori. *Beyond Essence: Ernst Troeltsch as Historian and Theorist of Christianity*. Cambridge, MA: Harvard University Press, 2008.

Petuchowski, Jakob J. "Jewish Prayer Texts of the Rabbinic Period." In *The Lord's Prayer and Jewish Liturgy*, edited by J. J. Petuchowski and M. Brocke, 21–44. London: Burns & Oates, 1978.

Pfeifer, Hans. "Die Gestalten der Rechtfertigung: Zur Frage nach der Struktur der Theologie Dietrich Bonhoeffers." *Keygma und Dogma* 18 (1972): 177–201.

Podmore, Simon D. *Kierkegaard and the Self before God: Anatomy of the Abyss*. Bloomington: Indiana University Press, 2011.

Polkinghorne, John. *The Way the World Is: The Christian Perspective of a Scientist*. Rev. ed. Louisville: Westminster John Knox, 2007.

Polyani, Michael. *Personal Knowledge*. Chicago: University of Chicago Press, 1958.

Presbyterian Church (U.S.A.). *Book of Confessions: Study Edition*. Louisville: Geneva, 1999.

Prüller-Jagenteufel, Gunter M. *Befreit zur Verantwortung: Sünde und Versöhnung in der Ethik Dietrich Bonhoeffers*. Münster: LIT Verlag, 2004.

Quistorp, Heinrich. *Calvin's Doctrine of the Last Things*. Translated by H. Knight. London: Lutterworth, 1955.

Rasmussen, Larry. *Dietrich Bonhoeffer: His Significance for North Americans*. Minneapolis: Fortress, 1990.

Rendtorff, Trutz. *Theologie in der Moderne*. Gütersloh: Gütersloher Verlaghaus, 1991.

Renz, Horst, and Friedrich W. Graf, eds. *Troeltsch-Studien: Über Religion im Prozeß der Aufklärung*. Gütersloh: Gerd Mohn, 1984.

Rieske-Braun, Uwe. *Duellem mirabile: Studium zum Kampfmotif in Martin Luthers Theologie*. Gottingen: Vandenhoeck & Ruprecht, 1999.

Ritschl, Albrecht. *The Christian Doctrine of Justification and Reconciliation*. Translated by H. R. Mackintosh. Edinburgh: T&T Clark, 1902.

———. *Instruction in the Christian Religion*. In *Three Essays*, translated by P. Hefner, 219–92. Philadelphia: Fortress, 1972.

Robertson, Archibald, and Alfred Plummer. *The First Epistle of St. Paul to the Corinthians*. International Critical Commentary. Edinburgh: T&T Clark, 1911.

Robinson, Marilynne. "Dietrich Bonhoeffer." In *The Death of Adam: Essays on Modern Thought*, 108–25. Boston: Houghton Mifflin, 1998.

Rorty, Richard. *Objectivity, Relativism and Truth*. Cambridge: Cambridge University Press, 1991.

Rose, Matthew. *Ethics with Barth: God, Metaphysics and Morals*. Farnham, UK: Ashgate, 2010.

Rossow, Francis C. "The Hound of Heaven, A Twitch upon the Thread, and Romans 8:31–39." *Concordia Journal* 23 (1997): 91–98.

Rummel, Erika, ed. *The Erasmus Reader*. Toronto: University of Toronto Press, 1990.

Runia, Klaas. "Eschatology in the Second Half of the Twentieth Century." *Calvin Theological Journal* 32 (1997): 105–35.

Sanday, William. "The Apocalyptic Element in the Gospels." *Hibbert Journal* 10 (1911): 83–109.

Sauter, Gerhard. *Eschatological Rationality: Theological Issues in Focus*. Grand Rapids: Baker, 1996.

———. *What Dare We Hope? Reconsidering Eschatology*. Harrisburg, PA: Trinity Press International, 1999.

———. *Zukunft und Verheißung: Das Problem der Zukunft in der gegenwärtigen theologischen und philosophischen Diskussion*. Zurich: Theologischer Verlag, 1965.

Scheiber, Karin. "Calvin und die Freiheit." *Neue Zeitschrift für Systematische Theologie und Religionsphilosophie* 52, no. 2 (2010): 193–207.

Schleiermacher, Friedrich D. E. *The Christian Faith*. Translated by H. R. Mackintosh. Edinburgh: T&T Clark, 1928.

Schmid, Heinrich. *The Doctrinal Theology of the Evangelical Lutheran Church*. 3rd ed. Translated by C. A. Hay and H. E. Jacobs. Minneapolis: Augsburg, 1961.

Schmidt, Karl Ludwig. "Basileia." *Theological Dictionary of the New Testament*, edited by G. Kittel and G. Friedrich, translated by G. W. Bromiley, 1:579–90. Grand Rapids: Eerdmans, 1964.

Schnabel, Eckhard J. *Der erste Brief des Paulus an die Korinther*. Wuppertal: Brockhaus Verlag, 2006.

Scholer, David N. "'The God of Peace Will Shortly Crush Satan under Your Feet' (Romans 16:20a): The Function of Apocalyptic Eschatology in Paul." *Ex Audito* 6 (1990): 53–61.

Schrage, Wolfgang. *Der erste Brief an die Korinther*. Evangelisch-katholischer Kommentar zum Neuen Testament 7/3, *1 Kor 11,17–14,40*. Neukirchen: Neukirchener Verlag, 1999.

Schwartz, Hans. *Eschatology*. Grand Rapids: Eerdmans, 2000.

Schweitzer, Albert. *The Mystery of the Kingdom of God*. Translated by W. Lowrie. New York: Dodd, Mead, 1914.

———. *The Quest of the Historical Jesus*. Translated by W. Montgomery. London: A&C Black, 1911.

Schweitzer, Eduard. *Lordship and Discipleship*. London: SCM, 1960.

Schwöbel, Christoph. "Last Things First: The Century of Eschatology in Retrospect." In *The Future as God's Gift: Explorations in Christian Eschatology*, edited by David Fergusson and Marcel Sarot, 217–41. Edinburgh: T&T Clark, 2000.

Scroggs, Robin. "Ernst Käsemann: The Divine Agent Provocateur." *Religious Studies Review* 11, no. 3 (1985): 260–63.

Sherman, Robert J. *King, Priest, and Prophet: A Trinitarian Theology of Atonement*. London: T&T Clark, 2004.

Smythe, Shannon Nichole. *Forensic Apocalyptic Theology: Karl Barth and the Doctrine of Justification*. Minneapolis: Fortress, 2016.

———. "Karl Barth in Conversation with Pauline Apocalypticism." In *Karl Barth in Conversation*, edited by W. T. McMaken and D. Congdon, 195–210. Eugene, OR: Wipf & Stock, 2014.

Spence, Alan. "A Unified Theory of the Atonement." *International Journal of Systematic Theology* 6, no. 4 (2004): 404–20.

Sponheim, Paul R. "Kierkegaard's View of a Christian." In *Kierkegaard's View of Christianity*, edited by Niels Thulstrup and Marie Mikulová, 182–91. Kierkegaardiana 1. Copenhagen: C. A. Reitzel, 1978.

Sprute, Jürgen. "Religionsphilosophische Aspekte der kantischen Ethik: Die Funktion der Postulatenlehre." *Neue Zeitschrift für systematische Theologie und Religionsphilosophie* 46, no. 1 (2004): 289–305.

Steckel, Clyde J. "Confessions of a Post-Eschatologist." *Theology Today* 64 (2007): 139–44.

Steinmetz, David. "Calvin and Patristic Exegesis." In *Calvin in Context*, 122–40. Oxford: Oxford University Press, 1995.

———. "Calvin and the Divided Self of Romans 7." In *Calvin in Context*, 110–21. Oxford: Oxford University Press, 1995.

Stendahl, Krister. "Your Kingdom Come." *Cross Currents* 32 (1982): 257–66.

Stewart, James S. "On a Neglected Emphasis in New Testament Theology." *Scottish Journal of Theology* 4, no. 3 (1951): 292–301.

Stuhlmacher, Peter. *Paul's Letter to the Romans*. Translated by S. Hafemann. Louisville: Westminster John Knox, 1994.

Stump, Eleanore. "Petitionary Prayer." *American Philosophical Quarterly* 16, no. 2 (1979): 81–91.

Tanner, Kathryn. "Eschatology without a Future?" In *The End of the World and the Ends of God: Science and Theology on Eschatology*, edited by J. Polkinghorne and M. Welker, 222–37. Harrisburg, PA: Trinity Press International, 2000.

———. "Justification and Justice in a Theology of Grace." *Theology Today* 55, no. 4 (2004): 510–23.

———. *Theories of Culture*. Minneapolis: Fortress, 1997.

Tertullian. *Adversus Marcionem*. Edited and translated by E. Evans. Oxford: Oxford University Press, 1972.

Thielicke, Helmut. *The Evangelical Faith*. Translated by G. W. Bromiley. Vol. 2. Edinburgh: T&T Clark, 1978.

———. *Theological Ethics*. Translated by W. H. Lazareth. Philadelphia: Fortress, 1966–69.

Thiselton, Anthony. *The First Epistle to the Corinthians: A Commentary on the Greek Text*. Grand Rapids: Eerdmans, 2000.

———. *The Last Things: A New Approach*. London: SCM, 2012.

Thomas à Kempis. *The Imitation of Christ*. Translated by A. Croft and H. Bolton. Milwaukee: Bruce Publications, 1949.

Thomas Aquinas. *Summa Theologia*. Edited and translated by the Fathers of the English Dominican Province. London: Burns, Oates & Washburne, 1920–42.

Thompson, Geoff. "From Invisible Redemption to Invisible Hopeful Action in Karl Barth." In *Messianism, Apocalypse and Redemption in Twentieth Century German Thought*, edited by W. Cristaudo and W. Baker, 49–62. Adelaide: ATF, 2006.

Thulstrup, Marie Mikulová. "Kierkegaard as an Edifying Christian Author." In Sponheim, *Kierkegaard's View of Christianity*, 179–82.

Tillich, Paul. "The Meaning of Providence" [Romans 8:38–39]. In *Shaking of the Foundations*, 104–7. New York: Charles Scribner's Sons, 1953.

———. "The Theologian (Part 1): 1 Cor. 12:1–11." In *Shaking of the Foundations*, 118–29. New York: Charles Scribner's Sons, 1953.

Torrance, T. F. "The Atonement: The Singularity of Christ and the Finality of the Cross; The Atonement and the Moral Order." In *Universalism and the Doctrine of Hell*, edited by N. M. de S. Cameron, 225–56. Carlisle, UK: Paternoster, 1992.

———. *Calvin's Doctrine of Man*. London: Lutterworth, 1949.

———. "The Concept of Order in Theology and Science." In *The Christian Frame of Mind*, 16–28. Edinburgh: Hansel, 1985.

———. *Divine and Contingent Order*. Oxford: Oxford University Press, 1981.

———. *Incarnation: The Person and Life of Christ*. Downers Grove, IL: InterVarsity, 2008.

———. *Juridical Law and Physical Law*. Edinburgh: Scottish Academic, 1982.

———. "Justification: Its Radical Nature and Place in Reformed Doctrine and Life." *Scottish Journal of Theology* 13, no. 3 (1960): 225–46.

———. *Kingdom and Church: A Study in the Theology of the Reformation*. Edinburgh: Oliver & Boyd, 1956.

———. "The Modern Eschatological Debate." *Evangelical Quarterly* 25 (1953): 45–54, 94–106, 167–78, 224–32.

———. "Revelation, Creation and Law." *Heythrop Journal* 37 (1996): 273–83.

———, ed. and trans. *School of Faith: The Catechisms of the Reformed Church*. London: James Clarke, 1959.

———. "Theological Rationality." In *God and Rationality*, 3–28. Oxford: Oxford University Press, 1971.

Triglot Concordia: The Symbolical Books of the Evangelical Lutheran Church. Translated by F. Bente. St. Louis: Concordia, 1921.

Troeltsch, Ernst. "An Apple from the Tree of Kierkegaard." In *The Beginnings of Dialectical Theology*, edited by J. M. Robinson, translated by L. De Grazia and K. R. Crim, 311–16. Richmond, VA: John Knox, 1968.

———. *The Christian Faith*. Translated by G. E. Paul. Minneapolis: Fortress, 1991.

———. *Kritische Gesamtausgabe*. Edited by F. W. Graf et al. Berlin: de Gruyter, 1998.

———. *Religion in History*. Translated by J. Luther Adams and W. E. Bense. Edinburgh: T&T Clark, 1999.

———. *The Social Teaching of the Christian Churches*. 2 vols. Translated by O. Wyon. Louisville: Westminster John Knox, 1992.

Turretin, Francis. *Institutes of Elenctic Theology*. Vol. 2. Philipsburg, NJ: P&R, 1994.

Ulrich, Hans G. "The Messianic Contours of Evangelical Ethics." In *The Freedom of a Christian Ethicist*, edited by B. Brock and M. Mawson, 39–63. London: T&T Clark, 2015.

Unnik, W. C. van. "Jesus: Anathema or Kyrios (1 Cor. 12:3)." In *Christ and Spirit in the New Testament*, edited by B. Lindars and S. S. Smalley, 113–26. Cambridge: Cambridge University Press, 1973.

VanDrunen, David. "The Context of Natural Law: John Calvin's Doctrine of the Two Kingdoms." *Journal of Church and State* 46 (2004): 503–25.

———. *Divine Covenants and Moral Order: A Biblical Theology of Natural Law*. Grand Rapids: Eerdmans, 2014.

———. *Natural Law and the Two Kingdoms: A Study in the Development of Reformed Social Thought*. Grand Rapids: Eerdmans, 2010.

———. "The Two Kingdoms Doctrine and the Relationship of Church and State in the Early Reformed Tradition." *Journal of Church and State* 49 (2007): 743–63.

Van Engen, John H., ed. *Devotio Moderna: Basic Writings*. New York: Paulist Press, 1988.

Vanhoozer, Kevin. "Effectual Call or Causal Effect? Summons, Sovereignty and Supervenient Grace." *Tyndale Bulletin* 49, no. 2 (1998): 213–51.

Visser 't Hooft, W. A. *The Kingship of Christ: An Interpretation of Recent European Theology*. London: SCM, 1948.

Vogel, Heinrich. "Shortened Course of Instructions for a Soldier of Jesus Christ." In *The Iron Ration of a Christian*, translated by W. A. Whitehouse, 217–24. London: SCM, 1941.

Vögtle, Anton. "The Lord's Prayer: A Prayer for Jews and Christians?" In *The Lord's Prayer and Jewish Liturgy*, edited by J. J. Petuchowski and M. Brocke, 93–117. London: Burns & Oates, 1978.

Volf, Miroslav. "Enter into Joy! Sin, Death, and the Life of the World to Come." In *The End of the World and the Ends of God: Science and Theology on Eschatology*, edited by J. Polkinghorne and M. Welker, 256–78. Harrisburg, PA: Trinity Press International, 2000.

Wainwright, Geoffrey. *For Our Salvation: Two Approaches to the Work of Christ*. Grand Rapids: Eerdmans, 1997.

Walls, Jerry, ed. *The Oxford Handbook of Eschatology*. Oxford: Oxford University Press, 2008.

Walsh, Sylvia. *Living Christianly: Kierkegaard's Dialectic of Christian Existence*. University Park: Pennsylvania State University Press, 2005.

Way, David V. *The Lordship of Christ: Ernst Käsemann's Interpretation of Paul's Theology*. Oxford: Clarendon, 1991.

Weaver, J. Denny. "Atonement for the Nonconstantinian Church." *Modern Theology* 6, no. 4 (1990): 307–23.

———. *Nonviolent Atonement*. 2nd ed. Grand Rapids: Eerdmans, 2011.

Weber, Max. *The Protestant Ethic and the Spirit of Capitalism*. New York: Charles Scribner's Sons, 1958.

Weber, Otto. *Foundations of Dogmatics*. Vol. 2. Translated by D. L. Guder. Grand Rapids: Eerdmans, 1971.

Webster, John. *Barth's Ethics of Reconciliation*. Cambridge: Cambridge University Press, 1995.

———. "Discipleship and Calling." *Scottish Bulletin of Evangelical Theology* 23 (2005): 133–47.

———. "Imitation of Christ." *Tyndale Bulletin* 37 (1986): 95–120.

———. "Reading the Bible: The Example of Barth and Bonhoeffer." In *Word and Church: Essays in Christian Dogmatics*, 87–112. 2nd ed. London: T&T Clark: 2006.

———. "The Self-Organizing Power of the Gospel of Christ." *International Journal of Systematic Theology* 3, no. 1 (2001): 69–82.

Weiss, Johannes. *Jesus' Proclamation of the Kingdom of God*. Translated by R. H. Hiers and D. L. Holland. Philadelphia: Fortress, 1971.

Wenz, Armin. "Natural Law and the Orders of Creation." In *Natural Law: A Lutheran Reappraisal*, edited by R. C. Ehlke, 79–96. St. Louis: Concordia, 2011.

West, Charles C. Review of *Dietrich Bonhoeffer: His Significance for North Americans*, by Larry Rasmussen. *Theology Today* 47, no. 4 (1991): 471–72.

Whaling, Frank, ed. *John and Charles Wesley: Selected Writings and Hymns*. Mahwah, NJ: Paulist Press, 1981.

Whitehouse, W. A. Review of *Juridical Law and Physical Law*, by T. F. Torrance. *Scottish Journal of Theology* 36, no. 3 (1983): 243–45.

Willard, Dallas. "Discipleship." In *The Oxford Handbook of Evangelical Theology*, edited by G. McDermott, 236–46. Oxford: Oxford University Press, 2010.

———. *The Great Omission: Reclaiming Jesus' Essential Teachings on Discipleship*. San Francisco: HarperOne, 2006.

Wingren, Gustaf. *The Flight from Creation*. Minneapolis: Augsburg, 1971.

Witherington, Ben, III. *Paul's Letter to the Romans: A Socio-Rhetorical Commentary*. Grand Rapids: Eerdmans, 2004.

Wolf, Ernst. "Das Letze und das Vorletze: Zum theologischen Denken von Dietrich Bonhoeffer." In *Die mündige Welt: Dem Andenken Dietrich Bonhoeffers*, 4:17–32. Munich: Christian Kaiser, 1963.

———. *Sozialethik: Theologische Grundlagen*. 3rd ed. Gottingen: Vandenhoeck & Ruprecht, 1988.

Wolfes, Mattias. *Protestantische Theologie und moderne Welt: Studien zur Geschichte der liberalen Theologie nach 1918*. Berlin: de Gruyter, 1999.

Wright, N. T. *Justification: God's Plan and Paul's Vision*. London: SPCK, 2009.

———. *Paul and His Recent Interpreters*. London: SPCK, 2016.

———. *What St. Paul Really Said*. Oxford: Lion, 1997.

Wright, William J. *Martin Luther's Doctrine of God's Two Kingdoms: A Response to the Challenge of Skepticism*. Grand Rapids: Baker Academic, 2010.

Würstenberg, Ralf. "Bonhoeffer Revisited." *Theologische Literaturzeitung* 131, no. 2 (February 2006): 129–40.

Yoder, John Howard. *Discipleship as Political Responsibility*. Scottdale, PA: Herald Press, 2003.

———. *The Politics of Jesus*. 2nd ed. Grand Rapids: Eerdmans, 1994.

———. *The War of the Lamb: The Ethics of Nonviolence and Peacemaking*. Edited by Glen Stassen et al. Grand Rapids: Baker Academic, 2009.

Zahl, Paul. *Rechtfertigungslehre Ernst Käsemanns*. Stuttgart: Calwer Verlag, 1996.

———. "A Tribute to Ernst Käsemann." *Anglican Theological Review* 80, no. 3 (1998): 385.

Ziegler, Philip G. "Christ for Us Today: Promeity in the Christologies of Bonhoeffer and Kierkegaard." *International Journal of Systematic Theology* 15, no. 1 (2013): 25–41.

———. "'Completely within God's Doing': Soteriology as Metaethics in the Theology of Dietrich Bonhoeffer." In *Christ, Church, and World: New Studies in Bonhoeffer's Theology and Ethics*, edited by M. Mawson and P. Ziegler, 101–17. London: T&T Clark, 2016.

———. "Secularity and Eschatology in Bonhoeffer's Late Work." In *Dietrich Bonhoeffers Theologie heute: Ein Weg zwischen Fundamentalismus und Säkularismus?*, edited by J. De Gruchy, S. Plant, and C. Tietz, 124–38. Gütersloh: Gütersloher Verlaghaus, 2009.

———. "'To Pray, to Testify, to Revolt'—An Introduction to Karl Barth's *The Christian Life*," introduction to *The Christian Life* by Karl Barth, 1–16. Translated by Geoffrey W. Bromiley. T&T Clark Cornerstones. London: T&T Clark, 2017.

———. "A Very Short Theology of Reconciliation." *Touchstone* 34, no. 3 (2016): 7–13.

Ziesler, Paul. *Paul's Letter to the Romans*. London: SCM, 1989.

Zwingli, Ulrich. "Of Baptism." In *Zwingli and Bullinger*, translated by G. W. Bromiley, 119–75. Philadelphia: Westminster, 1953.

———. *Sixty-Seven Articles of 1523*. In *Reformed Confessions of the 16th Century*, edited by A. C. Cochrane, 33–44. Philadelphia: Westminster, 1966.

Scripture and Ancient Writings Index

Author Index

Subject Index

CPSIA information can be obtained
at www.ICGtesting.com
Printed in the USA
LVOW11s2253200318

570586LV00001B/29/P